Under

the Editorship of

Marion Hathway

Director, Graduate Department of Social Economy

and Social Research, Bryn Mawr College

HERBERT H. APTEKAR
Executive Director
Jewish Community Services of Long Island

THE DYNAMICS OF CASEWORK AND COUNSELING

HOUGHTON
MIFFLIN
COMPANY

BOSTON · NEW YORK · CHICAGO · DALLAS · ATLANTA
SAN FRANCISCO · The Riverside Press Cambridge

*T*he great faiths of men, the great "schools" of philosophy and art, have been the influential perspectives within which men have been able to attain coherency. They have functioned as quasi-social devices by which query has defined its order and within which it has fed itself. They have also been castles of orthodoxy. Their borders have hardened into impassable fortresses, and the processes of query have dried into vested interests of the spirit.

Justus Buchler

*Toward a General Theory
of Human Judgment*

EDITOR'S
INTRODUCTION

As the complexity of modern society continues to press upon the individual and the family group, professional help with interpersonal problems of living is increasingly justified. Social casework describes this process of help when it is offered through a social agency serving individuals. The method of social casework is as old as the profession of social work. Its growth and development in a sense is the growth and development of the profession in which services to individuals account for the activities of more than eighty per cent of employed personnel.

Growth is rarely a painless process and the history of the development of the social casework method is no exception. The recent appearance of sharp controversy over philosophy and methods within the ranks of practicing social caseworkers and the division of the field into "diagnostic" and "functional" groupings of practitioners in various parts of the United States have been something more than growth pains. They have introduced a degree of difference among practitioners, administrators, and teachers which has been all-absorbing in some areas. To the editor of this series, whose major interest for many years has been in education for social work, the schism in social casework method has been divisive in the educational process. For this reason the inclusion of *The Dynamics of Casework and Counseling* in this series of basic books on social work methods and practices has great significance. The contribution of Herbert Aptekar to social casework theory seems to point the way to an emerging unity in practice and therefore to a greater degree of unity in the educational process.

The significance of the present volume is actually twofold. First, there is an objective analysis of the concepts and methods of social casework of the functional orientation with its reliance on the Rankian psychology and that of the diagnostic orientation with its reliance on the Freudian psychology. The nature of the controversy between the two has been clearly and sympathetically described by the author. He points out, incidentally, that the process of helping was not subjected to research methods in an effort to reach a reliable judgment between the two. It does little credit to the potentially promising field that the controversy could not be viewed objectively and submitted to a testing process. His analysis of common elements and differences is a first step in bringing together badly scarred warriors who have literally battled in certain localities to maintain the one position and to deny the other. There emerge unifying concepts of a dynamic process.

The second contribution of the book is an effort to further delineate the meaning of counseling and social casework, identifying the former with interpersonal problems of living and the latter with the offering of concrete social services of help to the individual.

Of Mr. Aptekar's two helpful contributions to social work practice, it is the thoughtful and constructive analysis of the split occasioned by partisan adherence either to the Rankian or the Freudian school which will have the greater influence. To some it has seemed that the "twain would never meet." Herbert Aptekar writes from an experience of over twenty years in social casework practice as a caseworker, supervisor, consultant, and administrator. His years of practice span the fields of family service, child guidance, and child placement. He was for two years a member of the faculty of the University of Pennsylvania School of Social Work, and is widely known as an institute and conference leader in the field. He develops succinctly the impact of practice on his casework philosophy and describes how he came to re-examine the question. Trained in the functional school, he has been able through years of practice to test its teaching. Certain unanswered questions and his own scholarly mind have stimulated him to examine the essential elements of both functional and diagnostic procedure. This seems to the editor the first step towards an integrated practice that may in time utilize the best of the two schools of thought.

MARION HATHWAY

Looking at the field of social casework in evolutionary perspective, one is impressed with the sequence of stages through which this young profession has progressed within a period of less than half a century. During this time, under the leadership of Mary Richmond, the method of social diagnosis came into being and served as a kind of temporary foundation over which the whole structure of a profession was to rise. This method had hardly been promulgated, however, when it was superseded by the influence of another developing profession, namely, psychiatry. It was not long until the profession of psychiatry split into a number of schools, and this split led to a parallel one in the field of social casework. As a result, two principal schools of casework thought have developed, namely, the diagnostic and the functional; and up until now, the profession has been embroiled in conflict between them.

There is evidence, however, that this conflict is playing itself out and that both schools of casework philosophy are ready for further growth and development. Many present-day practitioners have found that in actual practice they must use the conceptions of both the diagnostic and the functional schools, and that to describe or analyze their own practice they must concentrate on aspects of it which have received very little if any attention from either of the two schools. Practitioners are and should be concerned with the details of personal change. But this is where both present-day schools have been found wanting. Each school has developed very adequate conceptions of personality, and each one has given attention to the larger forces that make for personal change. But neither school has submitted its practice to any kind of detailed scientific scrutiny, and the subtle but significant factors which tend to produce change have been set forth at times in a rather vague and generalized way, instead of being analyzed on an inductive basis. The detailed data of casework *can* be subjected to scientific investigation. One can start with actual facts and events and analyze them inductively. In so doing it is necessary to apply certain deductive principles. An analysis cannot take place without an orientation. Our trouble in casework, however, has been that we have analyzed almost exclusively on the basis of orientation and often without scientific data of any kind. With this, many who are oriented to practice rather than to philosophy alone can no longer be content. It therefore becomes necessary to turn to an analysis of the data of practice, and in such analysis to concentrate on what actually goes on between client and worker, in other words, on the dynamics at play between the two.

If one searches for common factors between the two existing schools, one is impressed with the fact that both of these schools want the practice to which their thinking relates to be dynamic in character. Both schools of thought seem to be in agreement that casework and counseling practice must be built upon this key conception of present-day psychology and both have tried to develop a conceptual structure which takes it into account. Neither school, however, has approached the problem of dynamics in a satisfactory way, since neither one has ever attempted any kind of detailed analysis of what actually takes place between client and worker through the examination of scientifically reliable data.

That neither school has attempted a scientific analysis of the interview, which is the medium of both casework and counseling, is significant in itself. As one person put it, "everyone likes dynamics." Liking and understanding, however, are quite different, and scientific analysis is still another matter. I believe that our understanding has reached a point where the possibilities for scientific analysis of what goes on in the basic unit of casework and counseling, namely, the interview, are at hand. Prior to such analysis, however, there must be definition.

Perhaps no word is more widely used today in casework discussions and writing than the word "dynamic," and perhaps no term has been less well defined. In fact, little attempt has been made by either school to define the term, and this, I believe, has led to endless hours of confusion and conflict. For it is on the basis of such a definition that likenesses between the two schools become apparent, and it is through such definition too that both schools will find it possible to break out of their present deadlocked positions and to move forward. This book attempts to define and to describe the more dynamic aspects of casework and counseling. Its orientation is one which looks forward to a new stage of casework thinking — a stage which I think can best be described through the use of the term "dynamic." Both of the existing schools must evolve and in so doing, both will find common ways of thinking and practicing. A basic focus of interest in such an evolutionary development, I believe, will be the conception of mutual influence through interaction between client and worker. This is a conception which both schools now use in a minimal way and one which both will have to develop further.

This book has been written as a steppingstone in this direction. It is my earnest hope that it will serve as a kind of catalyst in casework thinking, and that it will tend, in some measure to break up the stultifying state of affairs which now exists between the two schools. As one who has drawn heavily on functional thinking in the past, and as one, too, who has had satisfying and productive relationships with members of the diagnostic school, I have learned to beware of sectarianism in casework. There is no monopoly of casework truth. Neither the diagnostic nor the functional school can claim to possess such a monopoly. Both, if they are to be honest, must acknowledge common ancestry, and both must admit to common interests and common goals. How to clarify their common interests and goals is the problem.

I believe that common interests and objectives can be clarified, and that one way to do this is to look at the common
heritage of both of these schools. Both have "inherited" the
dynamic conception in human relationships, although both have
acted, at times, as though they have not. Both have actually
minimized the implications of the conception, although they use
the term in an undefined way at every turn. Both must now get
together, I believe, and look into its implications for both theory
and practice.

A word must be said here of the semantic problem one meets
in any attempt to reconcile or even to interpret the thinking of
the two schools. In their present state of exclusiveness, each
school has developed a terminology which is unacceptable to
the other. It is impossible to write about casework and counseling, however, without using the terminology of one or the other
school. But as soon as one does so he automatically labels himself, and perhaps just as automatically loses readers of the opposite orientation. One could try, of course, to create an entirely
new social work language. I doubt, however, whether the introduction of a new terminology at this point in social work history
would contribute much to mutual understanding.

How then can one overcome the semantic difficulties involved
in an essay such as the present one? Frankly I do not know. I
have labored long and hard on this problem and I am afraid
that the best I could do was to use the terminology to which I
am accustomed. I have tried to make my meaning clear to readers whose orientation is different from my own, especially since
I believe that very little of the literature of the school with
which I myself was allied in the past, namely, the functional, is
understandable to readers of any different persuasion, and that
very little attempt has been made by functional writers to make
their thinking clear to the rest of the social work world.

In relation to the semantic problem, mention might be made
of the difficulties that arise over the term "counseling." This
term is used today by both schools, and both use it synonymously
with "casework." This book differentiates the meaning of the

two terms, recognizing that caseworkers do counseling and that properly qualified counselors can do casework. It is generally agreed that ministers, educators, personnel workers, and others can do counseling on certain levels, although most caseworkers would want to differentiate what they do as "counseling" from that carried out by the members of certain other professions. Most caseworkers, however, do not differentiate what they do as "casework" from what they do as "counseling."

I have considered it important to make such a distinction, and many caseworkers may find it a troublesome one. I have found in my own experience, however, that I cannot give the same meaning to the two terms. In Chapter 4, I have developed some of the differences as well as the likenesses which I see between casework and counseling, without insistence that everybody else make the same distinctions which I myself think of as valid. I should like to say, however, that the distinctions which I make with regard to casework and counseling represent no one school of thought. Certainly they should be attributed to neither the diagnostic nor the functional school.

My own thinking today must be distinguished from that of the functional school. I do hold a fundamental respect for certain conceptions developed by functionalists, however, and I believe that they should be put into wider usage. Wherever I have used "functional" terminology, therefore, I have tried to make my meaning clear to the readers who are accustomed to a different conceptual system, just as I have tried to interpret the significance of certain diagnostic conceptions to functionally oriented readers. I recognize many positive values in these diagnostic conceptions, as this book will make evident, and I think that there is every reason why functionally oriented workers should try to understand their full implications.

I shall not pretend that I have solved the semantic problem involved in writing a book such as this one. If I have succeeded, however, in demonstrating certain similarities and certain potentialities inherent in both of the present-day schools, with all their linguistic differences, as well as their differences in practice, I shall be content. I do not believe, nor have I anywhere suggested, that the differences between the two schools are merely semantic ones. They are, in a very literal sense, differences of *orientation*. This leads to differences in training and practice. Neither school will modify its orientation, however, without some kind of conceptual understanding. As matters stand today the two schools have lost their power to communicate with each other. They must regain this power, but they will do so, I believe, only when they come to understand each other's language. This will lead to mutual influence which ultimately will affect the orientation of both schools.

Perhaps mention should be made here of the audience to whom this book is addressed. Originally it was intended as a monograph addressed to the rather limited group specifically concerned with the diagnostic and functional controversy in social work. As the book developed, however, it became clear that a work of this character could have value for students in the professional schools of social work and perhaps also for students in psychology who are interested in counseling. Certain revisions were made, therefore, in order to meet the needs of these two groups of students as well as the interests of professional social workers. It is the professional social workers who are especially interested in the problem of the split within the profession and its possible solution. Students coming into the field of casework and counseling today cannot escape from such a reality, however, and it is important that they become oriented in as objective a way as possible to the nature of the problem, to its genesis, and to present-day professional opinion about it.

I wish to acknowledge my indebtedness to those who read the manuscript in its original form and whose responses stimulated revisions which are incorporated in the present text. Several of the readers were functionally oriented, several were adherents to diagnostic thinking, and at least two may be described as being sympathetically *and* critically oriented toward both schools. I particularly want to express my thanks for valuable suggestions to Mrs. Ernestine Wertheimer of the University of

California School of Social Work, Dr. Morton I. Teicher of the School of Social Work of the University of Toronto, Dr. Nathaniel Cantor of the Department of Sociology and Anthropology of the University of Buffalo, Professor Everett Wilson of the University of North Carolina School of Social Work, Miss Ruth Fizdale of the Arthur Lehman Counseling Service, Mr. Norman Lourie of the Association for Jewish Children of Philadelphia, Mr. Jacob Hechler of the Pleasantville Cottage School, and Mr. James Hunt of the Family Service of Rochester, New York, all of whom read the original manuscript. Helen Harris Perlman of the University of Chicago, Gordon Hamilton of the New York School of Social Work, and Edith Lauer and Joseph Reid of the Child Welfare League of America gave me the benefit of constructive criticism and made important suggestions. Dr. Ernest Witte of the Council on Social Work Education also made a number of very valuable criticisms. Dr. Marion Hathway, editor of this series, was helpful beyond measure. Mention should be made here that part of Chapter 5 was published in the *Social Service Review* under the title "Evolving Concepts in Casework and Counseling."

Since some of the subject matter of this book may be considered "controversial," I wish to add that I myself want to take full responsibility for it. It would be quite unfair to several of the persons mentioned to identify their opinions or outlook with the views expressed here, and I hope that this will not be done. My debt to both those who agree with me and those who differ is a very great one, and I could not be content if I did not mention a few persons by name. I want to say, too, that my indebtedness extends to many other professional associates who cannot be named in this Preface. Perhaps in reading the book they will recognize some of their own contribution.

HERBERT H. APTEKAR

CONTENTS

1. The Evolution of a Profession 1

Two Types of Personal Help — The Origin of Professional Case-work — Early Diagnostic Interest — The Influence of Psychiatry — Freudian Theory — Otto Rank's Contribution — Summary of Freudian and Rankian Concepts — The Diagnostic-Functional Controversy — The Dynamic Concept in Casework and Counseling

2. Conflicting Orientations 41

Dynamic Passivity — Relationship Therapy — The Conflict Between Relief-Giving and Therapy — Interest in Function — The Need for Diagnosis

3. The Dynamic Problem 71

The Diagnostic Method — The Functional Approach — The Dynamic Conception — Conflict as the Focus — Orientation of the Worker — Responsibility in Dynamic Helping — Dynamic Practice — The Need for Synthesis

4. From Casework to Counseling 105

Casework, Counseling, and Psychotherapy Defined — Implications in the Definitions — The Role of the Agency — The Person, the Problem, and the Service — The Specific Character of Counseling — Dynamics in Counseling

5. The Coming Phase of Integration 132

An Evolutionary Point of View — Professional Synthesis — The Problem of Diagnosis — The Use of History — The Nature of the Casework Relationship — A Case Example — The Need for Research

6. Dynamic Theory and Practice 165

The Five Freudian Concepts — The Five Rankian Concepts — The Integration of Theory and Practice

7. Analysis of a Counseling Interview from a Dynamic Standpoint 200

Transcript of Interview — Application of Diagnostic (Freudian) Concepts — Application of Functional (Rankian) Concepts — Analysis of Dynamics — The Dynamic Focus

Supplementary Reading Lists 245

Index 259

1

THE EVOLUTION OF A PROFESSION

Practice in many advanced social agencies today divides itself into two major parts, namely, (1) the administration of concrete services through the application of casework method, and (2) counseling, or help with inter-personal problems, without the administration of any concrete social service. In fact, certain agencies are organized along departmental lines, with specific services such as child placement offered in one department, while a counseling service for parents and children who do not need placement is offered in another department. This type of agency organization gives recognition to certain differences between the personal help which might be derived from a social service administered with psychological understanding, and that which results from discussion of a problem and the exertion of personal influence. Whether or not a concrete social service is administered, there must always be discussion of a

1

problem and some type of personal influence on the part of the helping person. The discussion and the personal influence often take on a different character, however, when there is a social service to be concerned about, as well as a problem, and the center of interest which must be maintained by the helping person will also differ. The client's expectations when he is interested in receiving a service are different from those which he has when he seeks only the solution to a problem through discussion with another person, and the helper's obligations to his agency and to the community are also in each instance different. In both cases, personality factors are involved, and the helper must be concerned at all times with these.

Two Types of Personal Help

The differences between the two types of helping situation, however, are at least as great as the similarities, and it is therefore necessary to make a distinction between two types of help. Even where one person helps in a given situation through counseling only, and in another through a concrete service which he administers as well, it is important for that person to be aware of the difference in character between the two helping situations. Where an agency can help the worker to maintain a distinct focus of interest through departmentalization, there is much to be gained, and administrators of some of the larger social agencies have recognized this. In any case, however, recognition must be given to the existence of two types of help being given in social agencies today.

While these two types of help are sharply differentiated in certain places, in others they are not. In fact, such differentiation should be looked upon as a manifestation of an advanced stage of casework thought and practice. Until quite recently, no distinction at all was made between them; and in many places emphasis is still laid on the likeness of all forms of personal help rather than on differences.

Perhaps an explanation for this is to be found in the fact that casework — and counseling too, when it is practiced by psychologists and others — represents an evolving profession. There are those who believe that several of the existing forms of help — casework, psychological counseling, and psychiatry — will one day evolve into a single unified profession, and this is certainly quite within the realm of possibility. For the present, however, there are different forms of help, and a question that naturally arises is: How did they come into being? What type of evolutionary process led to the development of casework and counseling as we now know them?

Later we shall elaborate on the likenesses and differences between casework and counseling, and we shall describe the relation between the two (see Chapter 4). For the time being, however, let us attempt merely a thumbnail sketch of their historical development. Any detailed history of casework, or of counseling, would be outside the scope and purpose of this book, but it is possible to highlight some of the important factors which led to the present stage of development of these two forms of help.

The Origin of Professional Casework

In looking at the social context of casework and counseling as we know them today, one is impressed, first of all, with the fact that there are modern cultures in which these forms of personal help simply do not exist. What we in America know as social casework and counseling has no exact parallel even in certain Western cultures where there is a profession of social work and where psychiatry and psychology have flourished for some time. What we are dealing with, in other words, is a cultural phenomenon which has arisen in the course of English and American history and which must be understood in terms of its relation to many other facets of that history. It was a unique combination of political, social, economic, and intellectual developments which led to what we now know as casework and counseling, and these same cultural factors undoubtedly are involved in some of the present-day problems which we must grapple with in the helping professions.

The beginning of *professional* casework and counseling as we know it in America is associated with the publication of Mary Richmond's *Social Diagnosis* in 1917. Prior to that time — that is, during the last years of the nineteenth century and the beginning of the twentieth — there had been certain developments which made Miss Richmond's work possible. The Charity Organization Movement, which originated in London in 1869 and soon extended itself to this country, was initially an attempt to organize private charities intelligently so that waste and duplication might be avoided. In this movement, however, in which large numbers of volunteer helpers, the so-called "friendly visitors," were used, a great deal of stress was placed upon the wholesome influence which one individual could have upon another. Monetary assistance, whether public or private, was looked upon with disfavor, and was left largely in the hands of "paid agents" employed by the Charity Organization Societies. In addition to the paid agents, however, there were hundreds and hundreds of volunteers who made visits to the homes of the poor and brought whatever they could in the way of understanding, sympathy, encouragement, and general good will.

In the friendly visits, there was undoubtedly much advice-giving and use of persuasive method. The role of the friendly visitor was a kind of educational one, and the goal was improvement of character through personal influence. In the light of present-day psychological understanding the methods of the friendly visitors were somewhat gross. There can be no doubt, however, that some of them did exert a wholesome personality influence in difficult personal and family situations, just as many nonprofessional persons do today in friendly personal relationships. Social workers, psychologists, and psychiatrists are not the only ones who are able to influence others in a helpful way. Very often in a personal or a business relationship one person will have the most profound influence upon another. The way in which this takes place is often unknown to both parties. In other words, there is comparatively little consciousness or analysis of the factors at work in the relationship. This was true, too, in the case of the friendly visitors. Comparatively little attention was given to method, but there can be no doubt that a great deal of personal influence did take place in the relationships which these volunteers established.

At the turn of the century, friendly visiting was still quite prevalent. By this time, however, professional schools of social work were coming into existence, with much encouragement from the Charity Organization Societies, which felt a need for trained professional staff. This was an era in which an interest in psychology and in educational method was rapidly developing. William James' *Principles of Psychology* was published in 1890, Freud was at work on the development of psychoanalysis, John Dewey foreshadowed a new trend in education, and in general there was widespread interest in personality and relationship. It was no longer assumed that one person could easily exert a desirable influence upon another; instead, it was recognized that a great deal of psychological understanding, method, and skill were needed for the purposeful accomplishment of such a goal.

It was in such an atmosphere that professional casework arose. After considerable experience as the Executive Secretary of the Baltimore and the Philadelphia Charity Organization Societies, Miss Richmond taught at the New York School of Social Work and what is now the University of Pennsylvania School of Social Work, and then carried out for the Russell Sage Foundation the studies which led to the publication of her book, *Social Diagnosis,* the first major contribution to professional casework. It is significant that Miss Richmond's primary concern in this work is with *method,* and that her orientation, while primarily social, is mixed with a great deal of psychological interest. It is also interesting to note that the first truly professional focus of interest in social casework was in this area of diagnosis.

Early Diagnostic Interest

This early interest in diagnosis is not surprising when one remembers that social casework, in its very nature, is a field in which everything starts with a problem. Sometimes the real nature of the problem is unknown at the beginning. Even where the problem is clear to start out with, the solution is not known. It can only be arrived at, or "worked out" — a familiar phrase in the social work vocabulary. In order to "work out" a problem, however, one must first understand it, comprehend it, and be oriented to it. The problem, in other words, must take on meaning. In the attempt to understand any given problem, there must be some analysis of it, some translation into other familiar terms, some set of associations which can be brought to it. This is the way caseworkers function when they are confronted with a problem. They must come to a point where they can "see through" it. The frame of reference which is used in seeing through the problem may vary, but the necessity to understand it is universal. Moreover, one must understand not only the nature of the problem, as a social, economic, or psychological entity, but also the personal context of the problem, in other words, the personalities which are involved in it. No service can be administered effectively without such understanding. It was awareness of this fact which led Miss Richmond to her interest in diagnosis.

What was Miss Richmond's concept of social diagnosis? In her own words, social diagnosis is "the attempt to arrive at as exact a definition as possible of the social situation and personality of a given client." [1] Miss Richmond's entire book is given to elaboration of this definition, which, she later states, must involve consideration of the relation of the individual "to the other human beings upon whom he in any way depends or who depend upon him, and in relation also to the social institutions

[1] Mary Richmond, *Social Diagnosis* (New York: Russell Sage Foundation, 1917), p. 51.

of his community." [2] Miss Richmond was quite interested in the formalization of the diagnosis, that is, in a statement which could actually be put down on paper in definite form. She visualized a "diagnostic summary" with three principal headings, namely, (1) Difficulties Defined, (2) Causal Factors, and (3) Assets and Liabilities. Under these headings, the worker would set forth what he had learned as a result of his study of the situation.

> The diagnostic summary, or the diagnosis put in black and white, should give the content of a diagnosis in orderly form, although that form may have to be somewhat varied for different types of social case work. Most types will have to include, in addition to a general description of the difficulty, a statement of those peculiarities of circumstance and personality which differentiate the case under review from all others. Then should come an enumeration of the causal factors, so far as known, in the order of their importance. It is a help to clearness of thinking to set them down though they must be understood, at this early stage of treatment, to be only tentative. And last should come the just mentioned appraisal of the assets for reconstruction discovered in the course of inquiry — those within our client, within his immediate family, and outside. . . . Not only the assets but the special obstacles to be overcome and guarded against in treatment should be included. All of this must be dated and must stand, like a bill of lading, "errors and omissions excepted." There would be few more dangerous things than a social diagnosis that was not subject to review in the light of further facts.[3]

Miss Richmond's general attitude toward the diagnostic statement is perhaps best revealed in the last two sentences. She knew that the "facts" which were observed by the worker and those which he inferred were not always scientifically reliable.

> . . . the duty confronts us of making sure what are facts in a client's situation. Evidence which is reliable and which is sufficient in amount and cogency is the first requisite for

[2] *Ibid.*, p. 357.
[3] *Ibid.*, p. 360.

searching diagnosis; the second is clear reasoning to infer-
ences that shall further our purpose. The use of inference,
then, the act of passing from some fact, belief, or judgment
. . . is an important part of diagnostic skill.[4]

We thus see that one of the principal questions which confronted
Miss Richmond was the problem of *how* one arrives at a diagnosis. What is the basis of inference? How reliable is the worker's judgment? What are the "facts" on which it is based?

The attempt to arrive at a diagnosis was seen by Miss Richmond not as a single act of thought on the part of the worker,
but rather as a *process,* that is to say, a *sequence of steps* which
makes it possible for the worker to arrive finally at his definition
of a social situation and of the personality of the client. These
steps were characterized by "evidence, or investigation . . . the
critical examination and comparison of evidence . . . , and . . . its
interpretation and the definition of the social difficulty." [5] In
all, four phases were involved. These were:

1. The first full interview with a client.
2. The early contacts with his immediate family.
3. The search for further insight and for sources of needed
   cooperation outside his immediate family.
4. The careful weighing in their relation to one another of
   the separate items of evidence thus gathered and their
   interpretation.[6]

In the first interview, as Miss Richmond saw it, an attempt
should be made to get clues to further information regarding
relatives, doctors and health agencies, schools, employers past
and present, and previous residences and neighborhoods. Anything that could be learned directly or indirectly about the
genesis of the problem was looked upon as appropriate. In other
words, the interviewer did not simply wait for the client to tell
his story but was active in eliciting information, particularly
information regarding sources of further information.

In the initial contacts with the family, Miss Richmond saw

[4] *Ibid.,* p. 55.
[5] *Ibid.,* p. 62.
[6] *Ibid.,* p. 103.

a need not only for garnering further information which could be used for diagnostic purposes, but also for developing a relationship with members of the family since work with the family considered as a whole might be necessary. Miss Richmond felt that attention should be given to such factors as "family cohesion." How united is the family? How easily might it be broken up? She was interested too in such factors as capacity of the family members for affection, enjoyment, and social development, and in signs of ambition, achievement, and aptitude, particularly among the children. Interference of relatives and differences in race, nationality, and religion were to be noted. "An ability to discover, note, and use the assets for reconstruction marks the true caseworker." [7]

Outside sources of information to be used in making the diagnosis included social agencies and churches, doctors and health agencies, former and present neighbors, relatives, friends, former and present employers, schools, and public records. In consultations with such outside sources, Miss Richmond recommended that the worker seek history and that he go first to those sources which were likely to be rich in history.

The data thus secured were to be looked upon as the raw material for diagnosis. The diagnosis itself, however, consisted of *an interpretation* of these materials. Such an interpretation is arrived at through the careful weighing of evidence and critical comparison. Social evidence was defined by Miss Richmond as consisting of "all facts as to personal or family history which, taken together, indicate the nature of a given client's social difficulties and the means to their solution." [8]

In a chapter on the First Interview, Miss Richmond presents the objectives of the worker as follows:

1. To give the client a fair and patient hearing.
2. To establish, if possible, a sympathetic mutual understanding — a good basis, that is, for further intercouse.
3. To secure clues to whatever other sources of information

[7] *Ibid.*, p. 158.
[8] *Ibid.*, p. 50.

will give a deeper insight into the difficulties of his situation and their possible solutions.

4. To begin, even at this early stage, the slow process of developing self-help and self-reliance, though only by the tonic influence which an understanding spirit always exerts, and with the realization that later the client's own level of endeavor will have to be sought, found, and respected.[9]

Miss Richmond recognized that "the client's own hopes, plans, and attitude toward life are more important than any single item of information." [10] This was distinctly out of keeping, however, with her statement elsewhere that "we must break through the narrow circle of our client's own view and get into the wider one of those who know and understand him. We must depend upon the first interview for those clues which are most likely to supplement and round out his story." [11] Regardless of inconsistencies, however, Miss Richmond did set forth *a method* different from indiscriminate investigation. There was a goal in her "processes"; there was a genuine attempt to understand the client psychologically, and there was an effort to arrive at such understanding through an orderly and logical procedure.

On the whole, Miss Richmond's diagnosis was centered outside of the client himself, even though she did recognize the necessity to see and appreciate some of his own inner psychology. It was as though the worker, who saw himself as very separate from the client, stood off and exercised his own mental powers to arrive at conclusions which were to give shape to his own activities, which would then be carried out on behalf of the client. This was essentially what was wrong with Miss Richmond's way of diagnosing, and later generations of caseworkers found that they had to depart from it.

For no matter how different or how well trained the worker is, he must be *related* to his client if he is to be effective at all, and one cannot really relate to another person in the spirit of

9 *Ibid.*, p. 114.
10 *Ibid.*, p. 133.
11 *Ibid.*, p. 113.

a laboratory technician. One's likes and dislikes come into play as well as one's own inner needs in relationship, and the process of judging becomes something infinitely more complicated than the kind of objective decision-making which Miss Richmond envisioned. It is possible to diagnose in a relationship, but this cannot be done through a simple process of adding facts or of comparing them and weighing them. Later in this book (see Chapters 5 and 6) we shall discuss what goes into modern diagnosis. For the present we must be content with pointing out that Miss Richmond made the first extensive effort to analyze a casework process, and that in this objective interest centered on the problem of diagnosis there was the first truly professional approach in casework.

Miss Richmond's contribution has always been held in respect by modern caseworkers, regardless of their allegiance to any particular school of thought. There is a variety of reasons for this, one of which is the fact that it contains the germinal conception of self-determination, a key concept in the thinking of every social worker today regardless of his orientation. Well-trained workers of both the diagnostic and the functional schools of thought try to practice at all times with genuine respect for the client's right to self-determination. Their methods of carrying out their intention of letting the client determine for himself what path he shall follow may differ, but the concept is one which is certainly basic in the thinking of both schools. Miss Richmond had the conception and introduced it colorfully in her philosophy of diagnosis when she spoke of "developing self-help and self-reliance, though only by the tonic influence which an understanding spirit always exerts, and with the realization that later the client's own level of endeavor will have to be sought, found, and respected."

The concept of self-determination has become so important in modern casework philosophy that if one were to pick any single conception without which modern casework simply could not exist, it would undoubtedly be the idea that the client must determine what his own life will be like and that the worker cannot and should not try to do that for him. To students coming into the field of casework this is sometimes almost a shocking idea, since most people who take up casework as a profession do so because they want to help others. Helping others means entering into their lives, and this the student sometimes feels is synonymous with pointing up the right way to do things. Most social workers have a kind of natural educational interest. They want to give to others what they believe to be of value themselves. It is, therefore, often quite troubling to the student to learn that he may not be able to satisfy his impulse to give, as a caseworker, and that he must learn to play quite a limited role, as far as the life of his client is concerned.

For social workers of an earlier day this was not so. The right to self-determination, that is to say, the right to arrange one's own life as one sees fit, was not considered a cardinal principle, and earlier caseworkers therefore proceeded to give advice and to persuade clients, often against their own will, to follow a course of action which the caseworker saw as proper in a particular situation. People were asked to live together when they really did not want to do so, to go to schools they did not want to attend, to take jobs in which they had no interest, and so on. The fact that such efforts failed more often than they succeeded did not deter many caseworkers from pursuing their own goals. Miss Richmond did much to contribute to a different orientation of the casework profession, and her successors built up the principle of self-determination to the point where it became the most basic one in casework philosophy.

There probably are many reasons why professional caseworkers of every orientation accepted this aspect of Miss Richmond's philosophy. The concept of self-determination and the corollary concept of self-help are deeply rooted in our culture. From the days of the American Revolution we have cultivated an independent spirit in our political, economic, and social life. The growing child in our culture finds that the adult world wants him to be independent. In his early life at home and in school certain conformities are expected, but even here attempts are made to cultivate individuality. When the individual strays too far from accepted norms he can expect disapproval. On the whole, however, he can look for encouragement in the development of individuality, which is what we mean by "self-determination."

Such a cultural assumption, therefore, is accepted by most of us without question. We are ready to act on it, unconsciously, so to speak, and we expect others to be ready to act on it too. Every culture is built on certain values which are translated, through the culture, into a way of life. These values are instilled in the growing child, and by the time he becomes an adult he is willing to live by them. In our culture self-determination has become such a value. We speak of this value with pride, we teach it to our youngsters, and we make many honest attempts to live by it. Experience shows, however, that it is a value which is easy to violate. While claiming the right to self-determination for ourselves, we are not always ready to grant it to others. This is what happens in casework, where it is easy enough to accept the principle, but where putting it into practice is quite a different matter. In actual practice, caseworkers find that self-determination is a *problem* as well as a principle. It is a problem that they must be continually conscious of, for no matter how disposed they may be to grant the client the right to live his own life, the very nature of the casework situation makes this difficult to do. The caseworker is so situated that he can easily interfere with decisions made by his client — or make it appear that decisions are the client's and not his. The temptation to do this is perpetually present, and the strongest discipline is required to resist it.

Miss Richmond held the concept of self-determination and the idea of self-help and wove them into her philosophy of social diagnosis. In practice, however, the kind of study or "investigation" which she called for, and the kind of diagnosis which she advocated, left little room for client participation. Casework today is more attentive to the client, and the worker can no longer be content to make a diagnosis largely on the basis of information he receives about him. Certain objective information regarding the client's social situation is always available to the worker, and he will inevitably make certain judgments on the basis of this information. But he will also be conscious of the fact that this information will have no value whatsoever, if the client is not aware of the nature of the difficulty as the worker may see it, and if the client is not disposed to do something about the difficulty. Workers today know that they too are dependent on the client's will to self-determination. Therefore, no matter how objectively valid their judgments may be, they will have no casework value until they are understood and accepted by the client.

Miss Richmond's interest, as we have indicated, was a dual one. On the one hand it was a social interest, and on the other, it was a psychological one. The interest in the inner person (psychological) and also in the individual as he is molded by his environment (social) is apparent throughout her writings. The method she develops is therefore one which is intended to deal with the outer forces influencing the inner person — the neighborhood, family, school, job, and so on. Miss Richmond could not be content with an external focus, however, and so she returns to the proposition that "client's own hopes, plans, and attitude toward life" must be recognized. This interest is not essentially different from that manifested by present-day caseworkers, who on the one hand are concerned with the help which the client can get from a concrete social service, that is to say, an environmental influence, and on the other hand, really wish to deal at all times with the inner self — the character or personality of the individual. A recent publication, for example, states the following:

> . . . There seems to be considerable agreement that *treatment* falls into two broad categories, even though the two categories are variously defined. The goals of treatment in the two categories may be described as follows: (1) to support or maintain the client's current strengths by helping him mobilize capacity and resources to meet his current life situa-

tion, and (2) to modify the client's attitudes and patterns of behavior by increasing his understanding of himself, of his problems, and of his part in creating them.

From the limited data available, it appears that most cases in family agencies fall into the first category. The psychological and social value of this type of treatment by the family agency needs to be reaffirmed. The problems include those that require social planning and the utilization of resources. The social pressures on the family, if not relieved, can have extensive deleterious effects on the persons involved. The persons needing such supportive help may be either (1) those who are handicapped, physically or emotionally, or are incapable, because of youth or old age, of making suitable plans without help; or (2) those who ordinarily have capacity to manage their affairs but who, at points of severe pressure (such as illness, accident, death, loss of employment, migration, and so forth) are temporarily immobilized. The focus of the agency's help is on the specific reality problems that the family is facing, and on ways of reducing pressure and relieving undue hardship.

In the second category of treatment, the client is helped to examine his attitudes and characteristic ways of behaving. The purpose is to help him increase his understanding of himself; that is, of his attitudes and the part they play in creating his social difficulties. The discussions are focused on the client's current interfering attitudes, modes of behavior, and their inappropriateness. The persons for whom this type of treatment is appropriate are those who have sufficient strength and capacity for positive feeling to engage in this kind of self-examination. The treatment often includes helping the client utilize various agency or community resources for himself and for other family members.[12]

Our own dual interest, it may be seen from the above, still runs to the social and environmental sources of help, on the one hand, and to the psychological, on the other. Miss Richmond attempted to combine this dual interest when she suggested that there ought to be a profession called "sociatry" (instead of psychiatry), which indeed would be an apt name for much of

[12] *Scope and Methods of the Family Service Agency* (New York: Family Service Association of America, 1953), pp. 7–8.

present-day casework or counseling practice. The dual interest of present-day workers in the administration of the social services (casework) and help on a personal and problem level (counseling) reflects itself in many ways, one of which is the conflict between the two existing schools of casework thought on the essential question of self-determination. Most discussions of differences between the two schools fail to deal with the very basic problem which workers of both orientations must face in this respect. Self-determination is somehow taken as an accepted principle, whereas the truth is that it is an ever-present problem in casework, today as it was in Miss Richmond's day.

One reason why mere subscription to the principle of self-determination is insufficient is that none of us can ever be *completely* self-determining in the conduct of our affairs. We live with others and this means that we make concessions. What is our own will and what is the will of someone else is sometimes difficult to distinguish. The caseworker can be misled by appearances and feel that he is granting the client complete freedom to make his own decisions, whereas the client in actuality may not feel that he is the free agent the worker would like him to be. What the worker takes as free and self-determined decision can be straight compromise on the part of the client — a yielding to necessity rather than a free expression of his own genuine desire or will. Self-determination must be looked upon as a goal in casework. It cannot be considered as an accomplished fact. This is true for the worker who is diagnostically oriented as well as for the functional worker.

How basic this problem is may easily be seen when actual practice representing the two present-day schools is examined. What the functionalist sees as self-determination, the diagnostic worker may sometimes see as lack of willingness *to do for* the client. On the other hand, what the diagnostic worker attempts to accomplish through the exercise of his own knowledge and skill, the functionalist sometimes sees as a failure to grant the client real self-determination. For example, a client in need of financial assistance might apply to a functionally oriented agency for this and fail to receive the assistance because he did not meet certain conditions of eligibility. The functional worker explaining this situation might say that the client had the choice of meeting the conditions of eligibility or deciding that he did not want assistance under such conditions. The diagnostic worker, on the other hand, might say that the client had no real choice, that he did not participate in the decision as to what the conditions of eligibility might be, and that what was accepted as his self-determined decision was not that at all.

The same client applying to a diagnostically oriented agency might find that his need for financial assistance was or was not accepted. The worker, however, would be interested in diagnosing the nature of the difficulty and in so doing might come to the conclusion that the applicant needed employment, or perhaps some educational opportunity. Attempts might then be made to help him with this diagnosed need. Such endeavor might be criticized by the functionally oriented worker as a violation of the client's right to self-determination, since he was being given a service which he did not seek himself and one which stemmed from the worker's theory or appraisal of the situation rather than from any basic interest felt by the client.

Both critics in this instance would be partly right and partly wrong. For what both workers failed to do was to recognize *the problem* of self-determination inherent in the situation. The true casework problem is to *find out* what the client can or will do himself and what he can or will do only with the help of another person. This was the essential problem of casework in Mary Richmond's day, and it is today also.

Self-determination is as much a problem as it is a guiding principle in casework. The idea rests on a culturally accepted belief regarding the nature of man. But what it turns out to be in practice must be examined. It is easy enough to subscribe to the proposition that people should help themselves, that they should be self-reliant and self-determining. Like democracy, everybody in our culture believes in it. But translating the belief into action is a different matter. Here we find that the belief sometimes is more honored in the breach than in the observance. What is breach and what is observance, as far as the principle of self-determination is concerned, is not always easy to settle. This is especially true because the caseworker must often function in a setting where he carries out obligations to the state or to some other organized body and not just to the individual. And this applies to workers of both orientations. Both schools, diagnostic and functional, are agreed on the basic proposition that the caseworker should operate so far as possible on the principle of self-determination. What is self-determination in any given case, however, must be discovered. It should never be merely assumed.

A problem of this character could be dealt with only in a most rudimentary way during the very early stages of professional development. Miss Richmond, in fact, treated it only in incidental fashion. As the two schools of casework thought developed, they accepted the principle of self-determination as a basic one, but failed to recognize that this principle could not be put into practical effect without a great deal of effort on the part of both client and worker. As a principle, self-determination has a great deal of value for purposes of orientation. It becomes a real part of method, however, only when the worker can recognize what a problem it is to let the other person be self-determining.

Another concept inherent in Miss Richmond's work, and also one which is not unrelated to questions of diagnosis, is the idea of process. As we have indicated (page 8) Miss Richmond saw diagnosis in terms of process. In later years, however, this term came to take on quite a different meaning. In fact, today it represents one of the points of cleavage between the diagnostic and the functional schools. The term is seldom used by the diagnostic group. The functional school, on the other hand, sees all of casework as a matter of process.

Just what is meant by this term and why do the two schools differ on such grounds? When Miss Richmond used the term she meant to imply that diagnosis could take place only through a sequence of steps (see page 8) which followed one another in logical order. The steps she envisioned were of an objective, systematic character and they could be looked upon as a set of rules of procedure. These rules might be applied to the study of any case and to the formulation of the diagnostic statement. No one today follows these rules in any rigid way. Diagnostically oriented workers, however, do put a good deal of emphasis on the formulation of a diagnostic statement, while the functional school sees little value in this and relies instead on what comes out of the process. By process, the functional worker does not mean a sequence of steps, as Miss Richmond did, based on orderliness of procedure on the part of the worker. Instead, the fact that client and worker must be related to each other, from the very beginning of the case, receives stress. In the relationship there is a progression, much as there is in the development of a chemical or a physical process. As the relationship develops, emotions are expressed, and in the expression there is often a shift or change of feeling. Subsequently the difficulty may be looked upon in an entirely different light. In other words, the point of emphasis in the functional view of "casework process" is the changing or shifting of attitude which takes place as the relationship progresses. The change in attitude is what the functional worker wishes to concentrate on, and a great deal of the thinking that he does about his case centers on this. Many functionally oriented workers do not use the term "diagnosis" at all, and it is rare for a functional worker to formulate his thinking according to any diagnostic scheme. The reason for this is the belief that such steps are unnecessary and that change of attitude, which is the worker's essential purpose, can take place only in the process itself, that is, in the direct and continued contact of client and worker. Since it is not intended for direct use with the client himself, the formulated diagnosis is looked upon as having minimal value.

In present-day diagnostic thinking, diagnosis is looked upon as a prior condition for treatment, although it is recognized that some help can actually be offered to the client without a well-formulated diagnosis. In the functional approach, with its emphasis on casework process, there is the distinct idea that "treatment" is implicit in every single contact. The process, in other words, *is* treatment, and any diagnosing that goes on within it is looked upon as inextricably interwoven with treatment, and not as something which can be separated from it.

It is not our purpose at this point to resolve the differences between the two schools in this respect. What we wish to do instead is simply to indicate that the schools are grappling with an inherent problem here, just as they do in the case of the principle of self-determination. The inherent problems of casework arise out of the fact that there is always a minimum of two persons involved, the helper and the one who is to be helped. Because of this, the question arises as to what one person can do himself, without the other, and what must be done by both together. This question existed even in Miss Richmond's time, when comparatively little attention was given to the matter of client-participation. It became a much greater question with the introduction of psychiatric thinking in social casework, and today it emerges in various forms in the cleavage between the schools of casework philosophy.

The Influence of Psychiatry

Miss Richmond's work foreshadowed the period of casework history which was to follow within the next decade — namely, the psychiatric phase. In fact, within two years after *Social Diagnosis* was published, the whole field of casework was preoccupied with the contributions of psychiatry.[13] Much enthusiasm for psychiatry had developed during the First World War, and caseworkers now turned to this field with the hope that it might provide many of the answers to the perplexing problems which confronted them. Miss Richmond's writing, with its combined social and psychological emphasis, served in some respects as a

13 Cf. Jessie Taft, "The Relation of Psychiatry and Social Work," *The Family*, 7:199–203 (November, 1926).

kind of check on this enthusiasm, but it also tended to stimulate such interest. Those who felt that environmental factors were not receiving enough attention turned back to the investigatory method of *Social Diagnosis*, while those who recognized the importance of psychological factors tried to see what they could learn from psychiatrists. Most workers of this period recognized, however, that the inner person would have to become a focus of interest,[14] and that it was necessary to learn as much as possible about him.

Before the advent of psychiatry, social casework was viewed and practiced as an active art. The caseworker was always a *doer*. He investigated, he diagnosed, and he administered the concrete social service. Relief was given, placement was effected, and so on. The managing, executive type of person was often looked upon as the proper type of personality to do casework, and the more passive, following type of person was often considered unsuitable. This was not so in the field of psychiatry. Much of what the psychiatrist accomplished took place because he was a listener. He did not do anything in particular to his patient. Instead he followed the lead taken by his patient and tried to see what he could do to help the patient help himself. Since this was quite in keeping with certain aspects of social work philosophy, if not practice, it was natural that caseworkers should turn to psychiatry for help in developing a method.

On doing so, caseworkers found that the psychiatrists were by no means unanimous in their ways of looking at personality, in their helping philosophies, or in their methods. Throughout all of psychiatric philosophy and practice, however, there seemed to run a central thread, namely, the necessity for being more observant and less active in a manipulative sense. The psychoanalysts all listened while their patients talked, and in talking there was therapy. The methods of the pressure salesman, persuasion and advice-giving, which were so prevalent in the casework of an

---

[14] Virginia P. Robinson, *A Changing Psychology in Social Casework* (Chapel Hill: University of North Carolina Press, 1930), describes this shift of focus.

earlier day, became suspect. A more observant, listening, and following role was now seen as appropriate in casework. We thus find an article in *The Family* in October, 1924, which contrasts with many earlier articles in expressing the thought that the worker should put himself in the background and wait until the client is ready to talk.[15] This article states that the worker should "maintain a professional attitude and guard against emotion on her part or at least keep her emotions in the background." The example of the psychiatrist, in other words, was to be followed.

This trend of the twenties was paralleled, interestingly enough, by a trend toward much more relief-giving. Joanna C. Colcord, in an article published in March, 1923,[16] points out that families formerly considered "unsuitable for relief" because of moral judgments, e.g., cases involving desertion, venereal disease, or families of criminals, were now frequently granted relief on a budgetary basis. Miss Colcord states, "We have largely lost our fear of relief as a danger to strength of character, feeling with good reason that casework has developed adequate methods to avoid this danger." In other words, along with the reluctance to project one's own ideas, standards, and behavior on another, there developed a tolerance — a willingness to deal with and assume some responsibility for the misfortune of others. There was a relaxing of faith in one's own way as the only way, and of the attempt to impose one's own way on the person who sought help.

The conflict which caseworkers had to face in themselves at this point was indeed a deep-rooted psychological one, involving the most basic patterns in relationship. They had to grapple with the very basic question: How much giving can one do in relation to another? How much demand does one make of the person one helps? Psychiatry did not solve this unsolvable problem for caseworkers, but it did bring about an attitude of general tolerance which undoubtedly entered into the willingness to try to

15 Mary S. Brisley, "An Attempt to Articulate Process," *The Family*, 5: 157–161 (October, 1924).
16 Joanna C. Colcord, "Relief," *The Family*, 4:13–17 (March, 1923).

help new groups of clientele. In the attempt to help these new clients, the more passive methods of the psychiatrist seemed to have value. There was, however, a disturbing factor, namely, the fact that these clients needed relief and relief could not be administered passively. Caseworkers, therefore, found themselves in conflict, wanting to follow the approach of the psychiatrist, but finding that this approach could not be taken over totally and used without modification in their work with a relief clientele.

By and large, psychiatry did win out. All caseworkers moved in the direction of the psychiatrist, and by the end of the twenties, all trained caseworkers were at least partially oriented in psychiatric method and philosophy. It had to be recognized, however, that there was also little single-mindedness in the field of psychiatry. There was no one psychiatric method, but rather many. Psychoanalysis, which represented the most advanced psychiatry of the day, was a unified field for a short time, but it did not take long until Freud and some of his chief disciples began to differ and a variety of schools of analysis developed. Three of Freud's disciples, Adler, Jung, and Rank, had developed schools of their own, and social workers began to look into the contributions of each.

For some reason the thinking of Alfred Adler never obtained an acknowledged place in social work philosophy, although certain of his concepts, such as those of "compensation" and "inferiority," certainly were widely used by caseworkers in their early attempts to analyze personality difficulties. Adler was instrumental in establishing the first child guidance clinics in Vienna. During his lifetime, he wrote extensively, lectured widely in the United States and in Europe and attained a considerable popularity among psychologists, educators and others. His system of "Individual Psychology," however, never really took root among caseworkers.

Similarly, Jung's "Analytical Psychology," though it was studied by caseworkers who wished to orient themselves to psychiatric thought, had comparatively little effect upon caseworkers, although certain conceptions which are widely accepted by caseworkers today have their parallels in Jung's thinking. One might mention Jung's emphasis on the relationship with the therapist himself as a therapeutic factor, or again, his conception of the projection upon the therapist which is later taken back into the self. There is a teleological emphasis in both Adler's and Jung's thinking which certainly is in keeping with casework interest in the aims and purposes of the individual. Nevertheless, although both Adler and Jung have developed followers in the field of therapy, they have never played an especially important role among social caseworkers.

The two other analytic philosophies — the Freudian and the Rankian — had a different kind of influence upon casework, and today it is difficult to disassociate one's self from one or the other. Those caseworkers who are oriented to Freudian conceptions are classified as members of the diagnostic school, and those who adhere to the philosophy of Otto Rank are designated as functionalists. Actually, Freud and Rank were not responsible for the development of these two distinct schools of social casework. What they did was to develop two schools of therapeutic philosophy. In the field of psychotherapy, there have been a great many lines of development since Freud, Rank, Jung, and Adler made their original contributions, and the number of schools of psychotherapy in existence today is almost legion. In casework, however, all foment has simmered down to the point where there are at present just two important schools, the diagnostic and the functional, and these have come to be associated with the names of Freud and Rank.

It might have been much more appropriate to associate these two schools with the names of the caseworkers who were really responsible for their development and crystallization, rather than with those whose primary interest was in psychotherapy as such. The historical fact, however, is that the two schools of casework thought have come to be known as diagnostic, or Freudian, and functional, or Rankian. The diagnostic school does make use of Freudian conceptions in its view of personality and of treatment. With regard to diagnosis itself, it probably has drawn the more heavily on Mary Richmond's contributions. The functional school uses Otto Rank's personality theories, and most of its philosophy of treatment is derived from him. Most of Rank's influence upon the group which developed the functional approach took place before functional thinking as such actually came into being. The emphasis on the part played by the function of the agency in the helping process cannot be attributed to Rank, who saw treatment much more in personal and individual terms. Regardless of the appropriateness of nomenclature, however, there are certain distinct contrasts as well as similarities in the Freudian and Rankian philosophies, and it is important to look into these in order to develop an understanding of the diagnostic and functional schools. It will not be necessary to treat every conception developed by Freud or by Rank. Certain key conceptions, however, have had a profound influence upon the development of social work philosophy, and we shall give attention to these.

Freudian Theory

Let us first consider several of the basic concepts in Freudian theory. Our treatment of these concepts at this point will be no more than introductory.

Unconscious Mind

Perhaps the keystone of Freud's whole philosophic structure is the concept of *unconscious mind*. Through his experience with hypnosis and the study of dreams, Freud found a world of hidden mentality, which he chose to call "the unconscious." As a result of his experiments in hypnosis, he came to the conclusion that there were past events in the lives of his patients which they had forgotten — or at least so it appeared as far as their conscious memory was concerned. He found that his patients could remember such past events in a hypnotic state, but when restored to normal consciousness they again forgot them. This was a fact — an objective fact which Freud observed and which he could reproduce for any unbiased observer. Past events, forgotten under certain conditions, would be recalled under others. Whether or not the actual event was the same as the memory was not the important point. There was the fact of forgetting in the normal conscious state and of recall under a state of hypnosis. This was the fact that Freud, with true scientific spirit, was determined to explore. He proceeded, accordingly, to look into the *content* of this forgotten material, reproduced in a state of hypnosis, and found that it consisted of thoughts, feelings, and attitudes which were quite unacceptable to the conscious individual.

Hypnosis was not too satisfactory a method, however. Freud wanted, if possible, to find another way of producing such "unconscious" material. This led to his development of the method of "free association" in which the patient was instructed to speak out every thought that came to him, regardless of how trivial or how unacceptable it might seem. Lying on a couch, in a darkened room, with the analyst behind him, the patient would recall his dreams and say whatever came into his mind. In this manner, Freud found that "repressed" thoughts and attitudes were expressed, and that when such material was analyzed by the therapist, the "unconscious" content of the mind could be studied. This was done in a historical or biographical manner. Events in the patient's life were reconstructed. What was formerly unconscious was now squarely viewed in the light of adult consciousness. Childhood fantasies and traumatic experiences were relived, this time in relation to the tolerant physician, a "father-figure" rather than the real parent, who originally would have been unwilling to countenance them, and it was assumed that in this way the patient could be helped to assimilate into his total psychology that which formerly would have found a place only in the unconscious.

It is not our purpose here to criticize the method or the principal conceptions which Freud used to try to understand the unconscious. The important thing for us to note is that he discovered, or perhaps one should say rediscovered, unconscious workings of the human mind. (The conception was known even among the Greeks.) The concept of the unconscious was fraught with implications for further development of psychological theory and therapeutic practice. No matter how critical we may be of the idea of the unconscious as a *place* in the mind, or an entity in itself, the fact is that there are manifestations of the mind which go on without consciousness. Whether one calls these manifestations — the dream is a good example — "unconscious" or something else is beside the point. Such manifestations are real and they must be understood. Freud attempted to understand them, using a variety of conceptions which in time took on a life of their own and became part and parcel of psychoanalytic philosophy.

Many of the social workers who came into contact with Freud's conception of the unconscious, as psychiatry was being introduced into social work, recognized its value at once because it opened up new vistas for understanding the personalities with whom they worked. The son who professed affection for his father was no longer taken literally. Instead one began to wonder whether this son might harbor an unconscious hatred of the father. The wife who was outwardly devoted to her husband could dream of killing him, and this could mean that she unconsciously hated the one she consciously loved. The brother and sister who supposedly had the strongest kind of affection for each other could now be seen as rivals. Nothing was what it seemed to be, in the field of personality at least, and those who worked with human beings would have to begin to look beyond surface manifestations.

Ambivalence

A corollary conception, for which Freud must be given great credit, is the concept of *ambivalence*. Here again Freud was not the originator of this concept, but he probably did more than any other human being to give it great significance. Having divided man into two parts, as it were, Freud further noted that these two parts were often in conflict with each other. In other words, one could love and one could hate *simultaneously* — one could have fear and at the same time be very courageous. There seemed to be no feeling, in fact, which did not have its opposite, and the human mind seemed to be quite capable of containing these opposites — often without disturbance. In many instances, a person consciously felt one way and unconsciously felt the opposite. This had been clearly observed in pathological situations. Once the idea of unconscious mind was accepted, however, it did not require a far step to postulate a conflict between the two minds, so to speak. The sources of such conflict accordingly became an important area of study for Freud himself and for some of his disciples. Social workers who were just taking on a psychiatric orientation, however, were much less interested in sources than they were in practical implications of the important conception of ambivalence itself.

The Past

As we have indicated, Freud's early discoveries led him to *the past*, that is, into the patient's history. Many of the conflicts which he observed seemed to be conflicts between past experiences which were still alive in the psyche of the patient and present attitudes and behavior which seemed to go on as if the past did not exist. If one were going to treat a conflict of any kind, therefore, it was assumed that one should know the history of that conflict. If one worked with a child, then it was important to know what the parents did with the child to create or intensify conflict in him. If one worked with the adult, then one had to know his childhood experiences in order to know how he came to be the kind of adult that he was. One had to look for conflicts of the past to understand those of the present. The emphasis which Freud put upon the historical factor in the development of neurosis undoubtedly corroborated the feeling of many social workers, during the years when they were becoming oriented to psychiatry, that history-taking should be an essential aspect of the caseworker's job.

Transference

Another primary Freudian concept, taken over by the social workers who first came in contact with it, was the *transference*. In psychoanalysis, it was recognized at an early date that one could not treat the patient except in a relationship, and that in this relationship basic feelings had to be expressed. A projection of feeling (originally psycho-sexual in nature) onto the analyst, who served as a kind of substitute for the original "love-hate object" (parent-figure), took place. The feeling, in other words, was *transferred* to the analyst. This gave the relationship of analyst and patient a distinct character and distinguished it from more ordinary relationships. The whole self was involved in the transference, since the self was built upon this original relation to the parent. In the transference this original relationship was relived. This time the feeling did not have to take unconscious forms of expression. It could be brought out into the light of adult consciousness and be recognized as not really feeling for the analyst himself, but as feeling which stemmed from another source. The concept of transference had great meaning for caseworkers and was taken over by many as a conception which might be used to explain the relationship of client and caseworker.

Resistance

Associated with the transference in Freudian theory is the concept of *resistance* — particularly the resistance to interpretation of the transference. In order to realize the therapeutic potentialities inherent in the transference, the patient must become aware of the fact that he is projecting onto the analyst feelings of love and hatred which stem from another source, and he cannot achieve this realization without interpretation. Through the insight thus derived, the patient comes to see that while the feelings he originally had toward his parents may have been justified, the actions of the analyst should not call forth such feelings. Before he comes to accept this, however, he strongly resists such interpretation.

The thinking involved in all of this was taken over by social workers, who were quick to see *resistance* on the part of their clients to their own interpretations. For many reasons clients would refuse to accept the "insight" which caseworkers would try to give to them regarding the nature of their problems. These same clients would show resentment toward the worker, or sometimes an excessive dependence, and these were regarded as manifestations of the transference. If real help were to be given, the transference would have to be strengthened, or perhaps interpreted. In any case, the client, one could be quite certain, would resist the worker's interpretations and try to hold onto his own views.

While this need of the worker to "interpret" and of the client to "resist" led to many difficulties, it must be recognized that social work made tremendous forward strides under the influence of these primary concepts in Freudian philosophy and method. It had acquired a way of seeing more of the total personality of the client than it ever had seen before, and it had also acquired a new center of interest. Progressive caseworkers were largely united on this new center of interest, and the profession as a whole took on a distinct forward impetus.

The above concepts are but a few of the many which are to be found in Freud's writings. They are the concepts, however, which have the greatest significance for social work and which must be compared with the chief ideas in Rankian philosophy, to which we shall now turn.

Otto Rank's Contribution

While caseworkers were still quite united in their new center of interest and focus of activity, a new philosophy and a new psychology came to their attention — the philosophy and psychology of Otto Rank, who formerly had been an outstanding disciple of Freud. Rank had worked closely with Freud for a number of years and was chosen by Freud as the person best suited to explore and develop the cultural implications of psychoanalysis. He practiced as a lay therapist and wrote extensively on technical as well as cultural aspects of psychoanalysis while he was still closely allied with Freud. After a number of years, however, Rank found that his own practical experience led him to certain hypotheses and conclusions which differed from those of Freud. This produced a split in the relationship of the two men, which had been a very strong one, and after the split Rank proceeded to develop a philosophy and a psychology, as well as a therapeutic method, which differed greatly from those of Freud. There was a kind of transitional period in which Rank used Freudian terms and ideas to give expression to his own thought. He found, however, that he would have to discard practically all of the important Freudian concepts and substitute others. This he did, and in all of his later work a totally different set of concepts are used. Let us look into these concepts now and consider their implications for social work.

Will

Rank's key concept, and one which has caused perhaps more dispute among social workers than any other, is *the will*. Rank's concept of will is a practical one which is used to describe *the drive and intention and mobilization of the personality toward a given end*. It carries no connotations of good and bad or right and wrong, and it does not refer to any kind of supra-natural force. It is a completely naturalistic conception and one which lends itself to scientific investigation.

Before Rank, Wundt used the conception of will to mean "an integrating or synthesizing element in the psyche." [17] Recogniz-

---

[17] Cf. A. A. Goldenweiser and W. F. Ogburn, *The Social Sciences* (Boston: Houghton Mifflin, 1927), p. 76. William James and others also used the conception with essentially the same meaning. In her book, *The Psychology and Philosophy of Otto Rank* (New York: The Philosophical Library, 1953, pp. 100–101), Fay B. Karpf sees Rank's conception of will as stemming from Schopenhauer's Voluntaristic philosophy.

ing that the mind did not simply perceive or receive impressions from the outside world, but instead organized and synthesized such impressions, Wundt felt that a descriptive term for this organizing process was called for, and he chose the term "will," which he felt implied a creative synthesis. Rank's experience in working analytically with human beings led him to feel too that the patient could never be the mere passive recipient of the analyst's knowledge or skill and that an actual synthesizing process was taking place within the patient at all times. This would have to be so not only for the analyst's patients but for all human beings. In his study of anthropology, with a special interest in the creative aspects of culture,[18] Rank found confirmation that there was a directive, organizing, and synthesizing force in human beings, and he chose to call this force "will."

Counter-will

One cannot do justice to Rank's concept of will in a few words, and the term "organizing force" is only partially synonymous. In Rank's concept there is implied the same ambivalence which Freud gave recognition to in another way, and for an appreciation of this, it is necessary to see the implications of the complementary terms which Rank uses, namely, counter-will and denial. No one ever simply wills something. He wills and denies that he wills, for along with the willing goes a great deal of guilt. If will were more accepted than it is in our society, perhaps there would be less guilt for wanting something one's own way. We are often taught from the early years that our own way is the wrong way, and this teaching produces feelings of guilt. Aside from this, however, there is a guilt problem which Rank sees as inherent in the relation of man to man. In willing, in being individual, one separates one's self from the other person. Thus separateness comes about as a result of self-assertion against the other, or meeting the will of the other with counter-

[18] Rank spent more than twenty years in a study of creative manifestations, the results of which were published in his *Art and the Artist* (New York: Alfred A. Knopf, 1932).

will of one's own. In analyzing the development of will, Rank sees its origin as being negative in character, that is, a refusal on the part of the infant and child to accept the will of the adult. This refusal is counter-will, which should be differentiated from will in a positive sense. There is only one will, but there are two sides to it, positive and negative. One refers to the positive as "will" and to the negative as "counter-will." The individual gives expression to the negative in differentiating himself and to the positive in self-assertion which does not have differentiation as its objective.

The Present

Another essential idea in Rank's philosophy is the emphasis which he places on *present experience* instead of past. Rank himself was interested in the continuity of personality and recognized that the past cannot be artificially separated from the present. He insisted, however, that mere inquiry into the past of the patient or client could have no value in itself. Rankian philosophy recognizes that knowledge of the past can be helpful through understanding of the role which the past continues to play in the present. But the real past can never be duplicated. The present can be experienced, however, and through present experience in differentiating one's self from another, it is possible to understand the pattern of one's own will. Once the will is understood — once the individual has come into possession of it, so to speak — he can then be free to live it out affirmatively, or creatively.

Separation

Inherent in Rank's therapeutic philosophy is a positive outlook upon man's potentialities. Implicit in it, however, is a negative factor, namely, the factor of *separation*. Rankian philosophy does not deny that there is such a thing as a wholesome togetherness. In fact, it maintains that this is necessary for normal living. It also maintains, however, that there is a problem in being an individual and in realizing one's own creative potentialities.

In order to be an individual one must separate. Just as the infant first becomes an individual upon separation from the mother's body, so in a psychological sense individuality cannot be achieved without separation. Rank recognized that this has tremendous significance for therapy and accordingly put great emphasis on the end (or separating) phase of the treatment process. It is in this phase that the patient frees himself from the tie to the therapist. By separating he becomes individual. It is the task of the therapist, therefore, to foster constructive separation, that is, to make it possible for separation to occur with bearable guilt and with a full sense of one's own separateness or individuality.

Creativity

Man, as Rank sees him, is essentially a willing, doing type of being. He is capable of much *creativity* but often does not realize his own creative capacity. In neurosis, the natural creative tendency is used against the self, and the individual's potentialities are often wasted. The degree of creativeness which is to be found in different individuals varies enormously, but within his own limits every individual possesses the power to create. In some cultures and under certain conditions, creativity is encouraged. Since creative expression, however, involves the exercise of will, it is often blocked by outside and inside forces. Men want to live creatively, in fact, must do so for self-realization; but creating — being individual — being different — is too often equated with being bad. The group does not want the individual to separate himself, as he so often does in genuine creative behavior, and creative will is often blocked in this manner. The obligation of the therapist is to bring forth and to free creative impulse in the individual. It is an obligation to promote and to sanction that which must be looked upon as the birthright of every human being.

The above conceptions represent but a small part of Rank's total psychotherapeutic philosophy. They are the concepts, however, which serve as foundation stones in functional thinking. At this point, our treatment of these concepts is necessarily quite limited. Later we shall deal with them in greater detail (see Chapters 6 and 7).

Summary of Freudian and Rankian Concepts

Summing up, we might say that the chief conceptions of Freud which have been taken over and widely used by caseworkers are as follows: *Diagnostic*

1. Unconscious mind as a determinant of behavior.
2. Ambivalence in feeling and attitude.
3. Past experience as a determinant of present behavior.
4. The transference as essential to therapy.
5. Resistance as a factor to be dealt with in all helping.

The chief conceptions of Rankian thinking, taken over by the functional school and substituted for the above, are:

1. The will as an organizing force in personality.
2. Counter-will as a manifestation of the need of the individual to differentiate himself.
3. Present experience as a source of therapeutic development.
4. The significance of separation.
5. The inherent creativity of man.

These two sets of concepts represent the core, as it were, of the diagnostic-functional controversy. We shall therefore return to them at various points in this analysis.

The Diagnostic-Functional Controversy

Our analysis so far has pointed up certain basic concepts which have been used in the development of diagnostic and functional thinking. These concepts are not so radically different in character that they must necessarily lead to a great deal of conflict and cleavage. As a matter of actual fact, however, this is what has happened in the field of casework. There are two distinct types of casework practice today, two philosophies, two types of agency, and two distinct groups of adherents to one or the other approach. Members of the diagnostic and functional schools frequently wish to be known as individuals who have come under no influence from the other group. Many workers are proud that all their schooling, supervision, and work experience has been in a diagnostic or a functional setting, as the case may be. Articles and books written by members of one school are not read by those who are differently oriented, some of the professional schools of social work refuse to place students in agencies which are known to be partial to the opposite orientation, and even students who have not had the opportunity to become familiar with the two schools have been known to take a stand in favor of one or the other.

Such a state of affairs is advantageous to none, and the objective student will ask himself: What is responsible for it? Must it continue to exist?

Undoubtedly many personal and emotional factors enter into this kind of cleavage. One important factor, however, is lack of evolutionary perspective. In the intellectual history of the world, schools of thought have arisen in many areas. Even those which last for long periods of time undergo change, and many do not last. What happens is that they evolve, often merging with their opposites, so that new levels of thought and inquiry become possible. Instances might be drawn from almost any field. For example, Gardner Murphy, speaking of the development of psychology, states:

> Associationism and the Scottish school had quarreled through the latter half of the 18th century and the beginning of the 19th century without learning much from one another. The first half of the 19th century, however, found them borrowing so freely from one another that it becomes more and more difficult to be sure where one stops and the other begins.[19]

[19] Gardner Murphy, *Historical Introduction to Modern Psychology* (New York: Harcourt, Brace, 1950), p. 99.

Aside from the lack of evolutionary perspective, there is another factor involved in the cleavage between the two schools, namely, the lack of understanding of each other's language and basic assumptions. This is true for many experienced workers as well as for students, who, on becoming accustomed to the language and thought of one school, find it difficult if not impossible to take in the thinking of the other. ▬

Why is this so? Is there really such a distinct antithesis between the basic propositions of one school and those of the other?

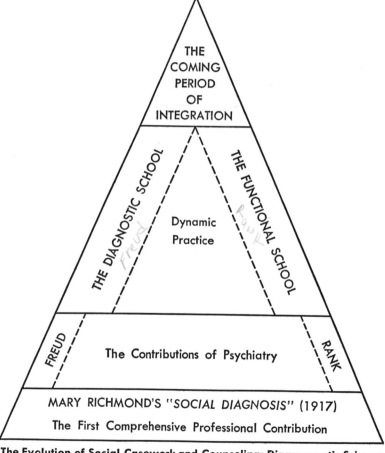

THE COMING PERIOD OF INTEGRATION

THE DIAGNOSTIC SCHOOL

THE FUNCTIONAL SCHOOL

Dynamic Practice

FREUD

RANK

The Contributions of Psychiatry

MARY RICHMOND'S "SOCIAL DIAGNOSIS" (1917)
The First Comprehensive Professional Contribution

The Evolution of Social Casework and Counseling: Diagrammatic Scheme

If not, just what is the substance of the diagnostic-functional controversy? This question cannot be answered in a few sentences. In order to answer it, in fact, it is necessary to consider not only the differences between the thinking of Freud and Rank, which we have touched upon in this chapter, but also the conceptual differences which developed at a later date. Subsequent chapters of this book will be largely concerned with an analysis of these differences. We shall also pay attention to certain likenesses, however, since it is on the basis of an understanding of what the two schools have in common that an ultimate reconciliation of the two points of view will take place.

The Dynamic Concept in Casework and Counseling

What both schools have in common is the dynamic content which inheres in their respective philosophies. Both attempt to explain why human beings act as they do, and both are interested in the fundamental problem of how one human being influences another. The way in which client and helping person interact with each other — the effect which the worker's verbal comments and the attitudes which he expresses non-verbally have upon the client, and vice versa — should be their essential focus of interest. Both schools have been content up until now, however, with philosophizing in very broad and general terms about this, instead of studying scientifically what happens in situations where one person attempts to help another. Both schools must move on to this type of study. When they do so, they will find that their outlook, and the practice which results from it, will be much more dynamic than it has been in the past.

What do we mean by the term "dynamic"? Why do we choose it as the term which most fully expresses the character of the best actual practice of today, if not all of the theory on which such practice is supposedly based?

By the term "dynamic" we mean to refer to the propelling forces which are involved in psychological and social change. The connotations of the term are causal. When two psychological streams come into interplay with each other, a kind of foment results, just as it does when two streams of water converge. Two different personalities — two different sets of attitudes — cannot meet without something happening. What takes place may not be significant change, nor will it necessarily be helpful. There will be considerable stirring, however, especially if the one person is really seeking help and the other is disposed to give it. A person generally does not seek help unless there has been considerable unrest within him. When he meets with the one who is to help him, therefore, the unrest which he has already experienced may be accentuated. One "stream of consciousness" is brought into play with another and a dynamic fomentation results.

This fomentation must be studied. The conditions under which it will yield desirable results, and those under which it will not, must be discovered. Obviously the two converging "streams" can negate each other, just as two firemen with hoses trained against each other can undo the beneficial work which each might have started. Dynamics in the realm of psychology and social situations are usually much more complicated than they are in the physical world, and they are therefore much more difficult to understand and control. It is not impossible, however, to analyze what goes on when two psychological forces converge. The conceptual systems which both schools have developed can be very useful in such analysis, as we shall try to show in Chapter 7.

We live in a changing world, and the problems which clients bring to caseworkers are always problems of change. Sometimes it is a matter of change taking place within an individual and resisted by those who may be subject to it in the world outside. For example, a young person may reach a point in personal experience where he is ready to leave his parental home and go to live elsewhere for schooling, work, or the establishment of his own home and family. His parents, however, may not be ready to let him leave, and much struggle may result. Either the parents or the young person, or both, may come for casework or counseling help in such a situation. Or the case may be reversed. An opportunity to leave home may be available, but the young person may resist it. In this instance, it is a matter of the inability of the person himself to accept change in the outer world. The perplexity which arises in such a situation may result in his coming for casework or counseling help. The caseworker or counseler is then confronted with a situation in which there has been a good deal of tension and unrest, and to this situation he must bring his own psychological orientation, which will be different from that of any of the other persons involved. This injection of a new and different orientation into the situation can be like pouring oil on the flames and it should be done with the same kind of caution. The help-taking and the help-giving situation, in other words, is one fraught with explosive potentialities.

By "dynamic" casework and counseling, therefore, we mean casework and counseling focused on change — change within or outside the individual — change which produces change. In the atomic age this has come to be known as the "chain reaction." Dynamic casework and counseling is a type of help in which client and worker start something, and a "process" or a sequence of events follows. This is literally what takes place in any casework or counseling contact.

This book is an effort to explore the dynamic implications of some of the conceptions which have been the preoccupation of social workers of both schools for the past decade or more, and to shift emphasis to a basic concept which has been inherent in the thinking of all who would call themselves professional. This, the *dynamic concept,* in fact permeates all of present-day physical as well as social science. It is a concept fraught with tremendous implications for both theory and practice, and one which, if understood in all its ramifications, can do much to bring theory and practice into harmony with each other. Theory and practice must be brought together — and they can be through analysis of the dynamic aspects of practice. When this takes place a new type of casework thinking — a type that can be called truly dynamic — will come into existence.

2

CONFLICTING ORIENTATIONS

In the late twenties and early thirties, just a little over a decade after the publication of *Social Diagnosis,* two schools of thought and two types of casework practice began to emerge. The publication of Virginia Robinson's *A Changing Psychology in Social Casework* [1] served as a kind of fomenting factor, bringing into conflict with each other the two rival orientations which had resulted from the assimilation of different parts of Mary Richmond's philosophy and the conflicting therapeutic philosophies of Freud and Rank. Originally the conflict between the two groups of caseworkers was not very strong. Those who were oriented to the diagnostic thinking of Mary Richmond and the psychoanalytic thinking of Freud still seemed to have much in common with those who could no longer see very much of value in Mary Richmond's method and

[1] Chapel Hill: University of North Carolina Press, 1930.

who favored the therapeutic philosophy of Rank. At first, it was as though both groups felt the appropriateness of maintaining a tentative and experimental outlook. Both were filled with enthusiasm for their newly acquired psychiatric orientation. They realized that they still had much to learn, however, and they were not ready to take authoritative or dogmatic positions. Within a very few years, however, definite convictions began to develop and two distinct approaches began to emerge.

Both groups had shifted away from an emphasis on the environmental or the social, and both looked to psychological or personality factors as a proper sphere of interest and activity for the caseworker. With the realization, however, that caseworkers had taken on two distinct ways of approaching problems of personality, two descriptive terms differentiating the two approaches, namely, "dynamic passivity" and "relationship therapy," came into usage. Dynamic passivity was the term used to describe practice which was primarily Freudian in orientation, although there was not much clarity with regard to the derivation of the term, while relationship therapy meant a type of practice built upon the philosophy of Otto Rank. Let us look into the kinds of practice which these two opposite conceptions described.

Dynamic Passivity

As we have indicated, dynamic passivity was a phrase used by many to describe a method of listening to the client similar to that which the Freudian analyst practiced. The implications of the term "dynamic" in this phrase were rather vague. It was believed, however, that a passive and receptive role assumed by the worker would stimulate or encourage further expression on the part of the client. The expression of one thought or feeling would lead to another and there would be a kind of unwinding of repressed feelings and attitudes. This unwinding would take place dynamically, that is to say, the client would do it himself, if the worker served as a receptive and accepting audience. This is quite a different conception of dynamics from that presented in this book. Our view of a truly dynamic social or psychological situation is one in which the factor of *interaction* between client and worker is of primary importance. The worker does not simply serve as a passive audience, but instead he responds quite actively to the client's presentations. He reacts to the client and the client reacts to him. Illustrations of this latter approach are given in Chapers 5 and 7. For the present, however, it is important that we understand what was meant by *dynamic passivity*.

In passively listening to what the client had to say, and allowing him to express his feelings, the caseworker who practiced dynamic passivity paralleled the approach of the Freudian analyst who gave his patient an opportunity to experience a "cathartic release" in a relationship with himself. The cathartic release of repressed feelings, it was recognized by Freudian analysts, was insufficient, and a living out of such feeling in relation to the analyst (abreaction) was considered necessary for therapy. Many caseworkers, however, were quite content with the mere expression of feeling — particularly the feeling of hostility. Repressed hostility was thought to be a principal cause of difficulty, and the expression of hostility by the client was therefore welcomed.

The worker's role in all of this was a passive one — a listening, following one. The client's role, on the other hand, was an active one — a talking, unburdening one. As he talked and unburdened himself of feelings of guilt, fear, hostility, and so on, a change supposedly took place within him. The person he formerly hated he might now love, or the one for whom he professed love he might hate or fear. Once expressed, once brought out of the unconscious, these formerly repressed feelings would not be so troublesome. They would no longer block the person who had until now been subject to them. Instead their very expression would have to be regarded as therapeutic. The worker's willingness to listen sympathetically and understandingly served as a dynamic factor. The client was encouraged by this attitude to talk more and more and in so doing to free himself of the secret, troublesome, and conflicting feelings which were the cause of all his difficulty. This procedure, which followed Freudian theory and method, came into common usage in case-work practice. It was not always called dynamic passivity and it was not always recognized as Freudian in origin. Few case-workers who followed this practice, however, doubted the value of a passive role on the part of the worker.

A notable exception to the passive role of the worker was history-taking, where Freudian philosophy was translated into a type of activity quite different from the role of the worker in the rest of treatment. Here the worker sought specific factual material, particularly with regard to the client's childhood and family experience. Workers who practiced this way often felt that the client had to talk about his past and about members of his family, since this was where the cause of the difficulty lay. The principle of determinism in psychic life was a guiding one for workers who practiced in this manner. Every psychic manifesta-tion had a cause, and the cause was to be found generally in a repressed experience. If allowed to talk sufficiently, a patient or client would bring this repressed experience into the light of day, and when this occurred, it would lose its potency. Proceed-ing on the principle that in removing the cause one would re-move the symptoms or the effect, caseworkers sometimes held lengthy interviews with clients which were devoted almost ex-clusively to discovery of the cause of the difficulty. The cause was seen as some incident or some experience which took place in the past, and as much understanding of the past as one could possibly get was therefore sought.

An extremely important factor in the practice of dynamic passivity was the *transference*. In the process of expressing important feelings, the client would often develop an affection for the worker who received all that he expressed with such acceptance and understanding. This seemed natural and accept-able enough to the worker, who had come to look upon the transference as a desirable phenomenon. Since it was hostility or aggression that had caused much of the client's trouble, a love experience could only be helpful, and the transference was therefore looked upon as a wholesome development. It was certainly to be regarded as one of the dynamic factors in dynamic passivity and without it one could not hope to have much influence upon the client.

With a positive transference, however, the client might be expected to experience genuine therapy. Positive feeling, supplanting a former negative frame of mind, would be expressed to the worker, who was seen in much the same light as the mother and father figures of infancy and childhood and loved in much the same manner. The difference lay in the fact that the worker as mother or father figure was non-condemning and fully accepting. The client could therefore love with greater safety and he could express himself more fully. There would be self-realization in this, because this time the client could love without suppressing hitherto condemned feelings.

Associated with the transference was the client's resistance, which required a great deal of the worker's attention. The client was seen as resisting the expression of hitherto repressed feeling, and as resisting the worker's interpretation of the nature of this feeling. Above all, the client would resist an interpretation of the nature of the transference, since he wished to make a real love object of the worker. Where the worker's role called for interpretation of the client's resistance, he of course could not remain passive. Aside from this, and from history-taking, however, the role of the worker was regarded as primarily a passive one by all who wished to translate Freudian philosophy into casework practice.

As an example of dynamic passivity we might cite the handling of a case in child guidance during the early thirties. Aaron, twelve years old, was brought for child guidance because of nocturnal enuresis. He was a shy boy who tended to withdraw from the more aggressive boys of the neighborhood and school environment. He was an only child, somewhat displeasing to his father who wanted him to show more "manly" characteristics. The mother was quite devoted to him, but she worked in addition to keeping house, and she could not give him all of the attention he seemed to want.

When Aaron was brought to the agency to see the worker, he met with a great deal of friendly interest. There was no reference whatever to the reason why he was coming, nor to what the agency or the worker might attempt to do for him. The worker wanted him to feel comfortable and free to talk, and responded in a warm way to the boy's willingness to tell about his play activities, the subjects that he liked in school, his favorite baseball team, and his other interests. Aaron spoke of such things with ease and the worker was content as long as Aaron kept talking. No attempt was made during the beginning period to interpret any part of what he talked about as related to his symptom, nor for that matter to what the worker saw as his basic problem.

In this instance, the boy's enuresis was seen as a conversion symptom through which he attempted to secure in an infantile way the attention of his mother who was not available to him during the day. The father's displeasure in the boy's lack of manly characteristics was seen as adding to his insecurity. The worker's task was therefore viewed as one of providing as much security through favorable attention as possible, thus making up for what was lacking in his home life.

Proceeding on this assumption, the worker said nothing at any time to Aaron which might be considered threatening. Instead he encouraged the boy to talk about anything that was of interest to him. This Aaron did, not infrequently with a view to what might be of interest to the worker too. He came each week, without fail, for a period of three years, excluding only the worker's vacations. Each time he would sit down after an exchange of greetings and relate some tale in which he himself played a heroic role. There were school fights in which he would emerge victorious and encounters with street gangs where he would succeed in outwitting them. When his mother or father came into these verbal fantasies, usually making some demand of him, he would have no trouble at all in satisfying or even exceeding the demand.

Few of Aaron's stories had anything to do with the future, and he brought out spontaneously very little material which related to the past. His mother had given a detailed account of his early years, but Aaron showed little interest in talking along such lines, although the worker did attempt to encourage this. Usually he gave an account of some exploit which supposedly had occurred during the week. Sometimes Aaron would proceed in a very eager way to tell his story and sometimes he would have a bit of difficulty getting started. Each interview, however, consisted of a recital of some supposedly current experience to which the worker would listen with a great deal of interest. As time went on an occasional question was raised by the worker with a view to encourage Aaron to elaborate or fill out his story. There was no challenge in these questions, however, and nothing to indicate that the worker did not take the boy's fantasies as the truth.

When the mother was seen she spoke about the positive feeling that Aaron had developed toward the worker, and she reported also that there was considerable improvement as far as his symptom was concerned. The boy gave no thought to ending the contact, nor did the worker, until the third year when it became apparent that the worker could not continue. The worker then spoke with Aaron about the possibility of his getting along without coming during the following year, and this suggestion the boy met with a great deal of resistance. He asserted his feeling that he did not want to stop coming, and the worker tried at this point to explain why he would like to come indefinitely as well as the reasons why it would be impossible to continue beyond a few months. Here for the first time difficulty arose between the worker and the boy who naturally regarded this turn of events as a kind of desertion. The worker tried to assure Aaron of his friendly interest, and pointed out that he himself ought to be relieved not to have to come. Aaron insisted that he did want to keep coming, despite the fact that he was getting on quite well now. His symptom had disappeared (this was known through contact with the mother but never actually discussed with the boy himself), but he felt he had made a friend and he wanted to continue the friendship. The contact ended, therefore, only when the worker's transfer to another position made it impossible to continue. There was some implicit understanding that it would have to end, but never any real and explicit agreement.

This case would be handled in a much more active way today by either a diagnostic or a functionally oriented worker. In the days of dynamic passivity, however, the worker was passive in a very literal sense of the term. In an interview of an hour with a boy like Aaron, the worker would sometimes make only two or three comments and these would often be quite noncommittal. Through smiles, frequent nodding, and general friendly demeanor the worker would show his interest and his accepting attitude. His activity, however, would sometimes be limited to this. Occasionally he would interpret the meaning of something the client might say, but would usually exercise a great deal of caution in doing so. The prevailing principle was to "keep hands off" as much as possible and to let the client cure himself by talking out whatever was troubling him. In some instances, as in the case of Aaron, this approach was undoubtedly helpful. When it was, the improvement that took place was frequently seen as the direct result of a transference, which enabled the client to live out formerly repressed impulses and feelings in an atmosphere that was friendly, yet neutral.

Relationship Therapy

Relationship therapy was a term used by caseworkers who were Rankian in orientation to describe a type of casework practice which was not radically different from the above, but which did differ in certain respects. The early Rankian workers did not distinguish relationship therapy from the practice of casework. In this they were not clear, any more than were the Freudian workers who also did not distinguish their practice from that of the analysts. Although the distinction between casework and therapy was lacking, relationship therapy was described quite succinctly by Dr. Jessie Taft, who stated: "Relationship therapy is nothing but an opportunity to experience more completely than is ordinarily possible, the direction, depth and ambivalence of the impulses which relate the self to the other, to outer reality, and to discover firsthand the possibility of their organization into an autonomous, creative will." [2]

Relationship therapy thus attempted to meet the client's problem by giving him an opportunity for self-expression, just as dynamic passivity did. However, it was not as much concerned with the historical cause of the difficulty as was the Freudian-oriented passive approach. Relationship therapy assumed that it was the *willing* person who was seeking the help of the caseworker or the therapist, and that he could not be helped unless his will was recognized and understood and its constructive aspects substantiated. This was what required understanding, acceptance, and corroboration. Denial of one's real will, pretending that one did not have a will at all, or guilt over any excess of will needed to be faced.

In relationship therapy it was assumed that one could enter into a relationship with another person who was seeking help — and be helpful — only if one understood the conditions under which therapy could take place. The therapist had to function in a situation in which the will in its changing forms and in its opposite aspects could be projected against a stable background. In order to achieve such stability, the conditions under which the therapist functioned had to be controlled. The time, the place, and the fee had to be set. Within this framework there would be a movement through a beginning, middle, and end phase of a relationship. In each of these the patient or client would express his will, often trying to change the conditions or to deny the true nature of the relationship, or the phase of it

[2] Jessie Taft, *The Dynamics of Therapy in a Controlled Relationship* (New York: Macmillan, 1933), p. 288.

which he was experiencing. While beginning, he might act as though he were ending. While ending, he might act as though he were just beginning. One day the time originally chosen might seem to him to be just right. On another day it might seem all wrong. Both feelings would be seen as reflecting opposite sides of the same will, since it is the will itself which is the constant center of interest for the Rankian therapist, rather than any particular momentary manifestation of it. Once these opposites were projected onto the therapist (expressed to him) he would not react to them literally, but would reflect them back to the client as manifestations of the same fundamental will. Then a comprehension or an "owning" of the will itself, in so far as it is concerned with the business of relating to others, at least, would become possible.

The aim of Rankian therapy is acceptance of one's will, acceptance in which one finds the freedom to be one's self. Neither the imitation of another self nor the mere yielding to the will of another is acceptable. One's own will must be discovered, in all its duality, and once discovered it must be granted freedom of expression in its integrated, that is to say, its constructive or creative form. The destructive will is always present and cannot be denied. But in an integrated will the constructive or creative will is dominant. Relationship therapy worked toward this end. In the course of relationship therapy it was assumed that a struggle would have to take place — a struggle in which two wills, the professional will of the worker and the personal will of the client, would stand at odds with each other. In the course of this struggle there would be a therapeutic development. Excess will would be given up, or the assertion of hitherto denied will would take place. In any case, the will itself was the central focus of interest.

It may be of interest at this point to look at the case of Aaron once again (page 45) and to consider some of the ways in which treatment of such a boy might have been different, had he been helped by a worker oriented to relationship therapy. First of all, let us consider whether it would be possible for the worker to take as passive a role as that which we have described. The answer to this question is that the worker in relationship therapy could *not* be as passive as Aaron's worker was. He would not simply listen to the boy's fantasies, but instead would give attention to *a structure* within which he and the boy were to work. The question of how long the interviews might continue, whether for a year or two or three, might be taken up in the very beginning of the case. An answer would not necessarily be reached, but a tentative time limit might be considered. Whether or not the interviews would always take place in the same setting might be discussed, along with any problems that this might cause for the boy. If a fee were being paid, attention might be given to this also. In any case, it is not likely that the worker would proceed without some mutual understanding regarding *the conditions* under which the help would be given.

Even the question of the nature of the relationship itself might have been taken up at an early point. Was this to be a friendship? If not, how would it differ from the friendships the boy has experienced in the past? Would the worker turn out to be like a teacher, or a minister, or would this relationship be something different from anything else the boy had ever known? Just what was the worker going to try to do for him, and why? What would the worker expect of him? Any or all of these questions might have been taken up in the early interviews by the worker oriented to relationship therapy.

Another important difference would be the worker's orientation to the will of the client. What use would the boy want to make of the worker? Was his approach to the worker a denying or evading one? Did he want to outwit the worker? Was he afraid of what the worker might want to do to him, that is, afraid of the worker's will? How much conscious understanding could he allow himself regarding the power of his own will to resist those who would make demands of him? Did he have any disposition to give in to the will of others? These questions would be ever present in the worker's mind, and he not only would try to discover the answers to them, but he also might actively bring to the boy his own understanding of what was going on between the two of them in this respect.

In other words, a great deal of attention would be given by the worker in relationship therapy to the part played by the will of the client *in this particular relationship*. The worker would not think in terms of a transference, positive or negative, nor would he be particularly concerned with resistance that the boy might show to any interpretation of particular feelings which he might have. Instead, the worker would be concerned with the nature of the "will struggle" which was going on between the boy and himself. Was the boy using verbal fantasies to keep the worker interested and thereby to avoid any real clash with him? Was there pretense and denial of his will in the sustained positive tone of the relationship? Would the worker have to do anything about this? Would he have to recognize the real nature of the boy's will — particularly as it expressed itself in relation to the worker — before any fundamental help could be given?

Perhaps enough has been said to point up the difference in approach in dynamic passivity and relationship therapy. Neither approach is followed in any rigid way by caseworkers and counselors today, since one has developed into the diagnostic and the other into the functional method. It may be of interest, however, to note that in both dynamic passivity and relationship therapy there is an attempt to get down to fundamentals. The worker in dynamic passivity was interested in diagnosing the cause of the difficulty and in substituting a situation in which the cause as he saw it would no longer hold sway. His method was to relate to the client in a warm, interested and supportive way and to let the client talk out his problem in whatever way seemed natural. The client did not have to face or grapple with the problem, *as such*. If his way of expressing himself was a roundabout one, that might mean that more time would be taken, but nothing would be lost. The therapy would proceed from within the client himself, in a positive setting provided by the worker, and it would take place with a minimum of interference or direction from outside. An unraveling would occur within the client, while the worker simply set the stage for it, and the core of the problem would be bared. Sometimes, as in the case of Aaron, little attention would be given to explicit recognition of the cause with the client himself, but instead an attempt would be made to create a situation in which there was no repetition of the cause of the problem. In any event, however, the worker would be oriented to what he regarded as fundamentals, rather than to symptoms.

This was equally true in relationship therapy, where in the attention given to the will of the client, an effort was made to deal with the most basic factor involved in the problem. Both dynamic passivity and relationship therapy were psychologically oriented. Both were based on newly acquired learning from the field of psychiatry in which most stress was placed on underlying causes. Both represented a move away from a focus of interest that was predominantly social, and both created a problem for caseworkers, namely, whether they would have to become psychotherapists in order to do the job which seemed to be called for by their respective theoretical orientations.

The Conflict Between Relief-Giving and Therapy

This problem was not so disturbing to many caseworkers as perhaps it should have been. Most caseworkers of this era really wanted to be psychotherapists; this was true for those who practiced dynamic passivity as well as for those who were oriented to relationship therapy. While possessing this kind of desire, however, most workers were actually quite actively engaged in giving relief and in administering other social services. They therefore experienced more than a little conflict over the area which was to get their major attention.

Many caseworkers attempted to reconcile their two conflicting interests, as Grace Marcus so ably showed in her book, *Some Aspects of Relief*,[3] by putting one at the service of the other. Relief would be used at times as a means of controlling the client

[3] New York: Charity Organization Society, 1929.

or subjecting him to the worker's therapeutic interest and was frequently spoken of as a "tool in treatment." At the same time, there was enough genuine interest in relief as such — especially after the beginning of the depression period — so that caseworkers as a whole could not be content to use it solely for purposes of practicing psychotherapy of one variety or another on unwilling recipients. As Dorothy G. Burpee of the Boston Family Welfare Society wrote in 1930,[4] in an article reviewing Miss Marcus's book, "One has but to listen in on almost any gathering of family caseworkers to realize that the two most disturbing problems uppermost in their minds are those of relief and the application of psychiatric principles in family casework."

In *Some Aspects of Relief,* Miss Marcus, who was vitally interested in the relationship of casework and mental hygiene, wrote that "Any attempt to appraise current relief practices is shortly converted into an appraisal of the methods being used to investigate, diagnose and treat underlying problems of physical health, family relationships, employment, etc., as problems which cause or contribute to the need for relief." What caseworkers were occupied with, in other words, was the problem of how they could relate their interest in psychotherapy to the practical tasks and services which clients sought from them. Few clients approached caseworkers at this date for psychotherapy. Most clients came for other services, but the worker was often caught in the conflict between his own interest in psychotherapy and the client's interest in concrete services, and many different attempts were made to reconcile the two.

In this attempt to reconcile these two opposite interests many agencies operated on the principle of "levels of casework." Thus an article by Florence Hollis, then of the Family Society of Philadelphia, recognized that 52 per cent of the applicants for family agency service came with only an economic need.[5] The

---

4 Dorothy G. Burpee, "Further Aspects of Relief, an Extended Review of Grace Marcus's *Some Aspects of Relief," The Family,* 11:58–61 (April, 1930).

5 Florence Hollis, "The Function of a Family Agency," *The Family,* 12:186–191 (October, 1931).

same article distinguished three types of service rendered by the agency, namely, economic help, environmental opportunities, and therapy. In a later paper,[6] Miss Hollis, who was by then with the Cleveland Associated Charities, stated: "Unfortunately the recently developed form of casework known as therapy is regarded all too often as something apart from the main body of casework." This article cites a case example in which the worker felt that the client, who needed help on an economic or opportunity level, could use the insight gained from therapy. An article by Marjory Boggs of the Cleveland Associated Charities [7] stated, "At this point in the evolution of casework, we seem to see the caseworker assuming roles ranging anywhere from single manipulative measures and ameliorative services to intensive individual therapy, but with a consciousness of purpose and objectives and a growing ability to articulate methods and techniques." Bertha Reynolds, in a report of a Committee appointed at the Milford Conference, which dealt with generic and specific aspects of casework, wrote in February, 1933,[8] "Social casework . . . has two poles of interest — the individual and his environment . . . the function of social casework is not to treat the individual alone nor his environment alone, but the process of adaptation, which is a dynamic interaction between the two."

These articles and others gave recognition to the non-psychiatric aspects of casework. That most caseworkers in the thirties were engrossed with the therapeutic aspects of their job, however, is confirmed by Florence R. Day, then of the Family Welfare Association of America, who wrote in March, 1937,[9] "I have the feeling that we overstress psychiatry as the one thing that has happened in the last ten years to affect casework practice."

[6] Florence Hollis, "Some Contributions of Therapy to Generalized Casework Practice," *The Family*, 15:328–334 (February, 1935).

[7] Marjory Boggs, "Present Trends in the Caseworker's Role in Treatment," *The Family*, 13:158–162 (July, 1932).

[8] Bertha Reynolds, "Can Social Casework Be Interpreted to a Community as a Basic Approach to Human Problems?" *The Family*, 13:336–342 (February, 1933).

[9] Florence R. Day, "Changing Practice in Casework Treatment," *The Family*, 18:3–9 (March, 1937).

It is interesting, too, that a psychiatrist addressing a State Conference of Social Work should speak as follows:

> The psychiatrist is quite suspicious about the trend toward therapy in social work because he wonders whether psychotherapy is not just a panacea for solving human ills. Social work, not being an independent discipline and being essentially a woman's profession, has tended to look for some one remedy for its problems. At one time it was legislation, then it was social reform, then it was education, then it was medicine itself, and now it is psychiatry.[10]

While workers in private agencies were thus concerning themselves with therapy in one form or another — dynamic passivity or relationship therapy — a development was taking place in another area which was to have a profound effect upon casework. During the decade of the thirties public relief agencies were developing all over the country, and in these agencies there was obviously little place for therapy as such. Widespread unemployment brought to the private agencies first, and then to the public agencies, a new clientele — a group of clients who formerly had been quite self-sufficient and obviously did not require therapy. The extent of need, and the hope that casework could play a part in meeting the need, brought casework into public view, and its aims and intentions could no longer be confined to the inner circle of a few professionals. As Dorothy L. Book, then of the Brooklyn Bureau of Charities, put it,[11] "Never before has the community at large been so interested in social work. With front page publicity daily, the entire community is aware of the situation, bringing a new influence into casework."

A community situation had arisen, in other words, with which neither dynamic passivity nor relationship therapy could deal. Thousands of able-bodied and mentally sound individuals and families needed relief, not psychotherapy, and the community

10 J. Kasanin, "A Critique of Some of the Newer Trends in Casework," *The Family*, 16:35–39 (April, 1935).
11 Dorothy L. Book, "Meeting the Pressure," *The Family*, 12:21–22 (March, 1931).

turned to social work with this problem. Social workers were unwilling to turn over the problem to business administrators, politicians, and others. Yet many were reluctant to give up the fascination and the personal satisfaction which they found in therapeutically-oriented casework. Hundreds of caseworkers did overcome their conflict, however, and entered the field of public relief.

The conditions of public relief made it impossible to practice passively. Case loads were high, ten- to fifteen-minute interviews were common, much factual information had to be secured, and there simply was no time to deal deeply or extensively with personality problems, even though the worker might be interested in doing so. How, then, were workers who wished to do more than a superficial job of relief-giving to serve their clientele effectively?

It was at this juncture that the Rankian orientation to the use of structure came into prominence, and a way presented itself of administering public assistance with psychological understanding. This way consisted of utilization of the many procedures — or the structure — of the public relief agency.[12] Just as the worker, in relationship therapy, was interested in the whole question of having an explicit understanding with the client regarding time limits, the fee, if there was one, and other limiting factors, so the public relief worker could now bring to the attention of his client a part of the structure within which he had to work, namely, *the conditions of eligibility* for public assistance.

The requirements for eligibility were set forth in the law and in many written regulations and procedures. Each worker had to be oriented to them and each client had to have an understanding of what he must do to prove his eligibility. The question of eligibility, in other words, was a mutual concern, though client and worker approached it from different standpoints. The client wanted the relief, and his will was directed toward getting

[12] Cf. Jessie Taft, "Function as the Basis of Development in Social Work Processes," *AAPSW Newsletter*, vol. 9 (1940), no. 1. See also Herbert H. Aptekar, "The Significance of Structure in the Practice of Casework," *The Family*, 24:375–381 (February, 1944).

it. The worker, on the other hand, might like personally to see the client get assistance, but it was his function to administer it only if the conditions of eligibility were properly met. His professional responsibility, in other words, was to recommend assistance once the client had done his share in providing the information necessary to establish his eligibility. Many clients, however, did not want to provide the information which was requested, and some would not accept the requirements for eligibility as being applicable to their particular situations. When this was so, a will-struggle would sometimes ensue between client and worker and there was a question as to who would yield.

The training problem in public relief work was therefore looked upon by the Rankians as one of orienting workers to the conditions of eligibility, as well as to the rest of the structural framework within which they would have to operate, and of helping them to understand what went on in a will-struggle which might develop with any client over eligibility requirements or some other similar structural factor. In order to transform such a will-struggle into something that might ultimately be helpful to the client, the worker would have to accept the fact that conflict would arise between his clients and himself and that it would be his responsibility to handle this conflict in such a manner that it would become easier for the client to give in, or to yield, on matters where he could satisfy agency requirements, but where he was determined not to for reasons of pride or fear. The feelings which the worker needed to understand were the feelings which blocked the client from doing whatever was needed by the agency to give him the assistance he wanted.

Important parallels were thus observed between the public relief situation and the practice of relationship therapy. Moreover, it seemed quite clear that if the worker in public relief could be oriented to the understanding of his function, to identification with it and to clear presentation and maintenance of it, then what the client might have to go through, as far as will-struggle was concerned, might be greatly facilitated. When the worker has conflict himself over such matters, it is difficult if not impossible for him to help the client get over his conflict. What needed to be taught, therefore, was how the worker could use whatever he knew and believed in about his function — and the conditions under which it could best be administered.

As we have indicated, much attention had been given by the Rankians, before public relief became so important in social work, to the problem of will. Less attention had been given, however, to function and structure and to the manner in which worker and client relate to or make use of them. With public relief experience, the emphasis was shifted and Rankian workers began to feel that the function of an agency, and the structure within which the worker operated, could be used advantageously in helping the client work out a will problem. Prior to this public relief experience, they had been conscious, to be sure, of the function or the services they were administering. Nowhere, however, did function and structure loom so large as in the public agency. Here everything was hedged in, so to speak, with law, regulation, policy, and procedure. In the private agency it was possible to overlook this aspect and to become immersed in the client's problem. In the public agency this was not so. Rankian workers therefore became tremendously interested in the exploitation of function and looked into the possibilities for centering attention on this aspect of the caseworker's job in almost every type of setting.

Interest in Function

Up until this time Rankian workers had never really distinguished between relationship therapy and casework. The two terms were used synonymously, and in practice too there was little distinction. With the new interest in function and structure, however, stimulated by casework experience with public relief, it became possible to make a clear-cut distinction between casework and relationship therapy. There were those persons who maintained that public assistance was not casework in any true sense of the term, and the possibilities for a new type of

casework which were inherent in it of course escaped them. But
to workers who had always been interested to some extent in
the utilization of structure, the public relief situation opened up
new possibilities. Since it was apparent that the very first decision which had to be made in the administration of public
assistance was whether or not the client was eligible, the *function*
of the worker was seen as one centering on the matter of eligibility. The client had to participate in establishing his eligibility,
and in doing so there was an opportunity for him to call upon his
own strength and to realize some of his own capability. Moreover, eligibility could be established only within a framework
of agency policy and procedures. These had to be made known
to the client, and this too was the worker's function. In arriving
at the final conclusion regarding the eligibility, responsibility
had to be shared. The worker was responsible for the presentation of agency policy and procedure; the client, for demonstrating
that his specific circumstances were such as to make him eligible.
Within this framework the different obligations of client and
worker emerged clearly, and this clarification of responsibility
permitted movement on the part of the client from an original
request or demand to the establishment of his eligibility for public assistance.

In order to see what was involved concretely, let us take a
typical example of an application for public assistance during
the depression period of the early thirties. Many families which
might never have applied for help under normal economic circumstances came to social agencies during the depression period
because of the breadwinner's prolonged unemployment. Many
such families owned their own homes and had accumulated savings. When savings were exhausted, however, and when borrow-
ing capacity too had been exhausted, there was nothing else to
do but to apply for public assistance. The head of the household
in many such instances was a person who was proud of his independence. He did not want relief. What he wanted was employment. He would apply for relief with the greatest reluctance.
When he appeared at the office of the public assistance agency

and was told that he would have to wait, sometimes with hundreds of other applicants, for hours before he could be seen, his resistance to taking relief was often intensified. He would insist that he did not want relief — all he wanted was a job. When given a four-page application form to fill out, he would complain of red tape and maintain that much of the information wanted was unnecessary in his case. He was particularly resentful of the fact that former employers, relatives, and others would have to know of his application for relief, and it was not uncommon for him to storm out of the office saying that he would starve or steal rather than comply with the ridiculous demands which the agency was making.

Calm and soft-spoken explanation to the effect that this was what was required of everyone would sometimes help, but in many instances much more was required. It was necessary to recognize the resentful feeling, and particularly the sense of frustration which the applicant was experiencing. What was being frustrated, of course, was the client's will — his will to be independent and respected. He wanted to be treated as an individual, but here he was regarded as a case — one out of thousands. It was natural for him to look on the worker as a much more fortunate person and to envy the fact that the worker had a job. It was natural, too, for him to personalize the situation and to feel that the worker was either for or against him. Being lenient in requirements would mean being *for* him. Insisting on compliance would mean being *against* him.

The client, in other words, was all set for a will-struggle, and when the worker confronted him with some of the necessities of the situation, he was often seething with bitterness and resentment.

How, then, could the worker approach this person in such a manner as to lessen his bitter feeling and make it possible for him to get the relief which, in most instances, he needed so desperately? The Rankian group felt that they had a way, and in public relief experience they were able to put it to the test. This way was to ask the worker to concentrate on one part of the total situation, to keep oriented to that part, and to let the client be responsible for the rest. The part the worker was to concentrate on was his *function*. He could not become involved in any extensive way in the psychology of the applicant, partly because of the practical conditions under which he worked, but also because of the limitations of his own knowledge. However, if the worker concentrated on what he could do — what he in fact had to do — and if he allowed the client the freedom to react in whatever way he chose, then he would be doing justice to all parties involved, namely, the state which determined the conditions of eligibility and which entrusted him to administer a function, the client who should meet with a minimum of interference in his personal life when he needed relief, and himself. He agreed when he took the job to administer public assistance carefully and knowingly; he did not undertake to serve as a therapist for all emotional ills. In carrying through with function, he would not be exceeding the limits of his own capacities.

This philosophy appealed to many who felt that much restorative power resided within the client himself, and that the more one left him alone, the more apt he would be to solve his own problem. It appealed also to many who felt that a will-struggle was necessary in any help-taking situation, and that the way to facilitate the working out of this struggle was to hold firm to a set of conditions which represented the function of the worker, thus allowing the client to distinguish what he might will from the necessities under which the worker must function. The conditions of eligibility in the public relief agency served as a clear-cut instrument which could be used in this way, and workers who were trained in the functional approach were glad to have them available, even when they personally did not identify with some of the eligibility requirements of the agency.

Many questions were left in the minds of workers who were not oriented functionally, about how the client came to feel that he was recognized or understood as a person, and how he worked through the will-struggle without some special assistance directed towards that end. The functional worker saw the client as engaged in a will-struggle, but did the client himself look on it that way? How did a simple or clear presentation of the function, or the worker's "holding to" it, enable him to work through the conflict over what he actually needed and the way he felt about taking it. There was question too about whether this approach did not take it for granted that the client's attitude toward the agency and the worker was necessarily negative. Weren't there some people who approached the help-taking situation in a more positive way? Did they too have to go through a struggle with themselves and with the worker? If so, did one approach them in precisely the same spirit as those who were openly negative?

Despite the many questions which were raised about the functional approach as it was practiced in the public relief situation, it did extend itself to other areas of practice.[13] The field of child placement looked into the possibilities for functional practice, and correctional work also explored the possibilities. In fact, every type of agency and every specialized service began to look at whether the function of the agency could be clarified, first for the worker, and then by the worker for the client. Through "clarification of function" it was felt that the worker and client would come into a truer relationship to each other. Each would know what to expect of the other, or would at least come to know, and this knowledge would facilitate the worker's administration of the service and the client's reception of it. How the worker would relate to the will of the client would be different in each different type of functional setting. Agencies of various types proceeded to work this out for their particular functions, and with this, the functional school of casework developed rapidly.

Up until the development of the functional approach, casework was practiced almost exclusively under agency auspices. But in spite of this the place of the agency in the profession was quite obscure. Certainly in dynamic passivity, and in relationship

[13] Cf. *The Journal of Social Work Process*, Pennsylvania School of Social Work, vols. 1, 2, 3 (1937, 1938, 1939).

therapy too, the agency played little part. Casework was a skill of a distinct personal character, and the agency was generally conceived of as a collection of caseworkers who offered their skill to those who came to a central source to seek it. With the advent of functional casework, however, the agency took on prominence. Workers began to look for their tools, so to speak, in the agencies in which they practiced, rather than in psychiatry. The functional movement, in fact, was looked upon by many as an anti-psychiatric development, since all of its emphasis was placed on understanding the agency and using its various parts, its structure, to help the client. In the functional approach caseworkers were advised to look in their own backyards, as it were, for their means of helping and to stop trying to borrow from other related professions. If the worker functioned in a child placement agency, for example, he turned to the structure of his agency and found that there were visiting regulations for parents, requirements for medical examinations, procedures for the distribution of clothing, and so on. In some child placement agencies the resources included temporary homes with policies regarding their use, as contrasted with permanent homes. In institutions there were additional structural factors such as a stated bedtime, a spending allowance, a time for athletics, and the like. All these structural factors were seen as having potential casework value. The worker could explain them; he was expected to identify with them so that he could really represent the agency or the institution when he spoke of them; he could keep discussion with the client centered on them, and by so doing, it was believed, could give the client an opportunity to work out the feelings he had about the service he was receiving. The client would do this by giving expression to his will (the way he thought the service ought to be offered). If he did not like a particular foster home or had complained about not being allowed to visit the home, for example, he would express himself regarding this, and the worker would recognize his right to do so. The worker would be mindful of the realities and would not negate his agency's way of working. Having expressed himself, and meeting with an affirmation of the agency's structure and the worker's function, the client might then work on whether his outlook really was a correct one. Was he too demanding or grudging? Wasn't the worker really fair? Wasn't it a matter of wanting things his own way, of his own unwillingness to yield? When the client could see things in this new light, his receptivity to the service and his willingness to use it constructively would come to the fore.

The instruments which the child placement worker would use in the functional approach were thus quite different from those which might be used by, let us say, a medical social worker or a public assistance worker. Each specific field of casework was regarded as having its own structure for the worker to utilize. In all, there was a function to be carried out; and in all, the worker had to keep oriented to his function. It was *the agency*, however, which provided the worker with his function and his structure, and it was the agency also (or some part of it) in relation to which the client was having his experience.

The agency was thus looked upon as a place where the client came to have an *agency experience* — not just a personal one in relation to the worker. Instead of practicing in a straight worker-client milieu, the functional worker operated in an agency-worker-client setting. The agency, which consisted of the board (representing the community), the administrator, and the supervisor, was always present, so to speak, and the worker had to relate to it and to his client simultaneously. The worker's relationship to the agency was seen as one characterized by *responsibility*. He had to identify with the agency and its purposes, be willing to represent it, and above all be willing to subordinate his personal interests to the requirements of the agency.

With so much emphasis placed upon the agency, it was perhaps to be expected that functionally oriented workers, for a certain period of time, would lose sight of the other important partner to the casework relationship, namely, the client. Not that the functional approach ignored the client and his need. Functional thinking, however, was not client-centered. Instead it was agency-centered. Because of this there were many pitfalls in it. The functional method does not work by itself. It requires an agency and a worker, and as a method it can be no better than the agency or the worker who practices it. When put into practice by immature and undeveloped personalities, or when used without sufficient diagnostic understanding, the functional approach will yield no more than any other approach to casework problems. In the policies and procedures of the agency, the inexperienced or immature worker can take refuge; and in the over-use of function which results, the client can have an experience in being not only misunderstood and mishandled, but even in not being recognized as a person. Function has value when it is personified, not when it is depersonalized. The worker who uses function must be a trained worker in the fullest sense of the term. His understanding of personality differences must be great, and his ability to apply this understanding in an individualized way — in a way that is right for the individual client — is a primary requisite in any successful application of the functional method.

When the functional method first came into prominence, there were many workers who were guilty of "clubbing" their clients with their function. Such workers would insistently maintain that the help which the client was seeking did not fall within their function, and on this basis often sent the client away without even giving him a thorough hearing. Taking the client's words literally, they would fail to see the real nature of his request and would turn him away. When, for example, the client said that he wanted employment and not relief, such workers might have referred him to an employment agency without considering fully his need for relief and what applying for it meant to him. Such referrals were made even though both the worker and the client knew that there was no possibility of his getting employment in this way. No skillful worker, whether functionally oriented or otherwise, would do this. The worker who was too literal about his own function, however, and the one who did not know how to look beneath what the client said to what he was actually seeking, did make this type of serious error.

In marked contrast is the approach of a worker who places a child with much attention to functional detail, but also with the understanding that comes out of identification with the child's view of placement; with a willingness to listen to his objections and to take them seriously, so that if a change in plans seems called for it might be arranged; and above all with a thorough study of the attitudes of all who are involved in the placement, namely, parent, child, foster family, and the worker himself. Such a worker will recognize that the placement can have many positive values for all concerned. He will also be aware, however, that there are negative and traumatic aspects. The experience of separation of parent and child will not be looked upon by such a worker as unqualifiedly a good one. Nevertheless, it is an inevitable and inherent aspect of placement, and the functional worker therefore believes that it should receive a good deal of attention. The skillful functional worker will not simply maintain, however, that it is his business to see the child and parent through the separation, but instead will watch for every indication of how the child and the parent are handling the separation. He will think of the actual separation experience, in other words, as one which will enable him to understand his clients, perhaps better than he could before, and he will be guided by what he sees in this area, as far as his future activities are concerned.

From these examples one can see that the prerequisite for any successful use of the *functional* method is what the *diagnostic* school has emphasized perhaps more than anything else, namely, the need for the fullest possible understanding of personality. Without such understanding the functional approach simply will not work. With it, function can be used not only to help the worker keep oriented to the nature of his job, but actually to serve the client, which is the only valid justification for its use.

The Need for Diagnosis

As we have indicated, one of the pitfalls of the functional approach is the fact that it can be practiced almost without reference to *the person* who is to be helped. In the hands of unskilled workers, the agency itself, its policies and procedures, can loom so important that the individuality of the client is forgotten. This need not be so, and in fact is not, when functional principles are applied by truly skilled workers. Functional literature, however, has given little stress to this matter, whereas diagnostic literature has put major emphasis on the understanding of personality.

If one believes, then, that an indispensable factor in the help-giving and help-taking situation is diagnostic understanding, a set of questions immediately arises. How does the caseworker, as contrasted with the psychiatrist, come to understand his client? How does he make his diagnosis? What part of Mary Richmond's method does he use? What part of his understanding must be psychiatric in nature? Does an understanding of all the implications of function help at all in diagnosis?

Assuming that there is no doubt of the need for diagnostic understanding, few caseworkers today will be content to proceed in their work without a formal or informal set of conclusions regarding the personality of the client, the attitudes he manifests in the casework situation, and in view of these, the adaptations which it will be necessary for the client or the worker to make in carrying out the service. During Mary Richmond's time such conclusions would have been formally and systematically set down, and members of the diagnostic school today believe that this should be done. In the heyday of *Social Diagnosis,* the data which the worker would call on for an understanding of his client were largely external, consisting of information about the client secured from employers, relatives, neighbors, and other outside sources. Today such information may or may not be obtained and used. On the whole, it would seem that members of the diagnostic school are more apt to seek such information than members of the functional school, perhaps because the latter place their emphasis on what can be known through direct contact with the client himself. Some functionalists have questioned whether it is possible to know anything about another person except in terms of one's own individual reactions to him. This is not the opinion of all, however, and in actual practice most functional as well as diagnostic workers do come to definite, transmittable conclusions regarding the personality, attitudes, and capabilities of the client.

The extent to which such conclusions are dependent on the psychiatric understanding of the worker will be related to the amount of such understanding which any given worker has. There is no aspect of psychiatric learning which cannot have value in casework or counseling. The more knowledge of personality the worker has, the more use of it he can make in his attempt to understand any given individual. Whether such understanding must take place within a single conceptual framework is another question. However, there are few who doubt the need for it.

The functional school has put all its emphasis on the understanding between client and worker which arises out of their direct contact with each other. Because of this, the set of conclusions, or the diagnosis, which the worker comes to, may be looked upon as a relative rather than an absolute one. It is relative to the function which the worker carries and relative to the worker too. In other words, it is assumed that under other circumstances, that is, with a different agency and a different worker, the parts of himself which the client shows might also be different. Moreover, the aspects of his psychology which a given client will manifest with the same worker at one time will be different from others which he will show at another time. Diagnostic judgments are looked upon as having temporary and relative value.

Diagnostically oriented workers, on the other hand, are interested in what might be called the core of personality. They want to know *what the client is like,* under a variety of circumstances, and they want to be able to classify him, if possible. Functional workers are less interested in classification. They want to know how the client behaves in a particular situation and with a particular worker. They believe that they can find out what they need to know about him by watching the way he acts when he comes for a service, and they assume that the service itself will have its impact on him. What they see, then, is not the whole person, but the part of the person which is active in taking the service. This is the part of the person which is believed to be most important for the worker to know. Other personality characteristics are apt to be considered irrelevant to the help-taking situation.

We shall not attempt to settle here the question of whether it is possible or necessary to comprehend the whole personality of the client. For the time being, let us be content to point out that one cannot do casework without diagnosing (in one important sense of the term, at least — namely, conclusion with regard to the personality and attitudes of the client) and that one also cannot do casework without administering a function of some kind. The two schools have not succeeded, so far, in analyzing and combining these two essential aspects of casework, nor is it likely that they will do so until the need for an understanding of function *and* diagnosis is recognized. When this occurs, both schools will have moved beyond their present status. It will no longer be possible to refer to them as functional or diagnostic, since they will both put their emphasis elsewhere, namely, on the dynamic interrelation between diagnosis and the administration of a function.

3

THE DYNAMIC PROBLEM

A s we have seen in the fore-going pages, one of the problems encountered by the objective student of the two present-day approaches to casework is the fact that each one deals, so to speak, with one half of the totality of casework and largely ignores the other. The diagnostic approach, to which we shall first turn our attention, attempts to overcome this difficulty through its division of casework into diagnosis and treatment.[1]

The Diagnostic Method

Diagnosis is the product of a set of activities on the part of the worker, activities which are concerned with understanding the

[1] Cf. Gordon Hamilton, *Theory and Practice of Social Case Work*, 2nd ed. rev. (New York: Columbia University Press, 1951), chaps. 8 and 9. See also, by Eleanor E. Cockerill, Louis J. Lehrman, Patricia Sacks, and Isabel Stamm (all of the University of Pittsburgh School of Social Work), *A Conceptual Framework for Social Casework* (Pittsburgh: University of Pittsburgh Press, 1953).

client and his social environment. Its aim is preparatory. Based on the fundamental assumption that the client cannot be helped unless the essential nature of his difficulty is comprehended, an effort is made in diagnostic activity to get at the root of the client's problem. Diagnosis, as seen by the diagnostic school, is a search for the causes of the problem which brings the client to the worker for help. The causes of the problem must be conceived of as residing both within the client himself (psychological) and outside of the client himself, that is, in the inter-personal and objective environment (social). Diagnosis is therefore concerned with understanding both the psychological or personality factors which bear a causal relation to the client's difficulty and the social or environmental factors which tend to sustain it.

The client's problem, or any problem, can be understood only through translation into terms which have meaning for the one who is to comprehend it. In other words, one must have a conceptual framework, a philosophy, or a science, for the comprehending. The diagnostic school of casework uses certain conceptions of Mary Richmond and of Freudian psychoanalysis as the primary ones in its conceptual framework, and all attempts to understand the client and his problem consist of translations into these terms. When sufficient information about the client and his social situation is obtained, a formal diagnosis, or translation of the specific information into generalized and conclusive terms which are part of the framework of diagnostic conceptions, is made. While formal, such a diagnosis is not necessarily final. A succinct statement of the nature of the problem confronting the worker is reached, however, and a great variety of manifestations of difficulty are narrowed down to a few comprehensible factors which now become the focus of the worker's interest and activity, or his "treatment."

Before proceeding further with the nature of diagnostic thinking, let us take an illustration of diagnosis as it might be carried out by a present-day worker oriented to the diagnostic approach in casework. We shall not attempt to give the development of the whole case; we shall simply pick out those aspects which have distinct diagnostic significance.

The parents of Donald, a sixteen-year-old boy, were referred to a guidance agency after he was brought to the attention of the police because of a series of acts of vandalism. Donald's father was a lawyer, and the mother had a doctorate in Fine Arts. There were two younger siblings, a brother of thirteen and a sister of ten. Both parents were eager for help and during the initial interviews gave a detailed history of the boy's infancy and later developmental years. From this history there emerged a picture of an over-severe father who related to the boy with a sense of annoyance and frustration, and an indulgent mother who could not set up or carry out any restriction on the boy's behavior. From the time of the birth of his younger brother, who was a very bright, conforming boy, Donald was regarded as a problem. He frequently beat his younger brother, sometimes unmercifully. As he grew older he started to throw things at his mother, who did not stop him. In school, too, he was known for many displays of aggression toward other students and teachers. Despite their son's serious difficulties in school, where he failed in his work although he had a high I.Q., and where he repeatedly fought other boys, the parents did not apply for help until he got into difficulty with the police.

Much information about the boy was secured from the school and police authorities. The results of intelligence and personality tests were on hand, and interviews were held with Donald himself as well as with his parents. As a result, the worker reached a tentative diagnosis as follows: *Anal-sadistic fixation with lack of superego development related to inconsistent handling on the part of parents, sibling rivalry, and failure to identify with harsh demanding father. On the social side, competitive situation in a large, formal school setting, with lack of sufficient opportunity for aggressive outlet, and demand for repression, intensifying the boy's need for sadistic expression.*

Based upon this diagnosis, a plan of treatment which included

Donald's transfer to a private military academy and insight therapy for his parents was worked out. Through the insight which the parents might gain into the nature of their contribution to the boy's problem, and through the opportunity to identify with masculine figures at a military school while being required to conform to strict discipline, it was hoped that Donald might be helped to get beyond his present stage of personality development.

Whether or not this plan of treatment could be effective, or whether it is a logical one following from the worker's diagnosis, is not our concern at this point. What we are interested in here is the nature of the diagnosis itself, which may be seen in this instance as both psychological, or rather, psychoanalytic, and social in character. Treatment in this instance was also planned along both lines.

The diagnosis and the treatment here are based upon a reasoning process on the part of the worker. They presume the acceptance of a philosophy or a set of principles regarding the nature of psychological and social problems. Implicit in this type of diagnostic thinking is a set of conclusions or generalizations regarding human behavior, which were previously reached, not by the worker himself, but by those who have formulated the conceptual framework which he uses in all of his thinking about personality and social problems. The concepts which the worker uses, in other words, are accepted largely on the authority and the transmitted experience of others who have been concerned with the diagnosis and treatment of similar problems.

In this very abbreviated description of the diagnostic approach, it should be noted that no particular attention is paid to the function of the worker or to the use of any structural factor within the agency itself as a means of helping the client. Diagnosis and treatment are worked out in what might be called a client-centered way. The worker and the agency, however, are not a significant part of the picture. We do not mean to suggest by this that the diagnostically oriented worker is not mindful of his agency, or that he never uses agency policies or procedures in his contact with the client. By and large, however, he does not use the function or the structure of his agency for any diagnostic purpose, nor is the treatment he plans, considered in its wider aspects, based primarily on the function of his agency. The diagnostic worker's relation to function and structure is incidental. His diagnosis and his treatment have a different center of gravity, so to speak.

The Functional Approach

Let us turn now to the functional approach and consider how the case of Donald might have been handled by a functionally oriented worker. Here too we shall merely point up the functional aspect and not try to set forth everything the functional worker might do. In the diagnostic approach we noted that the worker, first of all, obtained as much information as possible from outside sources and that he began by taking a comprehensive history from the parents. This the functional worker would not be apt to do. Instead, he would be concerned from the very beginning of the case with the problem of whether or not the boy and his parents really wanted help and whether they showed any real inclination to make use of him, or rather of his agency, in order to get it. In the initial interview, or interviews, there would be a testing out of this. What are they willing to do in order to get help? Are they willing to pay a fee, or do they seem to feel that it is society's problem, and that society should do something about it without making any particular requirements of them? Are they willing to come at what might be an inconvenient time for them? Will they travel a long distance? How much conflict over such matters do they show in discussion? Are they willing to proceed on a trial basis?

The functional worker gets his answers to such questions by telling the client what the agency can and cannot do. If it is a guidance agency, it usually does not arrange for placement in homes or institutions, and the worker might so inform the client, if he thinks the client might be interested in the possibilities for placement. If there is a fee he will discuss what it will be. The appointment time will be carefully considered with the client, as well as such matters as his travel distance and any obstacles there might be to his coming. What the functional worker wants to find out, in other words, is not the causes of the difficulty but rather whether he can contribute to its solution. Seeing his own function as a limited one, he wants to know whether the client can use it as an opportunity, as a possible way out of his difficulty. This is the basic question for the functional worker, and he tries to find the answer to it by giving the client a chance to see what taking help will be like.

According to the functional way of thinking, the client must make a choice, not just a superficial choice as to whether he likes a given agency or its way of offering help, but a fundamental choice as to whether he is going to remain just as he is, or whether he is going to change. If his decision is one in favor of change, he will be much more likely to accept the conditions of change with which the worker confronts him. If on the other hand he is very critical of the agency's way of doing things, or unwilling to accept the conditions of getting help which are set forth by the worker, then it is more than likely that he doesn't want to change. If this is so, then there is no point in pursuing him with a plan of treatment.

The functional worker attempts to arrive at an initial decision, then, as to whether the client really wants the kind of help he can give. He wants the client to participate in this decision, and he therefore tries to make it possible for the client to make his choice of taking or rejecting help. He does this by giving him as much information as possible about the kind of help he might receive and as much actual experience as possible in taking help, however little it might be, from the worker himself. In some instances, he will set up an exploratory period of several interviews, at the end of which he and the client decide whether to continue or not.

Is the worker's activity during this initial period diagnostic in character? Some functionalists maintain that it is not, and that, further, no diagnosis of any kind is necessary if one follows the type of approach to the client which we have outlined. If the client does not need help, they hold, a diagnosis in categorized terms will do no good. If he does want help, the essential question, in this view, is whether he can take it from the agency and the worker as he has come to know them through the initial interviews, and this can be answered only through actual experience in working together and not through a personality or social diagnosis.

Other functionalists differ from this view and in actual practice do very often speak of the client as a particular type of person. They see him as strong-willed or weak, rigid or flexible, volatile or inhibited, and so on. The functional school as a whole, in fact, has shown a great deal of interest in the study of personality. In its description of its method, however, personality considerations are played down, while functional or agency considerations are made the center of interest. Unlike the diagnostic school, the functional cannot be called client-centered. It is deeply concerned with the client, but the agency, its structure of policies and procedures, the worker's orientation to them and his skill in representing them, are considered primary and basic.

Here too it is clear that the worker makes use of a set of premises, which are transmitted to him on an authoritative basis. On this basis he develops a set of convictions, and whatever he meets with in the client is referred back to the original set of conceptions which he has taken over. The Rankian view of the will, certain conceptions about personality in action, and a belief in the rightness of division of responsibility are inherent in the functional worker's intellectual orientation and permeate his thinking. The function of the agency, however, remains central and all other considerations are related to it.

On the basis of what we have said so far about the two approaches to casework, it may be apparent why we said at the beginning of this chapter that each approach deals with one half of the totality of casework but largely ignores the other half. Diagnostic casework, with its client-centered emphasis, gives a minimum of consideration to the part which might be played by the agency and its function in arriving at diagnostic conclusions; and functional casework, when it does not deny the need for diagnosis altogether, often acts as though personality considerations were secondary and not the very core of casework. A question arises, therefore, as to whether the two approaches must be mutually exclusive. Can one diagnose in either Freudian or Rankian terms, or both, and still remain oriented to the function of the agency? Are diagnosis and function the only two significant aspects of casework, or are there others too?

The Dynamic Conception

Answers to the above questions are to be found, I believe, in a shift of emphasis away from both the diagnostic and the functional components in casework. Without denying that either one is of very great importance, it is possible to develop a third-dimensional view of casework — one in which both diagnosis and function play their rightful part, but one in which neither is predominant to the point where the presence of the opposite factor cannot be recognized. Such an approach to casework might be called *dynamic,* since its central point of emphasis must be neither the client, nor the agency, but instead the moving, changing, and developing interaction of one with the other. What forces does the client activate in the worker? What does he cause him to think? How does he make him feel? What action results? How does the worker appear to the client? What thoughts, feelings, and attitudes are activated within him? What mutual judging or diagnosing goes on? What respective use of function do the client and the worker make? In short, what interaction is originated in the client's and the worker's coming together? In what manner does it develop?

The mere bringing of a function to the client has no value, nor does the most skillful diagnosis, if the *dynamic interaction of client and worker* are ignored. Both the diagnostic and the functional approaches can be mechanical and sterile. Both also can be dynamic. They can only be so, however, when attention is shifted from the personality of the client, considered by itself, or the function of the worker, to the way in which client and worker are relating to each other. In a dynamic approach, in other words, the emphasis is on *both* client and worker, not one or the other.

It is the attention given to both the diagnostic *and* the functional aspects of the situation which characterizes the work of a dynamically oriented worker. To give attention to both simultaneously, however, is by no means an easy task. Concentrating on one aspect of a total situation is certainly much easier, even when one does it with respect to pure theory and not practice. To be continually aware, however, of the fact that there are two persons in every help-giving and help-taking situation, and to be conscious of the need for understanding of what *both* are like and what both are doing, is indeed a problem. It is a problem which is not insuperable, however, and it is a problem which the dynamic helper accepts.

In dynamic helping, such a problem cannot be skirted or evaded. It must be faced, and in facing it, the dynamically oriented worker takes upon himself a very considerable and many-sided task. What he must be prepared to do is to maintain a constant interest in the other person as well as in himself. He must be interested in and attentive to personality as well as function, and to the content of discussion as well as the process. He must be aware of divided responsibilities — those of the client as well as his own. In short, he must concentrate on the *dynamics* of the help-giving and help-taking situation. In so doing, he recognizes that there is never one single factor operating but that there must always be many.

The factors in efficient and effective helping are not located in the worker alone, nor in the agency, nor are they in the client alone. There can be a true helping situation only when those forces which are in the client himself are brought together with those which reside in the agency and the worker. The essential problem, therefore, must be understood as a problem of *bringing together* those forces which make for help and not as one of isolating each factor. The diagnostic and the functional schools have attempted to isolate helping factors, and this was undoubtedly necessary for the development of professional thinking. What must be done now, however, is to integrate rather than isolate, and for this it is necessary to go beyond either school and develop an approach which combines diagnostic and functional considerations in both theory and practice.

One of the inherent characteristics of casework is its *step-by-step* procedure. Just as a single note does not make a piece of music, so a single action on the part of the client or the worker does not make casework. This is the reason why Mary Richmond spoke of *a process* of study or investigation. It is one of the reasons, too, why the diagnostic school today recognizes the need for tentativeness in setting forth a diagnosis. It is also one of the considerations which permeates the functional approach. In the latter, some attention has been paid to the process or interaction which takes place within a single interview, as well as to the development in a succession of interviews. What is needed, however, is study of the *mutual influence* of client and worker. Who starts the ball rolling and how? What part is played by the client and what part by the worker? What effect does the worker's orientation — to diagnosis or to function — have upon the substance of the interview? What effect does it have on the development of the case? The client brings the same needs and desires, whether he comes to a diagnostic or a functional worker. The help he receives, however, often differs markedly. Obviously this is not desirable, and something should be done, if possible, to insure that he will receive essentially the same type of help, regardless of the philosophical outlook of the worker. The skill of particular workers will always differ. But the service the client receives does not have to differ to the extent that it actually does today.

It is the thesis of this book that the solution to the problem is to be found in the integration of diagnostic and functional considerations, and in the development of a common focus of interest, namely, *the dynamic interaction between client and worker.* There is nothing antithetical to either approach in this center of interest. An interaction between client and worker must take place, regardless of the starting point of the worker, and this interaction can and should be studied. Specific interviews should be analyzed to determine their diagnostic or their functional content. (See Chapter 7.) The non-diagnostic and the non-functional content of the interview should also be determined. The effect which the client's contribution to the interview has upon the worker because of his orientation, and the effect it has regardless of his orientation, should be studied. When this is done, the inherent factor of dynamic development through interactive influence of client and worker will undoubtedly loom large.

Let us examine the way in which the worker's orientation and the need and desire of the client are brought together to start the step-by-step progression which is casework. In order to do this, let us look into the general orientation of a worker in the field of child placement, together with the psychology of the applicant who wishes to place his child in a foster home or an institution. The placement worker is very fortunate in that he has a single clear-cut function to administer. He knows, however, that while placement is a desirable service for some parents and some children, it certainly is not good for all. It must be administered knowingly, and discriminatingly, and a decision must be reached in every case regarding its suitability.

A question arises, therefore, as to how the decision to place or not to place is reached. Can the worker do it on a straight diagnostic basis, deciding that it is right for certain types of personality and in certain distinct social situations? Can he do it on a straight functional basis, that is, on the assumption that his job is to place as long as the client can demonstrate his eligibility and as long as he makes a choice in favor of it? Every experienced placement worker knows that his job is really much more complicated than this would suggest, and that a great deal of his attention and his energy must be directed to other aspects of the total placement job. He knows, for example, that he necessarily

serves as a symbol in the client's mind — a symbol of *separation*
and all that it implies to any particular individual. When he becomes such a symbol, and when the client starts to relate to him
as such, something happens between the two persons which
would not necessarily happen if they were to meet under other circumstances. A distinct set of dynamics comes into play and the
worker's attention must be given to these.

Let us take a moment now to consider the dynamics of separation. When a parent comes to place a child, that is, to remove
the child from his own home, he knows that the physical close-
ness which has existed between the child and himself will have
to be broken up. They will have to separate physically, if not
psychologically. Usually the parent has a great deal of conflict
over this, and the worker must be geared to such conflict. He
must be attuned both to the desire to separate and to the inner
torment which such a frame of mind produces.

This does not mean that the worker is concerned with nothing other than separation. The implications of a separating experience have been dealt with quite extensively, particularly in
the functional literature on child placement, and it has appeared
in some instances that the placement worker is concerned only
with separation. Possible constructive or developmental aspects
of a child's experience in being separated from his parent have
been emphasized, and comparatively little attention given to the
destructive and growth-inhibiting aspects of a separation for
which the child particularly is ill-prepared emotionally.

The dynamically oriented worker is conscious of both destructive and constructive potentialities inherent in the separation experience. His essential problem is one of helping the client to
transform what feels like a destructive and painful experience
into one which becomes at least partially constructive. His emphasis, in other words, is on the *transformation* and not upon
the separation itself as inherently good. It is assumed, in fact,
that the separation experience will seldom come at a time when
the child is really ready for it, and that its consequences will be
traumatic. The worker is present, however, to help the child

work through the trauma which he experiences, and to transform what could be a completely destructive experience into one which is at least partially constructive.

In order to accomplish this, the child must have the opportunity to voice his protest against what he sees as an experience unfairly inflicted on him. He must see the positive interest and feel the support of the worker. He must know at all times what faith the worker has in his capacity to handle his feeling reaction to the traumatic situation and to take on new experience. In no instance does the worker assume that the separation itself will be good and that he need do nothing else but further it. He knows, in fact, that the child will have real problems in taking on the new personalities who are associated in his mind with the separation. Good as his own intentions and actions may be, he knows that the child seldom sees them as such. Intending to be genuinely helpful, the worker is seen as a threat and is often viewed with suspicion.

This means that there is *a dynamic* which operates in the relationship between worker and child, a tension, so to speak, created by the difference between the worker's actual orientation and what the child attributes to him. Before there can be any positive getting together of worker and child, this tension must be resolved. The worker must direct his attention, in other words, to the dynamic which is actually operating in his relationship with the child, and not to the factor of separation, as such. It is the separation experience which brings this dynamic into play. Once it is in operation, however, the worker will concern himself with how this factor actually operates in the relationship between the child and himself. He will recognize its existence in his discussions with the child and will not pretend that all is well between them when he knows it is not. He will not conceal his actual positive disposition, but neither will he fail to see how the child feels about him.

The dynamic operating between the worker and the child, in other words, must be talked about. Feelings, disposition, reality and the distortion of reality must be the substance of the discussion. When the worker proceeds in this manner, he gives the child a chance to work out all his feelings about separation and its aftermath, and to move on to new experience.

Conflict as the Focus

The worker must be willing to serve, then, as a symbol of separation with all of its advantages and obvious disadvantages for the client. But more than this, while maintaining his own role, he must allow his client to express all the conflict — all the will to place as well as not to place on the part of the parent, and all the will to be placed or not to be placed on the part of the child. He must work on this conflict, now seeing an advantage, and in the next interview probably a serious disadvantage. He must allow his client to come close to placement and then to turn away from it, if he will. The worker must further permit his client to personalize the experience and even to attribute the conflict to *him*, seeing the indecision as the worker's rather than his own. If the client's own parent or other authoritative figures would have condemned his action, he may see the worker as condemning what he wants to do. The worker, of course, is not indecisive and he does not condemn. He is identified with placement, and in his every word and every action he lets the client know this. The client must face all of his own conflict. He must act on his own while another (the worker) stands for the assumption of certain responsibilities which the client is not prepared to assume himself.

There is a distinct psychology of placement, in other words, as there is a distinct psychology related to any other service. The client will bring his own individual psychology to the situation in which the worker functions and to which he is oriented. The worker must *become oriented* to the behavior patterns of his particular client. The latter can occur only in experience with the client — experience in which the worker asserts one aspect or another of his own function, in response to that part of his own self which the client is expressing. A highly dynamic — active and reactive — process takes place, with *mutual* discovery, affirmation, and substantiation of the client's will as an end in view.

An even more complicated situation arises when there is a third person to whom the worker must be related. Here there are wheels within wheels, so to speak, and the worker must be continually attentive to the effect of his relationship with one person upon the other. An adult son or daughter, for example, may come to an agency to place an aged parent and of course will talk about his relationship with that parent. The parent must be party to the placement, however, and his attitudes will be more important to its success than those of anyone else. But parent and child seldom see eye to eye on such a matter. There is conflict between them which must be resolved before the placement can ever be effected. In this type of situation, the worker becomes the focus of conflicting wills. Both persons who are at odds with each other, and who certainly have a different stake in the social service which is to be rendered by the agency, bring their conflict to the worker. He is the same worker, but what he has to offer is seen differently by the two persons directly involved.

It would be possible to identify with one party to the conflict or with the other. The experienced and skilled worker who is dynamically oriented, however, will do neither. Both clients will project onto him their interests, thoughts, opinions, and feelings. They bring their reactions to the service which he is able to render, and he can bring to them the real facts about placement which they need to know. He can tell them what *he* can do, recognizing that an important question is whether *they* want the service which he has to offer and whether there can be any mutuality in their wanting it. How much together or how separate must they be in this? Can either move from his original position to see some of the outlook of the other? Can each one give in to the other sufficiently so that placement will become possible? Or must each hold onto the old view? The elderly person seldom looks for profound change in his way of living. The younger person may often feel that he is being blocked by his elderly parent in his efforts to live differently. Each has a different outlook, a different goal to achieve, and the question is whether placement will enable them to achieve their respective goals.

This is the type of conflict situation with which the worker must be concerned. As a caseworker he will not be interested in either person *just* as an individual. He will be concerned with the effect of the service which he administers upon a living social problem, a problem that arises because of social circumstances, one that either person living alone could not have. Social living often means living in conflict with others. The caseworker is trained to deal with conflict. It is one of the media in which he works. He has no need to deny it. He is, in fact, willing to become the focus of it because he knows only by so doing will there be any opportunity for a dynamic resolution of such conflict.

Orientation of the Worker

Dynamically oriented casework is both social and psychological. The term "social" implies that which involves more than one person; the term "psychological," that which takes place within an individual. Since the individual does not live in a vacuum, the content of much of his inner experience is "psychosocial." In other words, there is no real dichotomy between the social and the psychological. There is an aspect of experience, however, which belongs to and is characterized by the individual himself. A fearful person, for example, may be afraid of many types of social experience. The content of his fear may be social. It is *his* fear, however, and the fact that he is afraid must be regarded as a psychological fact. Some of his fear may be abated by removing its social causes. In a treatment situation, however, it is important to help the individual, if possible, to become less disposed to be fearful. This must be done through psychological understanding and not merely through a change of social circumstance.

Casework is social in origin and social in goal. The means which it uses to accomplish its purposes, in so far as they stress specific services, are also social. In the course of carrying out such services, however, there are always major psychological considerations. The social service must be given in such a way as to contribute to the resolution of conflict. Where more than one person stands in conflict with another and where the conflict becomes centered on the service itself, the worker literally stands *between* them. In this, he is not an arbitrator — he is not the one who decides. He is the willing recipient, however, of the feelings which are brought to him by the parties in conflict with each other.

For example, when a person comes to apply, let us say, for placement of his aged parent, the problems to be solved are problems of conflicting feelings as well as of social reality. Diagnosis, or understanding of the feeling manifested and of the way it is related to the personality of the client, is necessary. The aged person himself must be found eligible for the service from the standpoint of such criteria as his physical and mental status. But most important of all is the working out of conflict about the service which is sought.

No aged person starts out just wanting to be placed. Because of the guilt which the son or daughter feels for wanting to place the parent, that is, for wanting to be rid of him, and because of the guilt which the aged person feels for wanting to remain where he is not wanted, there is either overt or concealed conflict between the two. For the aged person himself who seeks stability, rather than change, there is often great fear of the new experience which the placement will force on him. This type of attitude must be expressed and understood. It can best be understood by the worker who is oriented to this particular service, the one who has responsibility for offering and administering it. Geared to the psychology of the placement situation and attuned to the type of conflict and the type of problem which is likely to arise in it, the placement worker can offer genuine understanding of such feelings and attitudes. He lives his professional life in this service, and he is thoroughly familiar with its attendant attitudinal conflicts. He expresses his understanding not just of the person, but of the service itself and of what taking it means. If the client moves toward the service, the worker's familiarity with its detailed aspects — medical care, visiting arrangements, food, sleeping arrangements, telephone calls, and so on — will enable him not only to present it in a realistic light, but also to see and even to anticipate the worries and fears and insecurities which there may be initially in moving into new conditions of life at an advanced age. In so far as the new conditions mean dependency, or the giving up of a former real or supposed independence, there will be a problem along these lines which needs to be worked on.

All of these detailed aspects of the psychology and the reality of placement of the aged (or any other similar social service) become the concern of the dynamically oriented worker before he takes actual action. As he takes such action he recognizes and reacts to every attitudinal factor which arises. He cannot "plan" placement ahead of time because these attitudinal factors can be dealt with only as they arise — only as the client proceeds toward placement or moves away from it. Such attitudes are activated by the presence or the imminence of the service. The individual himself cannot know beforehand what his attitudes are going to be. He knows them, and the worker meets with them, as the service is offered and administered.

Although firmly convinced of the values and the potentialities of his service, the dynamically oriented worker's attitude toward the use which the client will make of the service, and toward the benefits which he might derive from the process through which it is administered, is experimental and tentative. The outcome cannot be known beforehand. Whether or not the service will achieve its social purpose and whether or not the client will grow in making use of it can only be known as the service is offered, tried, and lived with. This does not mean that there are no indications regarding the client's eligibility for the service or the suitability of it in his particular situation. But these are never pure objective factors. Nor are they ever pure subjective ones. They are factors which emerge as the service is approached on the basis of the desire of the client. The worker who is geared to dynamics does not initiate a service on the basis of his diagnosis alone. He knows his service — every detail of it — and he is oriented to typical and atypical reactions to it. He assumes, however, that his client has both the ethical right and the interest to discover for himself whether or not a given service will be suitable for him. And he assumes, furthermore, that the client has the will to reject or to defeat the purpose of a service which he does not want. Finding out what he wants, not in the sense of getting a yes or no answer, but in the sense of working out with the client what he will apply himself to, is the worker's job.

The dynamically oriented worker thus concerns himself with personality and attitudinal factors, and with social as well as psychological considerations. As he works with the client he comes to certain conclusions regarding manifestations of inner conflict, and he is equally attentive to whatever conflict there may be between the client and others in his social environment. He observes the client's reactions to what he offers in the way of explanation or information regarding the agency, and he tries to keep aware of how the client may be feeling about him as a helping person. Within himself, he integrates these various observations, so that they all become part of his diagnosis. Whether or not he formalizes his diagnostic conclusions, he does consciously and purposefully arrive at them, and he shares them to the extent that he feels the client can understand them, so that they are not simply diagnostic conclusions but become a vital element in the helping process. The client, having an opportunity to know what the worker's impressions regarding his problem are, then has something new to work on. He has new possibilities for self-understanding and for re-orientation to the problem. Not that he will take over lock, stock, and barrel what the worker might say of the problem. Sometimes he will deny the worker's view completely, sometimes he will accept a part and reject other parts, and so on. In any case, however, there will be a frank and open sharing between client and worker.

We thus see that, in a dynamic relationship between client and worker, neither the diagnosis nor the function of the worker is used in a mechanical manner. Both are put into the relationship, that is, into the actual discussion, by the worker, who does not stop at this point but rather regards such activity on his part as a beginning. Something must follow, and it is his business to know what follows. The client must react in one way or another to his diagnosis, as well as to his function, and he must know the client's reaction. This will become the substance of subsequent discussion, which in turn will be followed by further diagnostic impression and further use of function. The dynamic contact builds itself up. One layer is added to another in pyramidal fashion and to the point where further additions are no longer necessary.

Responsibility in Dynamic Helping

The responsibility which the worker carries in this type of casework process is indeed different from that which is involved in any mechanical approach to the client and his problem. Since he does not take over the client's responsibility, the dynamically oriented worker is especially attentive to the responsibility which he does carry, that is, the responsibility for his own part in a shared process. This is indeed great.

There are of course various levels of responsibility ranging from a simple and external accountability in relation to a superior authority to an internal type of personal discipline and integration, upon which professional behavior is based. It is the latter type of responsibility which we refer to here.

Recognizing that the helping process is necessarily two-sided and that the client must carry responsibility for one part of it, while he is responsible for another, the dynamically oriented worker will give meticulous attention to the understanding of the process itself, since this is his responsibility and not the client's. He will not make himself responsible for the outcome of the process, however, since this is a factor for which no individual can be solely responsible. In his excellent discussion of this point Kenneth L. M. Pray states that the concept of control over the outcome of a process:

obviously places social scientific facts in the same relation to daily practice in social work as the sciences of anatomy, physiology, bacteriology, and chemistry may be said to have in relation to medicine, and for the same purpose, namely, to sharpen and strengthen the control of the practitioner over the objects to which his professional responsibility is addressed, that is, in social work, human beings in social relationships. . . . It also assumes in human behavior and social relations, the same sort of mechanistic and deterministic causal relations as science has devoted itself to discovering in the physical universe.[2]

The essential character of causal relationships in the social sciences is such that the type of control which it is possible to exercise in the physical sphere becomes quite impossible in the social or psychological realm. When one knows, for example, that a certain drug will kill a certain bacillus, the next step is to administer the drug so that the patient may derive the benefit. Even here, however, it does not always follow that removal of a cause of disease will always result in cure. Attendant circumstances are very important in many instances, and one cannot proceed on a strict basis of causal relationship following the formula of removing the cause and effecting the cure. Wherever human beings are involved, even in pure physical terms, causality tends to become complicated. Where matters social or psychological are concerned, the complications are compounded.

For this reason alone the assumption of responsibility for the outcome of a casework process becomes impossible. There is still another reason, however, why the worker should not regard himself as responsible for outcome, namely, the ethical one. On coming for help, no client ever turns over to the worker the privilege of taking away his capacity for self-determination. In fact, even if he wanted to, the client could not really do this, except within certain definite limits. He may ask to be taken care of in an institution, for example, and he may conform to institutional

[2] Kenneth L. M. Pray, "A Restatement of the Generic Principles of Social Casework Practice," *Journal of Social Casework*, 28:283–290 (October, 1947).

regulations and requirements. But no one can force him to enjoy institutional life or to make productive use of the opportunities which are made available to him. Only *he* can determine whether or not he will do this.

On ethical grounds, in other words, no caseworker should ever attempt to do for the client that which he can do himself. In so far as it is possible for him to manage his own life, the client should be given every opportunity to do so. This principle should hold in the initial determination of whether a case will be taken on or not, it should hold throughout the handling of the case, and it should be a guide for the determination of the ending of the case.

If the client plays such an important part, then, in determining, first of all, whether or not he should come for help, and then how much help he will take, how can the worker make himself responsible for outcome? He certainly can share with the client some of the responsibility for outcome (in so far as either or both can be responsible) but neither the client nor the worker can carry full responsibility for the outcome of a helping process. Both assume a measure of risk and both invest a great deal of trust in each other and in the process itself. The worker can go beyond this in that he can understand the process itself and can convey some of this understanding to the client. But he does not have the omniscience nor the omnipotence which would make him responsible for the outcome of the process.

What the dynamically oriented worker needs to know is not that this or that plan or type of treatment will produce a given type of result (assuming a degree of predictability unknown in social science), but rather that a helping process is characterized by certain stages, a certain continuity, and a certain polarity. There must be a beginning, middle, and end phase of the process, and the worker must be geared to these. He must recognize typical expressions, typical feelings and actions which occur in these phases. The fear of beginning, for example, will express itself in many devious ways. The fear of being caught in a situation one might not be able to get out of is very frequent in the middle phase. The end phase will often activate feelings about death; many clients, in ending, will speak of death in one way or another. The worker must be sensitive to the meaning of such manifestation. He must be able to translate them into some statement regarding their relevance to what the client is going through. Likewise, when the client has expressed himself in very positive terms in one interview, he will frequently give expression to the negative in the next. The following one may represent a mixture of both. The worker must be sensitive to this polarity. He must be able to discover the client's pattern and pace in movement from the positive to negative. He must distinguish between what is projection on the client's part and what is identification. He must recognize his own personal identification, when this occurs, and he must refrain from projecting personal interests. He must maintain a therapeutic standard in his own conduct while permitting the client the greatest possible freedom in self-expression.

The functional school has given the impression in some of its literature that holding to structure will in itself have a desirable effect, and it has discussed the responsibility of the worker in these terms. The worker who simply "holds to" his structure, however, and who has no concern with the effect of his action can hardly be called a professionally responsible person. The really responsible worker is one who is concerned with the effect of his every action. Insufficiently trained functional workers often rely on the use of structural factors, bringing them to the attention of the client in an insistent way and then waiting for something to happen. Little thought is given to the meaning of a time limitation, let us say, to the particular person, nor is there discussion of the client's reaction to what often seems to him an arbitrarily determined policy. The result is that the dynamic opportunities which should follow from the use of function or structure are completely lost. The client has a mechanical rather than a dynamic experience, and the worker simplifies his task to the point where he does not need to be concerned with human reactions. This is not the dynamic worker's conception of professional responsibility.

The dynamically oriented worker starts at the point where the worker who functions in a mechanical manner ends his task. He is not content simply to tell the client that the agency's policy is thus and so and to stop there. Instead he recognizes that the presentation of function or structure is a mere beginning and that what matters is the client's reaction to his presentation. He must learn what the client's reaction is, and he will look into it *with the client*. When he does so, he is engaged in a dynamic process, one in which the possibilities for transformation of attitude are opened up. The introduction of the structural factor is a mere beginning. What follows after the introduction is much more important to the dynamically oriented worker, who sees his responsibility as extending beyond the mere putting in of policy or procedure.

The dynamically oriented worker must carry responsibility for the control of the *conditions* of the process, such as time and place of interviews and amounts of money to be used. In this he is helped by the agency, which sets certain conditions within which the worker must operate, such as size of case load and number of hours available for it. If there is a fee, the agency will provide a scale based upon certain budgetary considerations. Relief, likewise, will be granted on a basis determined by the agency. While the agency can be most helpful in such ways, responsibility for the execution of control over his own part in the process must rest with the worker. This is an enormous responsibility and one which the worker cannot transfer to someone else. In the final analysis, it is worker and client face to face with each other who must grapple with the problem in whatever ways it manifests itself. The worker must carry responsibility for the controls which he puts into the process. They are his and not the client's.

In actual experience, dynamically oriented workers find that the degree of responsibility which clients can take and which they, in fact, want to take for their own problems, proves to be very great. Few people really want to have others manage their lives. When treated with the respect which goes into the worker's recognition that the client is the manager of his own life, most clients will respond with affirmation of this. The question of *how much* responsibility the client will take himself, and how much he wants the worker to take, then becomes a focal question. It becomes a subject of discussion. The answer is to be determined dynamically, that is to say, mutually. One works *toward* such a conclusion.

If the worker is responsible for his part of the process but not for outcome, who sees to it that there are favorable results? What is favorable result and what is unfavorable? The answers to these two questions rest on the fact that help is not a purely objective matter. The person himself must judge whether he is really helped or not. When he is, the worker will see this as the result of a process in which *two* persons participated and for which both have carried a measure of responsibility. Neither person alone could produce the outcome. Together both could — granted certain favorable external conditions over which neither has control.

Control must be distinguished from responsibility. Control is total; responsibility is partial. One can be responsible for the part, not for the whole. In the physical world one can sometimes control the whole, although even in this realm complete control is difficult to achieve. One can attempt it, however, say in the laboratory, without concern about social and psychological considerations. But in living situations, responsibility rather than control is called for. Control is always control *of* or control *over* something — mastery of it. Responsibility, on the other hand, is *for* something rather than *over* it. One cannot be responsible for the whole process. Still less can the worker alone be responsible for the results of the process.

Responsibility for outcome must be shared by client and worker. This does not free the worker from the most rigorous assumption of responsibility for his own conduct in a casework process. It does free him, however, and it frees the client too, from the type of control over the client's life which the client did not seek when he applied for a particular social service.

When one recognizes how much there is to be responsible for, without claiming control of outcome, it is surprising indeed that anyone should ever want to assert this type of control over the affairs of others. The dynamically oriented worker who is responsible for his own conduct at every stage of the helping process, sees literally hundreds of points at which he must take such responsibility. In even the shortest case, the question of what is his responsibility and what is the client's is uppermost in his mind. Moreover he does not keep this question to himself, but discusses it with his client. This discussion will lead to a tentative conclusion about this one aspect of the relationship of worker and client. In the course of development of the average case there will be many similar discussions, each one probably with a different content. In one interview it will be the responsibility of the parent which is the topic of discussion. In another it will be that of the sibling. In still another it will be that of the teacher or of the employer. Each of these discussions will be permeated with feeling. Often the client will insist (and it may be rightfully so) that someone else should have taken greater responsibility than he did — that is the reason for the difficulty. In some instances the client will assume too much responsibility, making himself responsible for factors completely outside of his own control. Anger, fear, and guilt will be expressed in relation to this central question, and the worker who would make expression of these negative feelings an end in itself will lose sight of the question of the client's responsibilities in relation to his own. Positive feelings will also be expressed and their expression also may be taken as an end in itself. Important as the expression of feeling may be, however, it is not helpful until it is seen in its relation to a crucial question, a question which needs to be worked out by worker and client. The crucial question is one of responsibility. How responsible will the individual be — for the feelings he has and for what he wants to do about the problem at hand?

This approach to human problems is a vital and dynamic one which calls for the utmost in skill and understanding. The psychology of particular services must be understood. The essentials of therapy must likewise be thoroughly comprehended. This assumes a thoroughgoing understanding of personality. Skill in management of one's own self in relation to the other — and in the handling of the difference between one's own outlook and that of the other — is required. The structure of the agency, as reflected in its operating policies and procedures, will assist the worker in this. The process which results from the coming together of the agency, in the person of the worker, and the client with all his differences from the agency, has a vital and dynamic continuity and is characterized by three essential stages, beginning, middle, and end. The worker must be able to adapt himself to the psychology of each phase. In doing this, he must stand responsible at all times for his part in this process, thus permitting the client to take responsibility for his. Constructive social and psychological change is the goal of such a helping process. The worker's interest is not focused on outcome, however, but on that aspect of casework which he alone can comprehend, namely, the dynamics of the process.

Entering into a dynamically oriented process with sensitivity to what the client must go through in every bit of movement, and with understanding of the dynamic factors at work, puts upon the worker a kind of responsibility seldom equaled in human relationships. The benefits to be derived can be as far-reaching from the standpoint of personality growth and development as the individual client allows them to be. In this type of casework, the service exists for the sake of the client. The worker's job is to make the service as effective as possible. In order to do this he calls upon the agency, first of all, with its resources in policy and procedure, upon his understanding of personality and the psychology of the service, that is to say, upon his diagnostic understanding, and upon his personal skill in the conduct of a relationship.

Dynamic Practice

Let us now return to the case example given at the beginning of this chapter and consider how the same situation might be approached by the dynamically oriented worker. In this situation, Donald, aged sixteen, was referred to a guidance agency because of acts of vandalism and was diagnosed as sadistic and lacking in superego development. These characteristics were seen as related to failure to identify with a demanding father. On the social side, Donald's adaptability to a conventional school setting was questioned, and plans for treatment included his placement in a military academy.

This was the approach of the diagnostic worker who, of course, was very careful in getting a detailed history and who did not proceed with treatment until all of the facts were on hand which might warrant a definite diagnostic conclusion.

In our discussion of the functional approach to such a case, we pointed out the lack of concern with history and fact-finding, and the emphasis given to such questions as whether the boy and his parents really wanted help and whether they could use the worker and the agency for this purpose. In order to find this out, the functional worker would present his function and observe the way the client reacted to it. He would then come to a conclusion as to whether or not he should proceed, and if his conclusion were affirmative, the case would continue. What would be done concretely to help the client would depend on the worker's function. If the client showed a disposition to get some other type of help, let us say placement, he in all probability would be referred to another agency and another worker whose function was to provide that type of help. If the client continued to demonstrate that he could make use of the worker and the agency in an attempt to achieve additional change, then the worker would continue with him for a period of time which had been discussed and under other conditions which had been agreed upon by worker and client.

This brief contrast between what the diagnostic worker and the functional worker might do in a given situation omits what either or both would do if they were dynamically oriented. The diagnostic worker does not have to restrict himself to the making of a diagnosis and manipulation of the environment. Nor does the functional worker have to restrict himself so that he simply holds to his structure and function and waits for the client to do something. Both can — in fact, they must — do a great deal more if they are to be genuinely helpful to the client. What they must do is to go beyond the gross diagnostic manifestations and the simple presentation of function to the much more subtle aspects of the case which are to be found in *the interaction of client and worker.* In this instance, for example, one of the questions which would arise immediately would be the worker's reactions to a boy who is sadistic, a father who is oversevere, and a mother who is indulgent. Does he react to all in the same way? This would not be likely. The worker might tend to shy away from a boy who is sadistic. If so, the boy himself would notice this in all probability, and the worker's tendency to withdraw would have an effect on what the boy would do and say. The worker, on the other hand, might not be troubled at all by the boy's tendency to violence, but might have a strong personal reaction to the father's excessive severity. In such an instance, the boy might find something in the worker's character which is complementary to his own, while the father might find a relationship with the worker quite dry and sterile. The mother might appear to be an admirable person to the worker who might meet her on a very positive level. She might react warmly to the worker's interest. But she might also be frightened by it and wish to withdraw.

The dynamically oriented worker observes all these manifestations, and he tries to find an answer to the question of what he does to the client, by virtue of what he is like himself, and what the client does to him, by virtue of what he is like. Needless to say, a great deal of self-understanding on the part of the worker is necessary, together with a great deal of genuine interest in what other people are like. Given these characteristics, the dynamic worker will observe himself and his client as they actually interact with each other and he will then redirect his activities accordingly. In this instance, the worker, on seeing that any one member of the family tends to withdraw from him, would ask himself why, and he might frankly discuss the point with the person involved. This frank discussion might enable the worker to get beyond the resistance he might have to the particular person, or it might enable the client to feel differently toward the worker. In any case, the next step would depend upon what had taken place in such a discussion. Client, worker, or both would *redirect* themselves on the basis of an experience they had together, namely, the frank discussion of the way they were reacting to each other.

A case such as the one we are considering is permeated with conflict. The boy, Donald, is in conflict with parents, school, and society, and it is therefore almost inevitable that he should come into conflict at some point with the worker. His parents obviously have a great deal of conflict over him, and this too must be a focus of the worker's attention. The worker thus finds himself steeped in a conflict situation, which he must face and work through to whatever extent possible. Such conflict is accepted by the dynamic worker as a professional challenge, and he is willing to keep it as a center of his interest and activity. He will discuss it whenever it manifests itself. He will observe the capacity of each person to work on it and he will not be afraid to become the object of it himself. He will also regard it as his job to facilitate the working through of conflict. In an instance such as this one, the boy might develop great conflict about the worker, wanting to exercise some of his sadistic tendencies in relation to him as well as to others, but feeling inhibited because of the worker's general understanding. This conflict would have to be faced, and in facing it, there would be an opportunity for the boy to arrive at no small measure of self-understanding.

The responsibility which the worker himself carries as he tries to work out such a conflict situation dynamically is indeed great. It is a type of responsibility, however, which rests on his capacity and willingness to see through to some logical conclusion the type of conflict situation into which he has entered and of which he has become a part. With this responsibility constantly in mind the dynamic worker observes his client and himself as their relationship together builds itself up. With each successive step in the process he redirects himself on the basis of what already has been achieved and what remains to be done in the progression of their relationship.

In the early stages of the case, for example, the worker would be concerned with the way in which each party made a beginning. Did he begin by impressing, by being agreeable, by being negative? Did he show a superficial conformity so as not to risk the worker's displeasure? How much frankness and how much receptivity did there seem to be? Was the beginning a gingerly one or a courageous high-dive? The answers to these questions could come only from discussion with the client about the experience which he was having. Again, as the relationship progressed and the problems of beginning seemed to be left behind, questions appropriate to the middle phase of the relationship would come to the fore. Does the client feel caught in a positive or a negative relationship with the worker? Does he want to get out of it? Does he want to prolong it indefinitely? The dynamically oriented worker does not rush his case to a conclusion, or set an ending on an arbitrary basis, but instead is willing to wait for a logical development to the point where ending is natural and almost inevitable for both the client and himself. This too is a matter for discussion; the worker will take up the question of ending with his client when, in the client's judgment and in his own, either a good part of what was to be accomplished is achieved, or it seems appropriate to substitute another course of action. A tentative time limit might be suggested at the very beginning of the case, but this would never be held to rigidly or arbitrarily, since the very essence of dynamic casework is adaptation and redirection on the basis of experience up to any given point.

In attempting to help a vandalistic boy or his parents, therefore, the dynamically oriented worker would never assume that a given course of action, or type of treatment, would result in real help. Nor would he simply offer his function and let the client do what he would with it. Instead he would get to know his client in the deepest sense of the word. He would be interested in psychiatric diagnosis which would give him some idea of the client's potentialities; he would attempt to work out with the client whether the social situation could remain stable or should be changed; he would enter into a relationship with the client in which conflict would be the focus of his interest and in which he would observe constantly the way in which the relationship was developing; he would discuss the development of the relationship with the client, and he would follow through with discussion of every changing phase in the process.

Is this approach contrary to either diagnostic or functional thinking? The answer would seem to be that it is not. Either the diagnostic or the functional worker can practice in this manner. In fact, both must do so, if they have due regard for what is inherent in human relationship. The dynamic approach does not negate what is valid in either the diagnostic or the functional method. It simply fills out what is lacking when overemphasis is placed on either diagnosis or function. In the dynamic approach both the diagnosis and the functional considerations are seen as important. One does not exclude the other. The dynamic practitioner utilizes and synthesizes both. Furthermore, he gives meaning to each, through his observation of the part that each one plays in the developing interaction which takes place between the client and himself.

The Need for Synthesis

We thus see that the dynamic problem is a problem of both diagnosis and function. It is a problem of self-understanding and self-discipline as well as a problem of understanding the other person. It is a problem of attention to and awareness of the many factors which come together in a help-giving and help-taking situation. The problem, however, goes beyond attention and awareness, since the dynamic helper must be a participant as well as the one who understands. The actual contact between client and worker is very different from the description of such a contact as it might be given by a non-participating observer. In a dynamic contact, the worker is both participant and observer.

The participant-observer (to use Eduard Lindeman's term) can be aware of dynamics which often are not apparent to the supposedly objective one. He is responsive to currents of feeling coming from the other person and can be aware of those emanating from within himself. If he is dynamically oriented, he will recognize that the two streams of feeling interplay with each other, and he will try to see in what ways they do so. He will recognize, moreover, that it is not only a matter of the interplay of streams of feeling, but that other factors including intellectual understanding and the sense of responsibility are also involved. All call for awareness plus the ability to enter into and participate in a process, not knowing what the outcome of such participation will be. One's own part in the process of help will be conscious, disciplined, and directed toward constructive potentiality. What will develop out of the dynamic *bringing together* of two forces, namely, the constructive attitude of the helper and the desire for help on the part of the client, cannot be known beforehand. But what is happening along the way, that is, in the help-giving and help-taking situation, can be known to the participant-observer.

The dynamic helper's job might thus be described as one of "on-the-spot" integration. He must synthesize the various aspects of his job, and he must bring this synthesis to the client in his own behavior. Out of chaos and conflict there must come clarity and direction. This can occur only when the helping person maintains an integrating and synthesizing attitude himself. He may be seen by the client in every conceivable light. Throughout the many changes of attitude which the client will undergo toward him, however, there must be an awareness of *synthesizing purpose*. This does not mean that the worker's emphasis is solely on the constructive, or that he cannot recognize or accept the client's need for destructive expression when this exists. However, the worker cannot be destructive or at loose ends himself. His attitude must be a constructive, that is to say, a synthesizing one.

On a wider level, the same need for synthesis can be seen in the case of a profession in conflict with itself. Neither the diagnostic nor the functional school has possessed the integrating power that is necessary to heal the breach which has existed within the past two decades in the field of social casework. What is needed to produce a constructive outlook on the part of the profession as a whole, therefore, is a philosophy which puts its emphasis on synthesis. The dynamic approach is one which tends to integrate. Each worker in each case integrates his diagnostic understanding and his functional identification. What can be done on the level of practice can and should be translated into theory. Such a theory, emerging from practice, will have a genuine synthesizing effect upon the profession as a whole.

4

FROM CASEWORK TO COUNSELING

During the nineteen-forties, the functional and diagnostic schools were quite involved in the process of differentiating themselves from each other. While this was going on, however, a complicated problem arose due to the fact that both schools took on a new interest — one spoken of as "counseling." Before they reached any agreement on a definition of casework, the new term came into widespread usage and it was quite impossible to tell from the way in which it was used whether counseling was casework, or therapy, or a form of help *sui generis*. Whether both diagnostic and functional casework should be distinguished from or identified with counseling, whether counseling was simply an old form of help with a new name, whether counseling and therapy were one and the same thing, and above all, whether there must be two types of counseling, just as there were two types of casework, were some of the troublesome problems with which caseworkers were now confronted. Comparatively few attempts have been made to answer these questions and in much of the literature one still finds the terms "casework," "counseling," and "therapy" used synonymously.

As early as the thirties the help given by caseworkers was occasionally referred to as "counseling." [1] The use of the term "therapy," however, with reference to problems of personal adjustment, was much more frequent. With the development of the functional approach, an effort was made to differentiate casework from therapy, but then "counseling" became widely used as a term designating any aspect of the worker's activity which concentrated on the element of personal problem. [2] "Counseling" became a substitute for both casework and therapy. It was somewhat removed from the administration of concrete services, but it was also vaguely associated in the minds of many with casework. All guidance services have been spoken of as counseling, although some child guidance clinics prefer to speak of the activities of their workers as "casework," emphasizing the *service* given to the parent in providing psychiatric treatment for his child. Occasionally the term "counseling" has been used to designate brief referral interviews carried out often by untrained workers, as in certain veterans' service centers, and at other times it has been used to signify a complicated form of therapy. [3]

Obviously a definition is called for — especially since the two

[1] Cf. Bertha C. Reynolds, "Can Social Casework Be Interpreted to a Community as a Basic Approach to Human Problems?" *The Family*, 13: 336–342 (February, 1933).

[2] Cf. Jessie Taft, ed., *Counseling and Protective Service in Family Casework* (Philadelphia: University of Pennsylvania, School of Social Work, 1946); Jessie Taft, ed., *Family Casework and Counseling* (Philadelphia: University of Pennsylvania Press, 1948); *Family Counseling Practice and Teaching* (New York: Jewish Family Service, 1949); M. Robert Gomberg and Frances T. Levinson, eds., *Diagnosis and Process in Family Counseling* (New York: Family Service Association of America, 1951).

[3] Cf. Carl Rogers, *Counseling and Psychotherapy* (Boston: Houghton Mifflin, 1942) and *Client-Centered Therapy* (Boston: Houghton Mifflin, 1951).

existing schools have been so vague about what they have called counseling. This book therefore proposes a definition differentiating counseling from casework and from psychotherapy conceived of as a whole. Elsewhere I have elaborated on the question of likenesses and differences among these three forms of help.[4] For our present purposes, let us try to cut through to the core and concentrate on certain inherent realities which must be taken into consideration.

Casework, Counseling, and Psychotherapy Defined

The problem of defining casework becomes a more complicated one as the years go on, and as casework practice becomes more subtle and intricate. Originally, there was very little problem because casework consisted of all the activities involved in the study, diagnosis, and treatment of specific, social problem situations. As time went on, however, and casework became more and more psychologically oriented, it became extremely difficult to determine what was essential and indigenous to casework, as practiced under any and all circumstances, and what was a special form that casework might take when it was practiced under some particular type of influence. Many definitions of casework have therefore come into the literature, and an actual chronological study of such definitions has been made.[5]

Casework: A Definition

For our purposes here, it seems appropriate to confine our definition of casework to those factors which tend to differentiate it from counseling or psychotherapy. In so doing, we must recognize that casework does have much in common with these other two forms of personal help. Despite many likenesses, however,

[4] Herbert H. Aptekar, "The Use of Private Psychiatrists in a Social Agency," *Jewish Social Service Quarterly*, 25:381–394 (March, 1949); also, "Casework, Counseling, Psychotherapy — Their Likeness and Difference," *Jewish Social Service Quarterly*, 27:163–171 (December, 1950).

[5] Cf. Swithun Bowers, "The Nature and Definition of Social Casework," *Journal of Social Casework*, 30:311–317, 369–375, 412–417 (October, November, December, 1949).

there is at least one important difference between what one does when employed as a caseworker and what one might do when practicing as a counselor or psychotherapist. This difference is to be found in the fact that in social agencies, where caseworkers have traditionally practiced, specific social services are administered, such as financial assistance, placement, and homemaker service. It is true that in recent years some social agencies have largely given up such services, while other social agencies have been created to offer psychological help alone.

By far the great majority of agencies do administer social services, however, and it is the caseworkers they employ who carry responsibility for administering them. This fact, I believe, differentiates casework from counseling and from psychotherapy. No psychologist, trained in counseling, knows *ipso facto* how to administer financial help, or to place a child, or to supervise a homemaker. Nor does any psychiatrist, by virtue of his medical training, have the understanding required to do these things. There is a special body of knowledge, pertaining to the conditions under which such help can be appropriately given in a social agency, which is necessary. Special skills are required, and a special psychological understanding that arises out of experience in administering social services. This knowledge, skill, and understanding of what goes into help-giving and help-taking, associated with specific social services, is casework.

Counseling: A Definition

Out of their wide experience in administering social services with psychological understanding, there developed among caseworkers, in recent years, an interest in what they could do to help people without any social service. Having observed that what they did, aside from their administration of concrete services was very much like, if not identical with, what the psychiatrist did, or the well-trained clinical psychologist, caseworkers began to look for a term which would describe the psychological aspect of their work, and the term "counseling" seemed to be a suitable one. The problem, however, was that this term had a wide variety of connotations, and it was soon found that it could contribute very little to an understanding of what the caseworker did, except perhaps through contrast. Synonymous use of the two terms proved to be confusing and a need for some kind of clarity soon arose.

How does "counseling" contrast with casework? What distinguishes it as a form of personal help? Who is qualified to do it? Unlike casework, counseling can be carried out privately, and without the need to call on agency resources. Relief funds, foster homes, and homemakers are not necessary. Instead, all that is required is a person who has a problem and one who is willing to share that problem and bring to bear upon it whatever skill he may have, so that a solution to it may be reached. Isn't this essential in casework, too, and if so, how can it be made the distinguishing factor? The answer is that while two persons meet in the casework situation too, one with a problem and one with skills necessary to solve that problem, still another factor must be taken into consideration and brought to bear on the problem by the caseworker, namely, the concrete service which he administers.

Counseling may be thought of, therefore, as casework without a concrete service. This condition, however, is a most significant one; its importance cannot be overstressed. In counseling, one is geared to a problem and not to a service. This means that the counselor need not be a caseworker employed by a social agency. His social agency experience, if he happens to have any, may contribute to his understanding of the problem, to his knowledge of the difficulties people have in taking help, and so on. The essence of counseling, however, is not to be found in the social agency. Casework, in so far as it involves the administration of concrete social services must be done in agencies. But the essential factor in counseling must be sought elsewhere. For it, one must look to the relationship between a person with a specific problem seeking help and a person with special experience, skill, and knowledge having to do with the type of problem on which help is wanted. Thus we have marriage counselors, employment counselors, school counselors, and so on. Each has a specific body of knowledge and experience which the other does not necessarily have. Each brings his special knowledge, skill, and experience to bear upon the relevant problem. Counselors generally do not attempt to deal with any and all problems, but instead with special ones toward which they are oriented. The essence of counseling, therefore, is to be found in the focus on a specific type of problem. Counseling is personal help directed toward the solution of a problem which a person finds he cannot solve himself and on which he therefore seeks the help of a skilled person whose knowledge, experience, and general orientation can be brought into play in an attempt to solve that problem.

Psychotherapy: A Definition

If casework is to be thought of, then, in terms of specific services, and counseling in terms of specific problems, what is the differentiating factor in psychotherapy? Obviously the person who gets real help, whether through casework as we have defined it, or through counseling, has an experience that may be called therapeutic. Both casework and counseling draw heavily on psychiatric understanding, and both accomplish results which are often as significant as those achieved through psychotherapy, as such. What, then, is the essence of psychotherapy? The specificity which is to be found in casework and counseling does not characterize psychotherapy, which has always been thought of as being more general in character. Originally a form of treatment for certain types of mental illness, psychotherapy has been extended so that it is not limited today to the mentally ill. When we refer to psychotherapy, however, we generally imply profound personality change. The use of a service or the solution of a problem is not what we mean by psychotherapy, although the client who really uses a service constructively, or takes help on the basis of a specific living problem, might undergo a significant personal development. He might use the service, however, or come to a satisfactory solution of the problem without undergoing psychotherapy, as such. Psychotherapy, in other words, is focused on personality change. The person who goes for psychotherapy generally recognizes the need for such change himself, and he seeks help in effecting it. He may or may not want help with a specific problem, and he may or may not need a social service. He does feel the need for change within himself, however, and he consequently seeks psychotherapy. The focus of psychotherapy, therefore, is the personality of the individual and the balance of forces within him. His fear, will, guilt, affection, hate must be brought into a different relation, so to speak, with one another. The fear-ridden person, for example, is helped to have less fear and perhaps to express more of his will. The person who has trouble in showing his affection, but who expresses his hatred at every turn, may be helped to live in a loving way and without fear that he may be destroyed if he lives out his affection for others. The one whose guilt is so great that he cannot act may be freed to express the strong, assertive part of himself. This is psychotherapy. It is concerned primarily with what goes on *within the individual* and with change which is to be effected through a relationship with the therapist whose attention is centered on the inner make-up of the individual.

It must be recognized, of course, that not all practice which is carried out under the name of psychotherapy has this balance of forces within the individual as its focus. Many psychiatrists, for example, work with certain patients on what we have defined as a counseling basis, but they in all probability would designate it as psychotherapy. In the practice of some agencies, too, it is often impossible to distinguish between counseling as carried out by psychiatrically oriented workers and psychotherapy as practiced by the psychiatrist. Psychiatry and psychotherapy should not be looked upon as identical. Originally, however, psychotherapy was the province of psychiatrists, and there are many today who believe that it should be exclusively a medical discipline. Others, including many psychiatrists, disagree with this point of view, and in actuality there are many non-medical psychotherapists practicing today. Much of their practice is what we have called "counseling" here. Some of it is psychotherapy in the sense that it actually is intended to result in a different balance of forces within the personality of the individual. Despite all the confusion caused by the imprecision of terms, however, if we are to look for the distinguishing characteristic of psychotherapy, the only place where it will be found, it seems to me, is in its focus on the balance of personality forces.

Implications in the Definitions

This type of tri-partite differentiation has much practical as well as theoretical value. While the distinctions which are made here are in no sense absolute ones, and while it must be readily admitted that there is much overlapping among casework, counseling, and psychotherapy, I believe that the synonymous use of the terms is misleading and quite contrary to the understanding of the general public. These terms have a history and are not easily shorn of their historical connotations. In the distinctions which I have made, I have tried to bear in mind the connotations which the general public brings to these terms and also their historical meanings.

As I see it, there are tremendous administrative and technical implications inherent in the distinction between casework and counseling. Certain agencies actually can be organized differently when the full implications of the distinction are recognized. By this I of course do not mean that a hierarchy is set up in which counseling is given status higher than that of casework. Quite the contrary is the case, at least as far as my own thinking is concerned, for I believe that if it were necessary to create such a hierarchy, casework would have to occupy the higher status because of the additional and more involved skills which are often required in the administration of concrete social services with full psychological understanding. Placing a child and working with full understanding of his parents or foster parents, and of the meaning of the placement to them, certainly requires no less in the way of training or special skill than counseling with the parents of a child living in his own home, as in child guidance. From my own personal experience I should say that it requires more. Where both concrete services and personal help without any tangible service are offered in the same agency, however, there are many important administrative advantages which may be achieved on the basis of such a distinction. Specialization in case loads and in supervision, based upon a distinction between the case requiring counseling only and that requiring a concrete service in addition, is both practical and economical. Specialized skills are developed by workers who concentrate, for example, on placement and home-finding, as contrasted with counseling for parents and children living in their own homes, and the client is the one who benefits.

As far as technical implications are concerned, it seems important to recognize that the actual content of the interview is often very different, where there is a concrete service which must be talked about by client and worker, from what it is when counselor and client are concerned with an inter-personal problem, but not with a specific and tangible service which the one is providing and the other receiving. The presence of the service means in addition that there are different diagnostic opportunities, different responsibilities which the worker must be conscious of, and as a consequence, different dynamics operating in the relationship.

There are some interesting implications from the standpoint of community organization in the distinctions which I have proposed. Wherever there is a multiplicity of agencies, questions arise regarding logical distribution of function. What should be done, for example, in the mental hygiene clinic of a mental hospital as contrasted with a family agency, or in a family agency as contrasted with placement services? Distinguishing psycho-therapy from counseling and counseling from the administration of tangible services can help to solve some of the knotty problems involved in such a community organization situation. This is true, too, in large agencies where departmental distinctions may be made on such a basis. Homemaker service, for example, may be separated from the marital counseling functioning, placement from child guidance, and so on.

If the distinction between casework and counseling seems troublesome to some readers, it might be well to emphasize that I do not wish to exclude anything from "casework." I wish merely to recognize that the worker has something extremely important to deal with when he is doing casework in the sense of administering a concrete service, such as placement or homemaker service, and this adds an element not present when he meets with the client on a straight counseling basis, that is, for the purpose of helping a client with a problem through discussion only. When the worker himself must *do something*, such as placing a child, what he does must be distinguished from talking about a problem. Historically, the word "counseling" was never meant to include such *activity* as the word "casework." "Casework" always implies activity, and "counseling" implies discussion alone.

What difference does the presence or absence of activity make? According to my way of thinking, it makes a great deal of difference to both client and worker. When the client is reacting to what the worker is doing, in a casework situation, and not just to what he is saying, much attention must be given by both client and worker to the doing, and it becomes a center of interest. How satisfactory is it? What are the client's reactions to what the worker is doing? Does the worker's activity arouse competitive feelings, feelings of inferiority, and others? Does the client feel that he or somebody else could do it better? Does he wish that whatever the worker is doing did not have to be done at all? These and many other possible reactions develop as a result of the fact that the worker is charged with doing something.

Where the worker is not actively doing something about the

problem himself, but is simply discussing it with the client, a different psychology prevails. The client may wish to make the problem the worker's; but it can never be that to the extent it can be when the worker is actually handling a big part of the problem himself, by providing a service which is at least a temporary solution to it. The counselor does not take this kind of responsibility for providing a means to a possible solution of the problem, and the agency cannot hold him accountable for, let us say, the money he spends, the length of time a homemaker stays in a situation, or anything of this character. But both client and agency have a right to expectations and a right to make requirements of the caseworker who does carry responsibility for such *doing*. When the worker serves as counselor only — when he simply discusses a problem with the client, but is not expected to act himself in relation to that problem, there will be enormous differences in the relationship with the client, in the supervision, in the development of special skills required for special services, and in various other respects.

Judging by the preference which many social workers now show for the term "counseling," used as a substitute for "casework," it is not impossible that the latter term will disappear in time. In that event it would still be necessary to find a way of giving emphasis to what the worker does in administering a tangible service, and to the value of the service itself as a helpful agent. The term "counseling" alone ignores this important aspect of what caseworkers now do. I do not mean to suggest that counseling is not a legitimate function for the social agency. It is my belief, however, that counseling in social agencies will remain a rather vague entity until it is quite rigorously defined and distinguished from other forms of help. Those who maintain that the client comes to an agency for *help* and that he does not care what the help consists of or who gives it to him, do not see the need for such definition. Those who are interested in wider implications of the use of the term, however, find a definition essential.

The Role of the Agency

While the agency can play a certain role in counseling, its role in that respect is different from the role which it plays in casework. This difference is an important one and must be recognized. In a casework process the agency's policies and procedures come up again and again. If financial assistance is being administered, for example, there are questions regarding the amount, the purposes for which it is to be granted, the conditions under which the client may become eligible, and so on. All of these are dealt with in agency policy and procedure. The agency, as a whole, has certain views about such matters which the worker must bring to the client. Likewise with a service such as child placement, there will be policies and procedures related to admission and discharge, visiting, medical care, clothing, schooling, requirements of the foster parent, and board payments. These will be discussed with the client repeatedly and inevitably, since they represent so important a part of placement. In one way or another the client will raise innumerable questions about all these aspects of placement. Interviews, accordingly, are permeated with such functional content. The worker will necessarily talk with the client about problems which he experiences aside from these aspects of placement. In fact, he will know that the placement cannot be of very great value unless problems associated with the need for it are the focus of a good deal of his contact with the client. There are personality and interpersonal problems in every placement situation and the worker must be prepared to recognize and deal with them. The work done along these lines may be called "counseling," if one prefers to use that term rather than "casework." If one does so, however, no particular emphasis is given to such a vitally important part of the placement situation as the very service or set of services which the worker is administering. To call the placement worker a placement counselor is to ignore the fact that he does more than counsel. He finds a home, he takes the child to it, he visits the child there, he provides clothing, he arranges medical examinations. Each of these acts carried out by the worker has great meaning to the child and to the parent, foster parent, and any others who may be involved. The worker must try to find out what his actions mean to each of the parties to the placement, and he proceeds on the basis of the understanding which he acquires. He must keep aware of the personality and inter-personal problems involved, and to whatever extent he is able to do so, he will contribute to their solution.

All of this contrasts strikingly with, let us say, parent-child counseling carried out with parents and a child living in his own home. Here the worker has no responsibility for finding a suitable home, no clothing budget to administer, no visits to be made regularly, and so forth. The counselor in this latter instance is concerned with only an inter-personal problem. The client wants nothing of him in the way of concrete service, no financial assistance, placement, homemaker service, or anything of such character. He wants a solution to his problem, a solution which he sees as taking place through discussion — he wants counsel, in short, and nothing more.

In this latter situation, the client will have some questions pertaining to the agency service, and these will be discussed with him. But the agency's part is not *inevitably* discussed in the way it is where casework services come into play. The reason why functional discussions — discussions of agency policy and procedure — are so prevalent in casework (defined, of course, in terms of concrete service) is that they are so relevant. The worker's answers to the client's questions about the agency's services will be an important part of their discussion, and exploration of the meaning of such questions will serve to help the client understand himself and his problems.

In counseling, the concrete service itself, with all its many implications, cannot stand between client and worker and cannot be the continued subject of discussion. Nor do the agency's policies and procedures make up more than a fraction of the content of the interviews. Instead, it is the client's *problem*, in its many different forms, that occupies the most prominent place. In casework related to the concrete service, the client's problem is of course a subject of discussion, but it is always the problem as related to the service. In counseling, it is the problem itself which is most prominent — the complaint regarding the child's behavior, the irresponsibility of the marital partner, the demands of the employer, the arbitrariness of school rules. There will be discussion of respective responsibilities of worker and client, and agency-determined factors such as the fee and the divided-interview procedure where two workers are involved will be kept in the foreground. But it is the client's problem which makes up the great bulk of the discussion, and it is the worker's personal skill which is the primary helping factor.

I should not want to minimize the importance of skill in casework. But in casework the worker's skill is complemented by the agency's policies and procedures to a much greater extent. The counselor is forced to rely more on his own resources, so to speak. The caseworker is supported to a much greater extent by agency framework. Many of the problems brought to the counselor could be brought to a private therapist and dealt with adequately. The problems dealt with by the caseworker — problems of relief, placement, and other tangible services — could not be handled by a private therapist. The resources of the agency are needed, and they will play a most important role in discussions between client and worker.

The Person, the Problem, and the Service

In counseling it is not the impersonal resources of an agency, such as relief or placement, that are being sought by the client. Rather, he seeks personal help with a specific problem — help which is largely therapeutic in nature. Casework help is therapeutic too, but it is first of all help to utilize an objective service — a service which has value for the client. In this respect the overlapping between casework, counseling and psychotherapy, which we have spoken of before, must be borne in mind. This overlapping may be diagrammed as shown on page 120. According to this scheme it may be seen how the caseworker by extending himself, so to speak, becomes the counselor; how the counselor, standing between the caseworker and psychiatrist, may extend himself into either field; and how the activities of the psychotherapist are related to those of both the caseworker and the counselor.

Despite much overlapping, however, there are essential differences of orientation between casework attached to a specific service and counseling on the basis of a recognized and defined problem. Psychotherapy as such is geared to the person rather than to the problem, although the way the person is reached very often is through the specific problem upon which his energies are being spent. Counseling has very little value unless it too gets to the person. But in counseling, specific problems of social relationship *always* predominate, whereas in therapy, as such, much more attention is given to the intra-psychic. Casework is ever mindful of the person and the problem. The service, however, always occupies a position in the center of the stage.

The problem, the person, and the service are all interrelated, so that it is difficult in practice to extract one from the other. For purposes of definition, however, it is important to do so, and from the standpoint of how the worker will function practically, it is important to know where his own orientation is likely to lead him. The orientation of counseling is toward a social and psychological problem, which brings counseling close to therapy and even makes it in some instances indistinguishable from therapy as such. If counseling is going to be done in social agencies, however, it seems highly important that emphasis be put on the *defined problem,* since only this will enable the client or worker to know where to start and where to stop. Agencies must differentiate their purposes from the standpoint of financial support and economical operation, and above all, must make themselves known to the client-community in terms of definite purposes. They cannot exist *as agencies* for so vague a purpose as to provide any and all kinds of help. Child guidance, for example,

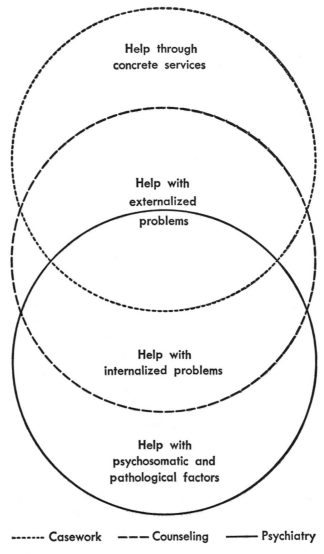

Help through
concrete services

Help with
externalized
problems

Help with
internalized problems

Help with
psychosomatic and
pathological factors

------- Casework   ——— Counseling   ——— Psychiatry

The Overlapping of Casework, Counseling, and Psychotherapy

must be distinguished from marital counseling. The agency which sets itself up to do both,[6] as though they were one and the same thing, will only confuse its workers and clients. By differentiating the two, both client and worker are enabled to function within a recognized framework. Each has a starting point and an ending point determined by the nature of the problem. The undifferentiated agency — the one set up to help with any problem regardless of its nature — is likely to find itself in a morass of problems to which its workers often are not oriented and in relation to which they have developed no special understanding or skill.

The Specific Character of Counseling

Counseling is specific. Generic skills are presupposed, but specific orientation on the part of the counselor is expected by the client and is helpful to him. The person who has a child-guidance problem does not go to the counselor for the aged. He wants to talk to someone who is oriented to *his* problem and not necessarily to others. Specialization implies the development of special skills, special adaptation, and special clear-cut focus. When counseling is carried out under these conditions it is something distinct from generalized therapy and therefore constitutes an understandable agency function.

The specificity of the counseling function need never be violated, even in so wide a field as family counseling. Here it may seem difficult at first to distinguish between marital counseling, let us say, and child guidance. In nearly every child guidance case, there is some point at which the client wishes to talk about the marital partner, and in many marital counseling cases there is a point where the client wishes to talk about a problem in relation to children. But this does not mean that the two are one and the same thing. While there is this kind of likeness in all counseling situations, clients do focus their problems at one spot

[6] Departmentalization in a multiple-service agency serves the same essential purpose as definition of function in a single-service agency.

rather than another. Sometimes they can come for help on one basis, whereas applying for help on another might be impossible. Furthermore, help taken in one area has a different significance from help taken in another. The person who comes for help with a difficult child may get help in the area of his relation to the spouse, but that does not do the child much good (except indirectly) and it does not necessarily help the person in his relationship with the child. It is true that, whether the difficulty is with the spouse or a child, the person must acquire understanding of himself if he is to accomplish anything at all, and this may lead him into psychotherapy as such. It not infrequently happens that a person who first seeks help on a counseling basis decides later to seek psychotherapy.

Counseling should bring about understanding of one's own self, but it should be focused on understanding of a particular difficult relationship. With such a focus, the person gets what he comes for and not something different, no matter how desirable the different thing may be. In so far as the help he gets in one area extends itself to other areas, that certainly is desirable. The attention of the counselor, geared to a specific type of problem, will not be diverted to other kinds of problem, however — nor need it be, if the counselor is able to exploit the potentialities which are inherent in mutual orientation on the part of client and counselor to a specified type of problem. Child guidance can become mixed up with marital counseling when this is not so, and marital counseling can be mixed up with child guidance. There have been instances of both in which a purpose has been achieved, but it is the wrong purpose — not the one which the client wished to achieve in the beginning. Even though generally helpful, such counseling is improper from an agency and a community standpoint.

Definition serves another purpose, and a much more dynamic one, namely, to clarify with the client what he is coming for, when he is in doubt, and to permit him to decide whether he will seek one type of help in contrast with another. There are times when coming to just this kind of decision can serve as the starting point — the initial dynamic — in a therapeutic process. Such definition is not something which the worker does by himself. The defining must be carried on with the client. The client, in coming to a decision with the worker as to what he thinks will be most helpful to him, starts moving in a particular direction. Definition thus has a great deal more than theoretical purpose. It is an essential part of the helping process. In counseling, it plays an especially important role because the decision whether counseling should be the form of help used, or whether it will be one type of counseling rather than another, is dependent on it.

When one emphasizes the generic rather than the specific aspects of counseling, the question arises why, if one works toward the growth and development of personality in all forms of help, it is necessary to distinguish them. Why not look on the job of the counselor, the educator, the minister, the psychiatrist, the child-guidance worker, the marital counselor, as one and the same thing? All are directed to personality growth and development. While all have this as an ultimate objective, however, it is obvious that each one has a different *immediate* goal. Different *means* are used to achieve it. In attaining the ultimate objective some of the same means are used by all. The immediate problem and goal, however, have great implications for counseling.

The client coming for help with a child who is adjusting poorly in school, or whose behavior at home is negativistic, or who has a physical symptom which may have a psychological basis, does not seek marital counseling. He may have a marital problem and he may have a distinct personality problem of his own. Moreover, in the course of the helping process he may become just as conscious of these problems as he is of the problem he presents in the beginning. Ultimately all problems are personality problems. But is it of no consequence that the child is adjusting poorly at school? This is the type of problem which is appropriate for the school counselor or the child guidance clinic. Most family agencies, particularly those which operate on an indiscriminate counseling basis, will accept this type of case rather than refer it to the school counselor or the child guidance clinic, if one is available. Acceptance of such situations as family counseling problems, however, tends to make the family agency a place where counseling of any and every type is offered. If specialized service is not available, there is justification for acceptance of such situations by the family agency. Where specialized counseling is available, however, it can be a most efficient and effective way of meeting such problems.

When the specific aspects of counseling are stressed, the child guidance worker does not represent himself as a marital counselor or as a general therapist, and the client who wants child guidance comes to him. The one who wants marital counseling goes to the agency and worker offering that. Different methods of counseling, appropriate to the particular type of help needed, can be distinguished when this is done. The client makes an important decision in the beginning regarding the type of help which he wishes to seek, and this decision then serves as a focus of attention. His ambivalence will invariably come to the fore with respect to this decision of his own. Whether the problem resides in him or in the other, or in both, is brought out, and the extent of the togetherness or the separateness likewise becomes an important phase of discussion. Questions of dependence and independence also clearly emerge, in fact, are brought out by this type of approach.

Counseling has evolved out of both casework and therapy. It is a form of help which neither the diagnostic nor the functional school claims as exclusively its own. Both schools must admit their indebtedness to the field of psychotherapy where counseling is concerned. But regardless of the approach to counseling, the likeness between this form of help and therapy, as far as method is concerned, and results too, must be recognized. For this reason, I think, there can be no doubt whatever that there are possibilities for some rapprochement of the two schools in the area of counseling. There is more difference, I believe, between diagnostic and functional casework than there is between diagnostic and functional counseling. The emphasis which the functional caseworker places on the service itself and the attention which he gives to its many implications are lacking in the realm of counseling, since the element of specific and concrete social service is lacking. On the other hand, the necessity for putting much emphasis on the personality of the client cannot be questioned in the field of counseling. Despite many other differences, both schools, in the realm of counseling at least, have shown a predilection for the therapeutic and a lesser kind of interest in the social. In the development of functional casework, the social factor came into prominence and the psychological or the therapeutic played a secondary role. In counseling, whether functional or diagnostic, the therapeutic factor again gains the ascendancy. In so far as counseling is practiced in agencies, the social aspect is present and to some extent there may be a social goal. In method, however, it is the therapeutic consideration which is predominant, and this is true for both schools.

Dynamics in Counseling

As soon as the predominance of the therapeutic factor in counseling is recognized, a question naturally arises regarding the dynamics of counseling as compared with casework. In casework, where the concrete service is present, the service itself with its inherent character and limitations serves as a constant dynamic factor. The client will be reacting, implicitly or explicitly, to all the implications of the particular service. If he has feelings that the money which he is receiving is insufficient, it will be necessary for the worker and the client to discuss this. If, in placing his child, he feels that there is too much risk, or that he will have to give up too much of his normal parental responsibility, it will again be necessary to discuss this. In other words, there is always a dynamic factor inherent in the administration of the service itself. It is impossible to administer a service without eliciting a response which has to do with the service. It is satisfactory or unsatisfactory, threatening or helpful — in any case, the very administration of the service must evoke response. Since this will be response focused on the service itself, one must think of the service as an initial dynamic. Administering it starts a chain of responses, and these responses become the concern of the worker.

In counseling, where the concrete service does not exist, there obviously cannot be responses to it. This means, therefore, that one must look to other factors which are dynamic in character. These may be quite similar to, but they are never identical with, certain of the dynamic factors which are to be found in the case-work situation. In placement, for example, if there are visiting regulations, the client will have his own opinions and feelings about the very existence of such regulations, and it becomes necessary for the worker to discuss the matter with him. When this is done the client will often modify his original opinions or feelings. But in counseling, where such a structural element simply does not exist, there certainly can be no discussion of it. The client's opinions and feelings will be focused on other matters and these must be the object of attention.

What difference does it make whether the client's interests are focused on one matter rather than another? Is it not a question, in any case, of recognizing the client's true feelings about what is happening between him and the worker, and does the content of the discussion make any real difference? My own answer to these questions is that the content of discussion does make a very great difference. Some functionalists deny this, maintaining that it is only the process which counts and that the helping process is fundamentally the same in all instances. I do not believe that this is so. The helping process cannot take place independently of a content of some kind, and the kind of content materially affects the process. The number of interviews, the spacing of interviews, and the conditions under which the interviews take place will all be conditioned by the nature of the service being given, and what takes place in these interviews (the content) will be appropriate or inappropriate depending upon the type of service.

One can grow through discussion and significant response to a problem which one feels in relation to another person — wife, child, parent, employer, and so on. Moreover, any development which takes place in relation to any of these will have *some* influence upon many other relationships. But being comfortable with one's self as a child is quite different from being comfortable with one's self as a parent. Being adjusted as an employer is different from being adjusted as an employee. Counseling is directed toward a particular problem of adjustment, and it may or may not have a significant effect on other areas of the person's total life. It is therefore the *particular problem of adjustment* which becomes the natural and logical content of the discussion between the client and the counselor, and the limits of such discussion are determined by the nature of the problem itself. In placement, for example, what the client likes or dislikes about the foster home, what he is permitted or not permitted by the agency to do by way of clothing his child, providing for medical care, and the like, will be appropriate subjects of discussion, as well as how he feels about his own competence as a parent who has placed his child. The discussion will occur within a placement framework, and the content of discussion will be largely determined by the placement situation. The growth which takes place on the part of the parent in the child placement situation will be growth stemming from his understanding of himself as a parent who must place his child. Placement itself in other words, will serve as an initial dynamic. Much will depend on it. Much will follow from it.

In child guidance or parent-child counseling, however, this cannot be so. Where the child resides in his own home, the content of discussion will be different and a different helping process will take place. The same *generic* element will play a part in counseling as in any type of helping process, but the specific factors will be different. The time factor will necessarily be different. The role played by the foster home and by the agency functioning *in loco parentis* will not be a subject of discussion, because these conditions simply do not exist in the counseling situation. Instead there will be much more specific discussion of particularly troubling aspects of the child's behavior and the parent's reaction to these. The parent's expectations of the counselor and of himself will be the subject of discussion rather than the agency's requirements of him as a parent. In other words, the whole helping process will have to be more *personally* centered, more a matter between the client and the particular counselor than a matter between the agency and the client. Changing workers in the midst of a counseling process is often much more difficult than changing workers in the casework process for this reason. The initial and sustaining dynamics are of a more personal character in counseling than they are in casework centered on a concrete service, and what the client goes through in the two different helping processes is different.

If one looks to factors such as time and fee, certain basic differences are again apparent. Where a concrete service must be administered, the frequency of contact, the time span of the total case, and even the time given to the individual interview can be directly related to the nature of the concrete service itself. The time span in a case in vocational guidance, for example, is very different from that required by a placement case. The fee, likewise, must be appropriate to the nature of the particular service. In all instances there will be a time factor and in many there will be a fee. How significant the particular time factor or the fee will be as a dynamic in the helping process, however, will depend upon the inherent nature of the particular kind of help which is being offered.

Counseling must thus be regarded as a special form of helping in which dynamic factors quite different from certain ones prevalent in the specific fields of casework play a very significant part. Since these dynamics are more personal in character — more client and worker centered than they are agency centered, counseling must be looked upon as being perhaps more akin to therapy, in this respect, than it is to specific types of casework. This does not mean that the caseworker who understands the generic nature of the helping process cannot become a good counselor. Experience demonstrates that not only can the skillful caseworker become a good counselor, but that training in maintaining a focus, such as is required in working with a concrete service, can be excellent preparation for counseling which also must be thought of as specific and focused.

Both casework and counseling, however, can be sterile and mechanical where there is an absence of the dynamic factors which are to be found in the *therapeutic* relationship. The caseworker or the counselor who is to relate helpfully to the client must have the capacity to relate *therapeutically* to his client, that is to say, he must have a knowledge of and a personal adaptability to the conditions under which psychological growth and development of the other person in a relationship can take place. He must develop an understanding of and a feel for the dynamics which are at work in the relationship between himself and the other person. If he functions as a caseworker administering a concrete service, certain of the dynamics will stem from the service itself and the agency through which it is being administered. If he functions, on the other hand, as a counselor working with specific problems of relationship rather than specific service, other dynamics will be more prominent. The worker, in any case, must keep himself geared to the dynamics which are in operation between the client and himself.

Analysis of the dynamic developments in any given helping situation is by no means an easy task. As counselor and client actually relate to each other, it is extremely difficult because of the attention given to the problem under discussion to keep aware of the dynamic factors at work. In casework, where the presence of the concrete service produces a constant dynamic factor, and where there must be much identification on the part of the worker with the service itself, it is much easier to keep aware of the way in which the service operates dynamically between client and worker. Where the contact is centered on a problem of relationship, however, and where the help given is much more a matter of personal skill than of agency service, the dynamic factors are more difficult to ascertain.

Even in counseling, however, there are certain dynamic factors at work which might be thought of as agency-determined. For example, in marital counseling, the procedure of having both marital partners see the same worker certainly operates dynamically. This procedure stimulates each person to put a certain content into the interviews, a content which is directly related to the fact that the other person is coming and telling his side of the story. If such a procedure is agency policy, then one is certainly justified in saying that an agency-determined dynamic operates here. This is a procedure which can be followed just as well in private practice, however, as it is in an agency setting, whereas in the casework situation, where the agency itself actually offers a concrete service, there are procedures which could not be applied in private practice, since the service cannot be offered privately. A private practitioner cannot set conditions of eligibility for financial assistance, because financial assistance is inherently an agency matter, and not a matter of personal skill only.

In counseling, therefore, one must look for the principal dynamic factors in the same place where one finds them in therapy, namely, in the relationship itself. One must look to the projecting and the identifying which the client does and one must look to the way in which the counselor uses the content of discussion. How does he respond to the client's putting of blame upon the other? How does he interpret discussion of the past? Does he share his diagnostic impressions with the client? What awareness of what is taking place in the process, that is, of the client's direction of movement, does he share with the client? What use does he make of the time factor? These are all matters of skill in counseling and they are all much less agency-determined than some of the dynamics which are at work in the casework situation, such as considerations of eligibility, visiting regulations, and so on.

Counseling must thus be viewed as a form of help in which the skill of the worker predominates as it does in therapy. In saying this, one does not minimize the importance of skill in the administering of any concrete casework service. In the latter instance, however, there are agency or functional factors which are much more prominent. In counseling, it is the way a client relates to a particular worker, and the worker to him, which determines whether the client will be helped or not. The principal dynamics must be sought in personal factors rather than impersonal ones, and agency function therefore plays a comparatively limited role.

The swing of the pendulum in the development of counseling must thus be regarded as a swing away from emphasis on function and back toward interest in the therapeutic. Counseling is a form of therapy. It is not the administration of a service, and it cannot be focused on a service, as any analysis of actual counseling interviews (even those of functionally oriented workers) will readily demonstrate. The contribution of functional thinking is therefore seen as a contribution to the development of casework as a method of administering services. With the development of counseling as a legitimate field of operations for social agencies, the functional approach has proved to have limited applicability and the emphasis of the diagnostic school upon the understanding of personality once more comes into prominence.

Neither the diagnostic nor the functional school, however, has done what must be done for a fuller understanding of counseling, namely, to carry out a full and detailed analysis of the dynamics at play in any counseling situation. This can now be done through the use of electrical recording devices in which counseling interviews are taken down verbatim. The verbatim recordings not only of isolated interviews but of a complete counseling process should be analyzed from the standpoint of an inquiry regarding the dynamics at work. When this is done, many of the matters which are presently the subject of dispute between diagnostic and functionally oriented workers will fall into proper perspective and a new phase of development will be at hand. This will be a scientific phase, that is to say, one in which theory will follow from inductive inquiry. It will also be a dynamic phase since the very dynamics of the helping process will be the subject of inquiry.

5 THE COMING PHASE

OF INTEGRATION

We come now to some examination of what might appear to be basic differences between the two schools of casework thought. In noting these differences, however, it is highly important that we do so in an evolutionary perspective. We must recognize first of all that the division of the profession into two schools of thought — diagnostic and functional — came about as a part of an evolutionary development. Neither school emerged full-blown, nor having emerged did they remain completely static. Both of these schools are in a process of development, which during the past decade or so was rather self-contained. Each school developed in its own way and with comparatively little reference to the other. Developments within the past few years, however, would indicate that this period of independent growth may be coming to an end and that both schools may develop much more in the future through greater recognition of each other.

I am aware of the fact that there are many who do not agree with this inference. Pointing out that the conflict is now more severe than ever, these people hold that the two schools of case-work cannot be integrated because their respective orientations are so different. Even the Committee which prepared *A Comparison of Diagnostic and Functional Casework Concepts* felt that there were "wide gaps in mutual understanding" when they started to analyze records, and stated that

> Certain apparent similarities between the two orientations of practice do not represent real likenesses when related to underlying premises. Within the context of the total philosophy and method of each group, these concepts have markedly divergent connotations. Attempts by the Committee to compare them as entities resulted only in obscuring basic differences.[1]

The Committee could do no better than to decide that the differences were greater than the likenesses and therefore felt that each group would have to present its own views separately. The report stresses the cleavage between the two schools, in both its form and its content, and gives little if any attention to the possibilities for integration.

An Evolutionary Point of View

An evolutionary philosophy looks upon this split in an entirely different light. Not only does it see the possibilities for integration inherent in the split, but it would maintain that intensification of the cleavage is a prior condition to integration. Instead of looking upon the difference as a bad state of affairs, or as a static and unchangeable one, the evolutionary point of view [2] looks upon

[1] Committee to Study Basic Concepts in Casework Practice, Family Service Association of America, *A Comparison of Diagnostic and Functional Casework Concepts; A Report*, ed. by Cora Kasius (New York: FSAA, 1950), p. 12.

[2] A point of view similar to that expressed in this chapter is brought out in two excellent statements: one a review of *A Comparison of Diagnostic and Functional Casework Concepts*, called "A Leap to Conclusions,"

it as an inevitable part of a growth process. The battle is often most intense just before it is finished. In an evolutionary process, likewise, opposites come into conflict with each other most vigorously at the point where they are about to merge. This point of change or integration, when it is observed in an individual, is sometimes spoken of as a "life and death struggle." Each opposing side of the individual's will-conflict asserts itself with more force than ever. Each refuses to give in to the other. In group processes of any type, this is no less so. There is no evolutionary process without struggle, nor is there any with incessant struggle. The stage of conflict precedes and is balanced by a stage of integration.

It must be admitted by proponents of both schools that the past decade has been a period of gradually intensifying conflict. Differences have been sharpened especially among the generation of workers who started with almost identical views. The differences which have developed have led these workers to a point where no real likeness is recognized and where it is proclaimed that nothing but professional divorce will do. Such professional separation may be necessary, but I, for one, cannot feel that it must be final or absolute. There cannot be two professions of social work. There must be one, and within the one there will be differences. But these differences are also in a state of flux and development. They are not absolute any more than the conflicting trends within an individual are absolute. They are rather opposite sides of the same fundamental life trend. No life process can exist without such opposites, which interplay with each other and make for evolutionary movement. In this evolutionary movement, which usually can be seen only in wide sweeps of time, opposite forces merge and separate and merge again. At first one

by Grace Marcus in the June, 1951, issue of *Trends in Social Work;* and the other, an article by Elizabeth Herzog and John Frings, "A Proposed Next Step in the Diagnostic-Functional Issue," *Social Casework,* 33:140–147 (April, 1952). Cf., also, Morton I. Teicher, "Anthropology and the Functional-Diagnostic Controversy," *Social Service Review,* 27:55–61 (March, 1953), and Helen Harris Perlman, "The Parable of the Workers of the Field," *Social Service Review,* 23:21–24 (March, 1949).

is dominant, then another. Neither remains completely separated, nor does either ever achieve total ascendancy over the other. Merging, when it occurs, is temporary in character and when it breaks up there is another split. This split also cannot be sustained beyond a certain point and is followed by merger again.

This view of the evolutionary process may be applied to the field of social work as well as to any other social phenomenon or process. Social work is one of the most dynamic of social institutions. Its nature is changing rather than stable. Adaptable to changing social forces — to changing times and circumstances — it must change itself more frequently and perhaps more rapidly than most other institutions. It cannot remain static. To do so would be to lose its value as a social institution designed to make other social institutions more effective.[3] As a social institution, social work should be thought of as having a function auxiliary to that of other moving and developing institutions such as the family and the school. Any static point of view within social work is therefore incompatible with the very nature of this institution.

This means that any attempt to maintain the separateness which obtains between the two schools of casework is a violation of a fundamental principle of social work. Such separateness comes about inevitably in a process of evolutionary development, and no one can take personal responsibility for it. But the evolutionary process that brings it about can also bring an end to separateness. The evolutionary process in social institutions can operate only in and through human beings. In no sense is it a mystical or supernatural force. It is rather because human mentality itself is evolutionary in character that human beings can project and identify an evolutionary process which has applicability to the understanding of ourselves, as well as of the rest of the physical and biological world.

All of this applies to the profession of social work. No profession should be looked upon as an entity in itself. Nor should it be conceived of as totally independent of other social phenomena.

[3] Cf. Helen Witmer, *Social Work* (New York: Farrar & Rinehart, 1942).

In like manner, it should not be looked upon as being in the grasp of some kind of supra-human force which controls it at every turn. A profession is made up of human beings and bears the stamp and character of the human beings who comprise it. If they see themselves as *evolving* beings their profession will reflect this evolutionary view. If, on the other hand, they deal in absolutes, the profession will take on the same character.

It is appropriate that social work look upon itself as an evolving profession. The diagnostic and functional schools in casework must also be thought of as evolving. Each is a manifestation of oppositeness within the profession. The evolutionary process can be retarded and it can be facilitated. It cannot be completely controlled. As participants in such a process, it is difficult for us to see the ways in which we retard or facilitate it. It is extremely difficult to step out of the framework within which we operate so that we may see what our own contribution is to the evolutionary process. But difficult as it is to do this, it is not impossible. In practice, we can function only within the framework of principle and of experience which makes up our own practice. Outside of actual practice, however, it is possible to observe the effects, upon the profession as a whole, of trends in which we ourselves participate. The split between the diagnostic and functional schools, in which all caseworkers participate at present, has had its value from an evolutionary standpoint. It has brought about a sharpening of principle which can only be looked upon as a contribution to the development of a profession. It has a negative side, however, which is manifest in efforts directed toward intensification of existing differences rather than toward unification.

Professional Synthesis

The profession must move on to a synthesis and it will do so when efforts are directed toward this end. Oppositeness in some new form will manifest itself, and there will be attempts to hold on to the old as well as to move on to the new. In any genuine effort to synthesize there must be less holding on to the old and more moving on to the new than there has been in the past.

What this means is that present differences must be stated with a view to eventual if not immediate synthesis, and with a readiness to take on that which has validity in a different point of view, or to discard that which has proved to be impractical in one's own. The scientific attitude, by which I mean an inquiring attitude, is not incompatible with either of the present opposing viewpoints. In fact, what is needed is cultivation of the scientific *attitude* in both. This does not mean proclaiming any principle as scientific and resting on it. It means a willingness to subject to the test of actual experience any principle or philosophical belief. In a field such as social work, only those principles which can be proved to be of practical value in helping may be said to have validity. Social work is meant to help others. It is not a way of securing self-gratification through the maintenance of principle.

There is much evidence that social workers of all times have been very ambivalent in their desire to help. The wish to help is counterbalanced by the wish not to help, and the latter can easily move into the ascendancy with justification and rationalization of every conceivable character. As professionals we are perhaps less subject to our own nature than were the helpers of the pre-professional period, but we are not without a similar ambivalence. Helping others is personally demanding. We wish to do it, but we also think of what it will require of us. The most giving person has his moments of selfishness. It is for this reason that giving professionally must have its limits. Those who protest that they wish only to give, thus denying their own ambivalence, very often take refuge from actual giving in a maintenance of principle which makes less personal demand of them.

The inner need of the professional for balance in his social relationships must have its expression just as it must with every other human being. Too much giving will not do, nor will no giving at all. One side of the conflict must balance the other. There is a difference, however, between professional and nonprofessional giving. This lies in the type and extent of responsibility which the giver takes for his giving. Both of the existing schools, as we have seen, have been concerned with the question of responsibility for helping. One of their important differences would seem to lie in what they will take responsibility for doing or not doing themselves and the extent to which they will hold the client responsible. The question of responsibility is tied up with the question of ambivalence. One can give or help responsibly only when one's own ambivalence is taken into possession, so to speak — when one does not claim to be totally giving, but instead recognizes the need for balance.

The problem of the extent to which the social worker can help is a problem which has been implicit in all of social work thinking for a good many years and is one which, in my judgment, cannot be settled on principle alone. An answer to this problem can be arrived at only by asking questions such as the following: How much does the client want to be helped? What can the worker be satisfied to do? What are the minima, as far as help is concerned, with which agencies can be satisfied? How much helping of the individual client should there be to justify community support? Does the community want more thoroughgoing help than agencies are prepared to give? Do clients seek this?

These are questions which lend themselves to actual research, although little effort has been made along these lines. Answers to such questions are not dependent on any school of thought, so much as they are on scientific study. The thinking which has been advanced by the opposing schools of thought with regard to the responsibility which the worker should assume can be tested through research just as other principles can be. If this is ever done, any worker who is interested in a scientific outlook should be prepared to modify or discard principles which have no scientific foundation. This is the attitude which the profession must manifest in a stage of synthesis. It is an attitude which has been lacking in the past, but hopefully will not be lacking much longer. In the separating phase which the last decade represented, the maintenance of one's own point of view may have been essential. In the phase of professional development which is yet to come, a sufficient security with one's own point of view may make it possible to risk scientific testing. To approach the problem of its own conflict in such a manner would represent genuine modesty and responsibility on the part of the profession.

Aside from the question of scientific study, however, there are a number of areas in which the difference between the two schools of thought turns out to be difference of emphasis rather than total difference, and it is important that this be recognized. This is no denial of the different orientation of the two schools. It is simply an affirmation of the fact that where the difference is one of emphasis, its extent can be clarified objectively.

The Problem of Diagnosis

As an example, let us take the problem of diagnosis itself. How much difference is there in actuality? Some functionalists would maintain that they do no diagnosing. In practice, however, many functional workers make extensive use of a trial period in which client and worker have an opportunity to see, through the experience of actually working together, whether or not they feel it will be worth while to continue. These trial or exploratory interviews represent a period of study. A great deal of diagnosing, whether or not the worker is willing to call it that, takes place within them. Judgments based on living experience, as well as on pertinent information which may confirm or contradict that experience, are what make it possible for the worker to decide whether or not the agency, as he represents it, can be helpful; whether or not the client can make use of help, and if so, what kind. In making such judgments, the functional worker calls on a fund of knowledge concerning personality. In doing this he may use different conceptions from the diagnostic worker, but he nevertheless comes to certain definite opinions regarding the personality of the client. If he does not do this, he must function mechanically and not professionally.

The real difference, according to my way of thinking, is not one of whether there should be diagnosis or not, but rather one regarding the content of the diagnosis. As stated in *Scope and Methods of the Family Service Agency*,[4] the study process of the diagnostically oriented worker

> varies in the number of interviews required, the number of family members or collateral sources interviewed, and so on. Its purpose is to acquire sufficient knowledge and understanding of the problem, of the client's life situation, and of the psychosocial factors operating, to determine what kind of help the client requires and wishes to use, and what resource is best able to meet his needs. Casework consideration leads to (1) a psychosocial diagnosis and (2) an evaluation of the type of help that is appropriate in the particular situation.

In their study, *A Conceptual Framework for Social Casework*, members of the faculty of the University of Pittsburgh School of Social Work have presented the diagnostic phase of casework in terms which, in my judgment, point up certain essential similarities as well as the differences between the diagnostic and functional approaches:

> The caseworker, in initiating the social casework process, is confronted by a person he does not know, with a problem of an undesignated kind. Willingness on the part of the caseworker to acknowledge his initial ignorance of the precise nature of the client and his problem, coupled with the caseworker's emotional freedom, open-mindedness and the rational wish to understand, in order to help, make it possible for the client to become productively related to the study process as a step toward the solution of his problem. The rational necessity for inquiry, since the caseworker is not omniscient, provides the basis for helping the client to deal with his resistances, fears and unrealistic expectations in this situation. Courtesy, respect, acceptance of the client as an individual and a noncondemnatory attitude toward him reassure the client by demonstration and constitute the climate in which his real problems can emerge.

4 New York: Family Service Association of America, 1953, p. 17.

Involvement of the client in the study procedure through such an interacting process between client and worker is essential if the study is to produce the information which is needed for adequate diagnosis and definitive treatment. It thus is basic not only for treatment within a given agency but also for referral elsewhere. Since study involves understanding of the client's situation as he sees it and knowledge of the situation as it actually is, inability on the part of the client to participate in either of these aspects of study will constitute an initial obstacle to be worked through.

The essential qualities of the caseworker outlined above plus the involvement of the client are not sufficient, however, to ensure a competent study. The caseworker must possess a clearly defined body of knowledge about human development and social experience which serves as his frame of reference and guides the process of study.[5]

A frame of reference drawn up by the Pittsburgh group for the initial stages of the casework process includes many suggestions regarding the behavior of the individual which might be observed by the worker, and also many aspects of the client's problem which might be communicated verbally.[6] The diagnostic activity of the worker is thus systematized in a way one does not find in the functional approach. Most functional workers, however, would take little exception to the idea that the worker must learn a good deal from the client himself through observation and verbal communication. The mind of the worker entering into a beginning contact with the client is not a *tabula rasa*. Nor can it be oriented solely to the agency. The functional or the diagnostic worker wants to get to know and understand the client as well as he possibly can. Where the two schools differ, therefore, is on the question of how the worker gets to know the client. What items of information can be used? Must all understanding proceed from the worker's and the client's direct contact with each other? Can the worker know the client

[5] Eleanor E. Cockerill, Louis J. Lehrman, Patricia Sacks, and Isabel Stamm, *A Conceptual Framework for Social Casework* (Pittsburgh: University of Pittsburgh Press, 1953), p. 10.

[6] Cf. Florence Hollis, *Casework Diagnosis — What and Why*, Smith College Studies in Social Work, XXIV, no. 3 (June, 1954), pp. 1–8.

only through his reactions to the way the worker presents himself? Can he diagnose scientifically only if he uses a formal list of items to be studied?

The truth is that it is possible to get to know the client through direct observation and verbal communication, and that one can also get to know him through formal study with certain definite objectives in mind. The client will spontaneously tell a good deal about himself, if the worker is a willing and receptive listener. He will gladly answer questions about himself, if the worker is disposed to ask them in a spirit of genuine helpful inquiry. He also will make it possible to secure information from others, if he feels that it will be used to his benefit. The worker therefore need not depend on only one way of getting to know his client, and in actual practice seldom does so. This is true for functionally oriented workers as well as those whose approach is diagnostic.

Disagreement between the two schools on the question of diagnosis thus becomes largely a matter of disagreement about the basis on which the worker comes to significant conclusions about the client. Both certainly do come to such conclusions. One insists on doing it formally and through the use of a definite diagnostic scheme. The other believes that such conclusions must be arrived at through actual direct contact with the client. Is it impossible to combine the two? I do not think so. In fact, the one approach interferes so little with the other that the two may really be regarded as complementary to each other. What the one misses, the other fills out.

By this I do not mean that functionally oriented workers need only to add a diagnostic scheme to their work, or that diagnostic workers need only to start presenting their function to the client and observing his reactions. The functional-diagnostic controversy cannot be settled so easily. On the basic problem of diagnosis, however, it seems clear that the issue is one regarding the *method* of diagnosis, rather than anything else.

The method of diagnosing, in both instances, involves *observation* of the client. What one observes depends, of course, upon what one is prepared to look for. The functional worker tends to look for the direction in which the whole person seems to be moving. The diagnostic worker, on the other hand, tends to look for data regarding the person. He is interested in the details of the person's life experience. This becomes evident when other aspects of the diagnostic approach, which are designated as essential in a true diagnosis, are considered. The Pittsburgh faculty group states the following:

> Diagnosis is the organization and interpretation of the facts uncovered by study and provides a definition of the total phenomenon and an understanding and interpretation of its behavior and development. It aims to determine cause and to predict how the organism will behave under definable circumstances.
>
> Descriptive facts about the "what" of the individual's functioning (psychologically, physiologically and socially) are acquired in the study process. These are functional manifestations of the individual-environment constellation on the basis of which certain inferences about structure and capacity of the individual are made. These inferences are systematically expressed by the existing classifications with respect to psychological, physiological and social structure. Behind these classification systems are more speculative inferences with respect to ultimate causality (causal constellations) and the causal weighting to be attributed to internal and external factors.
>
> Since psychological, physiological and social factors define man's needs and problems, an adequate diagnosis requires consideration of all of these factors. There is a system of classification with respect to deviation from social norms (unmarried mother, dependent child, unemployed man, etc.). There is a system of classification of physical disturbances (heart disease, cancer, etc.) and there is one for the classification of psychological phenomena (psychoneurosis, psychosis, etc.). Although there has, as yet, been devised no system of classification which reflects and fuses the multidimensional aspect of the phenomena with which social caseworkers deal, they are committed to the concept of the interacting nature of the person and his situation.
>
> Facts do not automatically communicate their significance to the worker. An interpretative or diagnostic act is in-

volved. This act, essentially, is one in which the facts as gathered are reviewed in the light of known inductive generalizations, thus leading to tentative conclusions with respect to case or classification.[7]

We see here that a rigorous, formal, and *comprehensive* procedure is demanded. The functional school would differ with this, not only with respect to the value of formality in diagnosis, but also on the question of comprehensiveness. The question would be raised whether a worker can really know as much as is implied here, about a given client, and also whether it is necessary to know all that is implied in order to render a service adequately. The functional school would also differ on the question of whether a diagnostic judgment must be based on as wide an understanding of causality as this statement requires.

These are significant differences and they cannot be dismissed lightly. The basic fact remains, however: namely, that the essential difference, with respect to diagnosis, is one of method. It may be presumed that the diagnostic school would not object to what the functional worker does along diagnostic lines. It objects to what it considers the lack of adequate diagnostic study. Objections might be raised to the setting forth of diagnostic impressions in Rankian terminology, but certainly not to any attempt on the part of the functional worker to get to know or understand his client. This common interest remains. The essential difference, therefore, is one of method.

Under the heading "The Diagnostic Process — Some Principles," the Pittsburgh group has this to say:

> *Diagnosis must define the phenomenon as an organic whole.*
> The study process answers the question of "what" in a fragmentary way, makes no effort toward integration and, therefore, remains descriptive. Diagnosis consolidates these fragments into a constellation (syndrome). This constellation defines the "what" but may not imply knowledge of cause or development.
> *Diagnosis must deal with the problem of causation (i.e., find the causal constellation).*

[7] *Ibid.*, p. 14.

Diagnosis attempts to answer the question of "why" by identifying first, the operational dynamics immediately responsible for producing the syndrome and secondly, by attempting to identify the fundamental forces (circumstances) which have set these dynamics in motion. The effort to secure the greatest individualization is always in the direction of establishing the cardinal differences between entities. The maximum distinction is attainable only through differential causation (causal constellation).

The diagnosis must reconcile all the known data acquired in the study.

The diagnostic conclusion establishes the connectivity between the data which, at the outset, appeared unrelated. Problems of differential diagnosis arise when the data seem explainable in terms of more than one hypothesis. This is due either to insufficient data or erroneous interpretation of it and should lead to further study of the area of conflict.

Diagnosis (i.e., classification) must result in accurate individualization through the process of comparison of entities with respect to both their similarities and dissimilarities.

Classification and individualization are not opposing processes. On the contrary, individualization is the result of a descending chain of classifications which, by progressive delimitation, achieve the maximum of specificity.[8]

The essential questions raised here are *what* and *why*. What is the nature of the problem and why? The functional approach substitutes another question, namely, *how?* How does the client see his problem? How does the worker, oriented to his particular function, see it? How do client and worker relate to each other? How can the client make use of the worker? The diagnostic worker might maintain that these are questions of treatment and not of diagnosis, to which the functional worker would reply that diagnosis and treatment cannot be separated. The diagnostic worker wishes to diagnose primarily before he treats. The functional worker maintains that one cannot diagnose without trying to help. The question as to *when* one diagnoses therefore takes on some prominence too.

[8] *Ibid.,* pp. 14–15.

Regardless of their opinions, however, as to the method of diagnosis, or the question of when it is to take place, workers of both schools do agree on the necessity for coming to conclusions regarding the personality of the client, his capacity to take help, and the kind of help he can take. Such judgments may be couched in different language, and they may differ in character to some extent. In many instances they do not differ in substance any more than a medical diagnosis made in French would differ from the same diagnosis in German. The diagnostic school uses a system of Freudian personality concepts, and the functional uses Rankian concepts. This makes it necessary for the objective student to be bilingual, so to speak. Substantive facts can be recognized as such, however, in any language.

Where real differences are concerned, such as those mentioned above, argument could continue as long as attention is focused on such differences. If the center of interest is shifted, however, and if attention is given instead to the dynamic factor in diagnosis, then it may be readily seen that the two schools have much in common in the realm of diagnostic thinking. Fundamentally, neither wishes to ignore the need for a type of diagnostic activity which is essentially dynamic in character. As Helen P. Taussig put it, in an article on treatment as an aid to diagnosis,[9] "Diagnosis directs treatment, and as treatment progresses the diagnosis shifts and develops, and treatment must be redirected." This "redirection" takes place at almost every step of the helping process. As the client brings forth new content in his discussion, questions such as these must arise in the mind of the diagnostic or the functional worker: What is the meaning of what is being said? Why is the client saying it? What does it mean to me as a worker? This is the dynamic aspect of diagnosis and no one claims that casework can take place without it. Regardless of how such questions might be answered, the worker who raises them is engaged in an attempt to know his client better than he could initially. His initial impressions, whether formalized or not,

[9] Helen P. Taussig, "Treatment as an Aid to Diagnosis," *The Family*, 19:289–294 (January, 1939).

must be modified in the light of subsequent developments. Having used his initial diagnosis, he then observes the way in which it serves as a dynamic factor in further development of the case. This can be done by the worker of either orientation and it can be done in essentially the same way.

The dynamically oriented worker, as we have seen, will not go off by himself, or to his supervisor, and say, "Now I will diagnose my client." Those who practice dynamically, whether functionally or diagnostically minded, maintain that diagnosis cannot be carried out in this manner, nor can treatment. They see diagnosis and treatment as parts of a whole, which cannot be broken up in practice as it may be in theory. Those who might wish to discard the idea of diagnosis altogether would discard one of the bases for dynamic development between client and worker. This is something which neither school really wants to do. What they both want and need to do is to become more dynamic and not less so. This means using diagnostic thinking, of whatever variety it may be, toward a dynamic end. Nothing in either the diagnostic or the functional philosophy runs counter to such use of diagnosis. It is my belief, therefore, that in a shift of emphasis from the question of how the diagnosing is to be done to the question of how the worker can use his diagnosis dynamically, the two schools will inevitably find that they have much in common.

The Use of History

Let us look into another difference between the two schools, namely, that with regard to history. The diagnostic school is historically oriented, whereas the functional school places its emphasis on the significance of the present experience of worker and client. The diagnostic school wishes to know the *cause* of present difficulties. It feels that such knowledge will enable the worker to remove the symptoms by destroying the cause, as in medical practice. In medicine, however, it is a present cause of a present difficulty which is removed. Past causes cannot be dealt

with as such, because all life processes are irreversible. Knowledge of the history of an illness will sometimes enable one to
understand what present causes may be operating and in this
manner facilitate the treatment. The diagnostic school uses history in this manner. It is interested in what history can teach us
about present causes. It does not claim that the course of history
can be reversed and that causes which operated in the past can
be eradicated at their source. The best that it can do is to deal
with present causes as these are understood through historical
inquiry. The essential question, then, is whether present causes
can be understood only through history or whether there are
other ways in which such causes may be understood.

The diagnostic school does not claim that history is the only
way to understand the causes of behavior, nor do all functional
practitioners claim that one cannot arrive at an understanding of
causes through history. However, there are many levels of causality. Both the functional and the diagnostic schools are interested in those causes which can be dealt with *now*. How any
given client uses the service or the relationship with the worker
will depend on his past. All clients come with patterns of behavior established in the past. These project themselves into the
present. In trying to discover how these patterns were established, one may come to understand the patterns themselves. The
functional school maintains that patterns of behavior may be
understood in terms of their present operation, the way they
function and the purposes they serve in the present. The pattern
must be allowed to project itself. When it does so it may be understood directly. The past can often be conjectured from the
way it operates in the present. In any case, the important thing
is that the worker allow the present pattern of the client to express itself. Both schools are agreed on the necessity for this.

Once a pattern of behavior is projected it is then understood
by the worker in terms of his total understanding of personality.
It is not just the worker's understanding of the particular client
who is involved here. It is the worker's understanding of the
particular person in terms of what he knows about *people*. The

only way anyone can form a judgment about another person is by applying concepts and principles which he believes to be valid. This implies that the judgment is necessarily limited to the extent of the knowledge or experience of the one who is to do the judging. Can one know another as he really is, or as he sees himself? I do not think one can except by translating into one's own accepted concepts and principles whatever the other projects. If one looks upon concepts and principles as identical with the objects to which they refer, then one's "knowledge" will be absolute. If one sees concepts and principles as having relative and different meanings for different individuals, then one's judgment will be taken as reflecting one's own conceptual framework and what is valid in it, or valid for one person at a given time, rather than as something absolute or valid in any framework at any time.

It is not factual knowledge of the past which is important so much as what an individual thinks about his past. In so far as he presents facts, which lend themselves to verification, or opinions or feelings about the past, which do not correspond with the actual facts, these will be translated by the worker into his own way of thinking about personality. This is what both the diagnostic and the functional worker do. It is the only thing that anybody can do.

What both diagnostic and functional workers must deal with, therefore, is not history *per se*. It is their own opinions, and those of the client, about his history. History-telling and history-taking may or may not have positive values for both client and worker. If not used as an escape from the present, but instead as a means of elucidating it, and if understood in this light by client and worker, there can be real value in the attention given to history. The dynamic emphasis is on the attention given, and not on the history itself. It is on the mutual or the different interest of client and worker in the history. The dynamically oriented worker is scientifically skeptical about the "facts" which emerge in case histories. These "facts," he feels, must be understood as reflecting attitudes, and it is the attitudes of the client as they come into interplay with his own professional ones which hold significance for him.

Do we have total difference, then, between the two schools on the value of history? I do not think so. We have partial difference and difference which lends itself to clarification. Dynamically oriented workers in both schools use history. Both are interested in the attitudes reflected in history-telling. The one engages in formal history-taking as a prerequisite of treatment. The other believes that history may follow another type of beginning. The one calls for thorough and comprehensive history in the beginning; the other accepts partial and spontaneous retelling at any point in the casework process. Both assume, however, that an account of the past generally carries great feeling and that this feeling can be dealt with. What both schools must be interested in basically is the relation of history to feeling. This is the dynamic question and it is a question that both schools must explore further.

We thus see that in the realm of history, too, the two schools may not be so far apart as it sometimes appears. Their differences in this area are partial, not total ones, and as such they lend themselves to further exploration.

The Nature of the Casework Relationship

A third sphere of difference between the two schools is that pertaining to the nature of the casework relationship. Is it one characterized by struggle or by support? The diagnostic view of the part played by relationship in casework has been concisely stated as follows:

> The primary medium through which casework help is extended is the relationship, between the caseworker and client and/or between caseworker and persons in the client's environment. The caseworker brings to the relationship an attitude that is basically a supporting one; it is consistently accepting, strengthening, encouraging, responsive, and enabling.

The caseworker endeavors to keep the relationship predominantly on a positive level and on a reality basis. The client, however, may direct negative feelings toward the caseworker, either (1) because he is reacting appropriately to reality pressures, to his feelings about having to ask for help, to some oversight on the part of the worker, or to inability of the agency or the community to meet legitimate requests; or (2) because he is reacting inappropriately, in response to the transference situation. In either event, the caseworker responds to the reality situation and endeavors to keep the negative feelings at a minimum.

Because of a variety of factors the client may have no, little, or much awareness of *how* he is using the relationship, although he must have an understanding of the purpose of his contact with the agency. The caseworker has the professional responsibility to be aware of the various elements in the relationship, and to control it properly; that is, to use it in behalf of the client's welfare.

The client gains emotional support from the relationship itself. The quality of the worker's attitudes and feelings creates, for the client, an atmosphere that enables him to examine his difficulties and to begin working toward solutions. The worker's technical help, both in exploring the problem and in working with the client toward its solution, is not separable from the relationship. Techniques and relationship form a constellation; both must be correct if the client is to be helped.

In addition to the basic qualities the caseworker manifests in the relationship, which are always present, others are called into play for specific purposes. For example, a quality of permissiveness, that is, of approving the expression of impulses and the satisfaction of emotional needs, may be appropriate in one case; a quality of control, that is, of disapproving certain behavior, appropriate in another; and a quality of neutrality, that is, of not allying with either side of an inner conflict, may be appropriate in other instances.[10]

There can be no doubt here that the emphasis is on the positive and sustaining factors in the relationship. The diagnostic worker is seen as one who puts the giving and loving qualities

[10] *Scope and Methods of the Family Service Agency* (New York: Family Service Association of America, 1953), pp. 16–17.

which he possesses into his contact with the client, except in those instances where the situation demands that he use the negative, that is, the restricting or controlling side of himself. The same essential view is expressed by Gordon Hamilton, who in a chapter entitled "The Use of Relationship" states: "The social worker must be a person of genuine warmth with a gift for intimacy. He must be willing to enter into the feeling experience of another, willing to listen to the other's view of his problem, and willing to go patiently along with him in his struggles for a solution." [11] The emphasis here again is on the positive, although Miss Hamilton recognizes that the client "struggles for a solution."

This view of the casework relationship contrasts with the functional, which is known as one that puts primary stress on "the will struggle." While in actual practice many functional workers do maintain relationships with their clients which are predominantly positive, very little of the literature has stressed this aspect. Instead it has pointed up the struggle which must go on between client and worker. The client is pictured as needing to "come to grips with" his problem, and it is believed that in order to do this he must project it onto the worker. The worker must be made responsible for it, so to speak. When he has thus put out his problem, that is, when he has made of it something which exists outside of himself, something which he sees in the person of the worker, he can then work on it, or struggle with it, until he comes to some kind of solution. He is seen as being apt to do so when he recognizes that the problem is not the worker's responsibility, but that it is his, and that he must do something about it. The worker does not deliberately antagonize, but he enters into the fray and lets himself be used as someone with whom the client must struggle. While the client struggles with him, the worker maintains and affirms his function in everything he says or does. His function is the reality which contrasts with the client's view of him.

[11] Gordon Hamilton, *Theory and Practice of Social Case Work*, 2nd ed. rev. (New York: Columbia University Press, 1951), p. 28.

In yielding to the demands of reality, which are seen as more powerful in the long run than his projections, the client makes a choice "between growth and the refusal of growth, life or the negation of life; when the organism, in short, chooses to live and turns its energies from the negative fight against what is, to the vibrant immediacy of what it can do, no matter." [12]

As stated by Miss Faatz:

> There will be the gathering towards the center of the first crisis, when the one seeking help tests his own strength against the helping person, feels the greater strength on the outside, halts ambivalently, struggles, then yields to it, and from it discovers he gains a new release toward forward movement.[13]

And further:

> The will of the client is bent upon discovering where there is a weak spot, and if it can be found he will go through it — perversely, to be sure, for what he requires above all else (if the life impulse has any strength) is that he should not succeed in this endeavor. To this outer strength he craves to yield the too-tight organization of himself, but this does not happen until he has pitted his own will and yielded in the process.[14]

Here in contrast with the diagnostic emphasis on the positive character of the casework relationship, stress is given to the negative.

These two divergent concepts of relationship may therefore seem to be quite irreconcilable, but are they? Does the functional worker never support his client, and does the diagnostic worker never struggle with his? As we have seen, neither the diagnostic nor the functional school really claims that this is so. Obviously there are points in the progression of any case where there must be struggle, and other points where there must be support. In reality, diagnostic and functionally oriented workers do both.

[12] Anita Faatz, *The Nature of Choice in Functional Casework* (Chapel Hill: University of North Carolina Press, 1953), p. 53.
[13] *Ibid.*, p. 119.
[14] *Ibid.*, pp. 120–121.

They have given comparatively little attention, however, to where they must engage in struggle and where they must support, and this is the reason why they, in a sense, have misrepresented themselves. They have pictured the casework relationship as white or black, and the truth is that there are many shades of gray in it.

In a dynamic approach to this problem, the question of where one struggles and where one supports is the essential question. It is not a matter of doing one or the other, but rather of doing both at different times or in some instances simultaneously. The important question is what follows from what. What is the effect of either the struggle or the support upon client or worker? At what points does the client or the worker shift from one role to the other because of the dynamic effect which the supporting or the struggling has had?

These are basic questions in relationship and they are questions for workers of both schools, not just one. In turning to the dynamics of the client-worker relationship as a focus of interest, both schools will find not only how much they have in common but how much they still need to explore in order to understand what actually takes place in this relationship.

A closely related problem which also might lend itself to objective study is the problem of activity or passivity on the part of the worker. Both approaches, diagnostic and functional, are active in some respects and passive in others. About what is the caseworker active, and about what is he passive? Although Freudian caseworkers originally were much more passive than were the Rankians, both the diagnostic and the functional schools today advocate activity in some respects and passivity in others. The diagnostic group calls for activity in eliciting history and particular types of content, such as discussion of feeling toward other members of the immediate family, which it believes to be of therapeutic value. It is perhaps more passive in matters of direct relationship between client and worker. The functional group, on the other hand, pays a good deal of attention to how the client feels about the worker at any particular time, and the worker will generally talk with the client about this feeling. The functional worker, however, has much less concern over the specific content which any person chooses to talk about. Wherever a specific service is involved and the worker carries responsibility for this, it is discussed. The agency's policies and procedures are discussed. Beginning, middle, and end phases of the relationship are discussed. But no other special content is considered obligatory. If the client wishes to discuss his family, he does so. If he prefers to discuss his employer, teacher, neighbor, or any other person, that too may be of his own determination, as long as such discussion seems appropriate to the function which is being administered. What the functional worker is primarily concerned about, however, is the present relationship between the client and himself.

Recognizing that any particular content may have meaning on several different levels, the dynamic problem is what meaning to select for further consideration and understanding. A client may speak of a harsh father-figure, for example. What he says may be taken literally, since the father might actually have been harsh; it may be taken as evidence of hostility toward the father, or as a wish for protection, or as a fear of being too harsh one's self, and so on. Any or all of these meanings may have validity in a particular case. The client often speaks of such a matter, however, because of its implications for the helping relationship itself. Is he hostile to the worker? Does he want more protection from the worker? Is he afraid of the worker's power over him? These are questions which are important to the dynamically oriented worker of either school, and his responses to any content which the client uses will be of this character.

While the theory with respect to content is rather different in the two different schools, however, practice is not always in keeping with theory. It is therefore important to examine actual practice in the two schools. Records ought to be analyzed in terms of the worker's response to any particular content. What does the worker actually say and do? What does he elicit? What comes spontaneously from the client? What is the worker's reason for a given response? This type of research [15] is entirely feasible, I believe, and if carried out objectively, both schools could undoubtedly contribute materially to our understanding of the real character of the casework relationship.

A Case Example

Let us now look at a case example in which the role of the worker in the casework relationship can be examined. The case is that of a seventy-four-year-old woman who was placed in a private home, after she could no longer remain with her sister, with whom she had lived for the past fifteen years, because of the sister's illness. Her husband had died twenty years previously and there were no children. Several cousins and a nephew who lived out of town were the only other living relatives.

Mrs. W was referred for placement while she was hospitalized herself. She had a cardiac condition, she was arthritic, and her hearing was very poor. In the hospital she was known as a very difficult personality. She complained a great deal about getting insufficient attention and felt that she should be treated differently from other patients because of her superior background. She came from a professional family, was rather well educated, and spoke in a somewhat haughty manner.

The hospital worker who had referred her to the agency had much doubt whether Mrs. W could adjust to a private home. She could not remain in the hospital much longer, however, and she did not seem to need institutional care. The initial problem, therefore, was to discover whether Mrs. W was interested in private home placement, whether she was suited for it on personality grounds, and whether she would be eligible for it in terms of physical care required.

In this kind of situation much objective information is needed. Before seeing Mrs. W, therefore, the worker secured detailed reports from the hospital, including a physical diagnosis and

[15] In his *Client-Centered Therapy* (Boston: Houghton Mifflin, 1951), Carl Rogers cites instances along these lines.

prognosis. Mrs. W's physical problems were long-standing and there might be further deterioration. However, she did not require hospital or institutional care. During the study period, the worker saw members of the family, including the sister with whom Mrs. W had lived and the cousins who could contribute to the cost of care, and they provided some of the information necessary in order to obtain the public assistance which would be necessary in arranging placement in a private home.

The worker evaluated all the information which had been received about Mrs. W and was able to conclude that neither her physical condition nor the personality factors which had been reported so far would necessarily stand in the way of placement. It was clear that Mrs. W would require much physical care because of her cardiac condition and that this would be complicated because of her poor hearing. But although she was reported as a difficult personality, there was no evidence of psychosis or other problems which would make placement in a private home impossible.

When it seemed clear that there were no definite contraindications to placement, provided that it was what Mrs. W wanted herself, the worker saw her and discussed the matter, which had been presented to her previously by the hospital worker as a possibility and by her cousins who wanted her to know that they were trying to get a home for her. At first Mrs. W took the position that a Home for the Aged was the only place for her. On hearing about private homes from the worker, however, she expressed great interest. Let us quote from the record [16] here:

> In seeing Mrs. W, I secured an increasing sense of her as a person who might fit into a private home placement situation. The somewhat abnormal personality picture which she presented at the hospital might well have been aggravated by the fact that she had to share a room with a senile person who was incontinent and by the fact that the atmosphere was Orthodox and this was alien to her. Mrs. W

[16] Mr. Arthur Farber was the worker.

certainly related to me in a positive way, showing decided interest in our placement program. She asked many questions about it: What were the financial arrangements? Would the public agency contribute? Would she live with another person? What kind of house would it be? How would the food be, etc. When I told her about another person who lived in the home which we might consider for her, she was quite accepting of this person's limitations. In addition she was able to tell me about her past, her relationship to her husband while he was living and the sister with whom she lived. She felt somewhat bitter toward her sister, and probably without justification. On the whole, however, I was impressed with her interest and liveliness and felt that we should explore things further.

The next step was a meeting between Mrs. W and the person with whom she might be living. This took place in the agency office. Mrs. W came in with one of her cousins.

She could hardly walk straight and she seemed quite distraught and upset. Her hair was disheveled and flying in all directions. She was over-heated and over-exhausted. In the strain and excitement, she talked almost incessantly. I felt it important to go over our regular procedures, although Mrs. W did not listen very much to what I or anybody else said. After she and Mrs. N spoke to each other alone, however, something seemed to happen and there was less confusion. With a good deal of spontaneity Mrs. N took some hairpins out of her own hair, and in a few deft motions, and with some demonstration of affection, she remarked on how beautiful Mrs. W's hair really was and she fixed it up so that Mrs. W looked so much more presentable. It was through several other of these little personal human re· sponses that these women began to get together. I then de͏̈ cided to accompany them to see the actual home.

When we arrived the other resident welcomed Mrs. W and even the dog took to her with considerable show of affection. Mrs. W's anxiety diminished and she no longer talked incessantly. Instead she began to ask a few intelligent questions. At one point Mrs. W said something humorous and Mrs. N looked back into her eyes and smiled with much positive feeling. Mrs. W's cousin was well impressed

with the house and he suggested that he would bring Mrs.
W to the home next week. We had agreed, however, that
Mrs. N would do this, since it seemed that it would be so
much more like a welcome to have the person to whose
home she was going actually call for her and bring her there.

After Mrs. W was established in the home, the worker visited
her and found that she felt quite warm toward him. She said
she had told her cousin that if she were forty years younger she
could consider marrying the worker. This was offered with
humor and a sparkle. Mrs. N, however, spoke of the great demands which Mrs. W was making, and the worker took this up
with Mrs. W. When he next visited, the worker found that
Mrs. W was making fewer demands and that she was very happy
about the attention Mrs. N paid her. The food pleased her and
she even complained with some humor that it was too much.

Over a period of a year the relationship between Mrs. W and
Mrs. N grew to the point where each one expressed great satisfaction in it. Mrs. W wrote to her sister that she no longer felt
angry and that she would be glad to see her. She also began to
write poetry and short stories which she sent to the worker,
who responded to them with warm interest. Throughout the
remainder of his contact with Mrs. W, the worker saw to it that
she received the medical care she needed. Aside from this, however, the worker brought to Mrs. W a sense of the agency's, and
not just his own, sustaining interest. As a consequence, when the
worker had to give up his contact with Mrs. W, she was able to
accept this and to relate to a new worker with much the same
positive spirit.

This is a case in which it was necessary to integrate both a
diagnostic and a functional type of interest. It would have been
literally impossible to help Mrs. W through placement in a
private home without the understanding of her physical and
emotional needs, which were revealed through careful and objective or extraneous study. It also would have been impossible
to proceed with any placement plan without Mrs. W's participation. The worker had to learn about her from others, and he

had to learn from Mrs. W herself whether she was really interested. Mrs. W could not know this herself until the function
was presented to her in such a way that she could have some
actual experience with it. What took place before the worker's
own eyes not only confirmed the judgment which he had previously made regarding Mrs. W's suitability for foster home placement, considered from an objective standpoint, but made it
possible to test out whether the particular placement was at all
feasible. Diagnosis and the test in action, on a functional basis,
actually went hand in hand here, and in no sense interfered with
one another.

It is interesting to observe in this case that one could not
judge just on the basis of past behavior what the client would
do in a future situation. The hospital worker felt, on the basis
of what she knew about Mrs. W's difficulties in the past and
her problem in adjusting to the hospital setting, that placement
in a private home might not be successful. The placement
worker, however, made his judgment largely on the basis of
how Mrs. W related to him and to the function. The picture
he secured of Mrs. W in this manner was a dynamic one. Initial
impressions were not taken as ultimate truth. Instead Mrs. W
was given an opportunity to discover for herself how she could
relate to the worker and to the person with whom she was going
to live. As she discovered this, the picture of her reaction pattern
changed. An inflexible and complaining individual became a
warm, responsive one who showed capacity for taking the good
with the bad.

As far as the casework relationship itself is concerned, it is
quite evident that a functionally oriented worker could be very
supporting and that the relationship between the client and
himself could be a very positive one. The positive in Mrs. W
herself was brought to the fore by the positive attitude of the
worker and the home owner to the point where she could begin
to write poetry and express the feeling in a letter to her sister
that she "no longer had reason to be angry." Mrs. W did not
need to have a negative experience with the agency in order to

utilize its service or in order to discover her own potentialities for constructive adjustment in spite of much adversity. The worker in this situation was attuned to the positive and he made his essential contribution to Mrs. W in this manner.

We thus see that the two theoretically opposed views of what constitutes the casework relationship are not irreconcilable in actual practice. Overstress on a single aspect is one of the dangers of theorizing in any field, and this seems to be particularly true in the realm of casework and counseling, where the realities are broad enough to encompass theoretically opposed propositions. No caseworker can get along without theory of some kind. But the living relationship, which is the medium in which casework and counseling takes place, never coincides with theory. Theory can help to give shape to it, and living experience can then contribute to the further development of theory. In order for this to take place, however, we must be willing to learn the lessons of actual experience. What *actually* takes place in the casework relationship must be submitted to scientific scrutiny. Out of such scrutiny will come a more reliable and comprehensive theory.

The Need for Research

Many factors of likeness and difference between the two schools will lend themselves to analysis in this manner. In speaking of the use of function, for example, what does one mean? What does the diagnostic worker do about his function? What does the functional worker do, concretely? How much of his discussion is concerned with function as such? How much does he make indirect use of function, reflecting it in his attitude and behavior within the actual interview, rather than dealing with it in specific comments? What does he do about time and other limitations? How much of his total response is based upon basic training rather than function as such? Similar questions might be applied in a study of diagnostic casework. How much history does the worker take? How much does the client give spontaneously? What diagnosing or planning does the worker do by himself, with the supervisor, with the psychiatrist? In what areas does the client lead while the worker follows?

Research along these lines would undoubtedly bring out many common factors between the two schools as well as factors of difference. Whether there is more likeness or difference in the area of counseling than in the administration of specific service should be established objectively, and this would help also in clarifying the relation of the schools to each other. In the work of the Committee which prepared *A Comparison of Diagnostic and Functional Casework Concepts,* the choice was deliberately made to exclude cases where the emphasis was on concrete service. "In order to provide at least a broad case of comparison, the Committee agreed to limit the selection of cases to those dealing with problems of personal or social maladjustment, ruling out those which called primarily for the provision of concrete service." [17] This, in effect, made the study one of counseling rather than of casework, or as it might have been thought of by the Committee, counseling as one form or level of casework. Although there would appear to be more likeness between the schools in the area of counseling than in any other, the conclusions drawn by the Committee were that the differences which emerged in personality concepts and in actual method were so great that they overshadowed any element of likeness which there might be. Certainly the cases selected for presentation by the Committee were radically different. None of these cases was analyzed, however, in the manner which I am suggesting. *A Comparison of Diagnostic and Functional Casework Concepts* clearly demonstrates that caseworkers in 1950 were more interested in bringing out their differences than in working toward integration of the profession.

Meritorious as this study is (and great credit must be given to the Committee for the beginning which it made in comparing the two schools), the fact remains that this study was limited to a group of family agencies and that no other function was included in the study. The important fields of public assistance,

[17] *Op. cit.,* p. 5.

child placement, and child guidance were untouched, not to mention others such as probation and parole and medical social work. If *casework concepts* are to be studied, other specific fields of casework will have to be represented, as well as the family field. When this is done, possibilities for integration not evident in family societies may well come to the fore.

Who is to carry out such study? Are there enough caseworkers who are interested in likenesses as well as in differences? Is the profession ready for this movement toward some kind of integrated status or must it further concern itself with differentiation? In what ways will casework in the fifties and sixties be different from what it has been in the thirties and forties? These questions will only be answered by the future. However, the evidence seems to indicate that the field of casework is ready to move beyond its present divided status and the possibilities for some kind of integration may be at hand. The renewed interest in research which has developed during the past few years [18] certainly gives great promise; and while research must not be confused with help, it is possible for caseworkers to study their own processes. Electrical recording devices, which have been tried in a few agencies, may prove to be very useful, if not indispensable. Records which have been written for purposes other than research have their drawbacks but are not entirely without value for this end. Some agencies have employed experts in research to study their own casework processes. It would seem, however, that caseworkers themselves must see the value of such research and must be willing to participate in it, out of obligation to the profession as a whole, if for no other reason. Willingness to do this will bring casework into the intellectual mainstream of the twentieth century.

---

[18] Cf. M. Robert Gomberg, "Criteria for Casework Helpfulness"; Elizabeth G. Herzog, "Preface to a Program of Research"; and John Frings, "Function and Operation of a Research Program"; all in *Diagnosis and Process in Family Counseling*, ed. by M. R. Gomberg and F. T. Levinson (New York: Family Service Association of America, 1951). Also J. McV. Hunt and Leonard S. Kogan, *Measuring Results in Social Casework* (New York: Family Service Association of America, 1950).

With the development of a research attitude on the part of caseworkers, there will be innumerable possibilities for movement of casework as a profession beyond its present status. Study might then take place within each of the two schools and comparisons on a broad basis and in detailed manner might be carried out with reference to the relation of principles to practice. Agencies, conferences, and professional schools might all participate in such study. If this occurs — and there is every reason to think that it can occur — endless possibilities for integration and for growth and development of the profession will emerge.

The interest in research which has been shown by many progressive agencies foreshadows a period of integration which must take the place of the existing dichotomy. For when one becomes interested in the possibilities for testing principles rather than stating them and maintaining them at all costs, then the blocking to an integrated point of view is removed. Much of the research which has taken place in social work so far has been concerned with agency programs and practice rather than with fundamental principles. There is no reason, however, why research cannot be extended into the realm of principle. The relation of principles to practice can be studied and without any doubt will be in the not too distant future. When this occurs the profession will be well on its way to a new stage of development — one which should be thought of as a stage of integration.

6

DYNAMIC THEORY AND PRACTICE

In the opening chapter of this book we outlined five Freudian and five Rankian conceptions, upon which most present-day theory and practice rest. The Freudian concepts which have played such a significant part in the development of casework theory and practice were identified as the following:

1. Unconscious mind as a determinant of behavior.
2. Ambivalence as a product of repression.
3. Past experience as a determinant of present behavior.
4. Transference as essential to therapy.
5. Resistance as a factor to be dealt with in all helping.

The five Rankian conceptions which were taken over by the functional school and used in the development of the functional approach were the following:

1. The will as an organizing force in personality.

2. Counter-will as a manifestation of the need of the individual to differentiate himself.
3. Present experience as a source of therapeutic development.
4. The significance of separation.
5. The inherent creativity of man.

We recognized that these conceptions represent only a part of Freudian and Rankian philosophy and psychology, and that they should not be thought of as the whole of either the Freudian or the Rankian contribution. We selected these particular conceptions, however, because of the fact that they are all dynamic conceptions and because of the belief that they are fraught with implications for the development of a truly dynamic approach to the helping process. Let us, therefore, take them once again and look into their implications for the development of a dynamic approach to casework and counseling.

The Five Freudian Concepts

1. *The Unconscious*

The concept of the unconscious has been a source of conflict between the diagnostic and the functional schools. Those who are diagnostically oriented look for the unconscious sources of behavior, while many of those who are functionally oriented maintain that there is no such thing as unconscious mind, and that even if there were, there would be little point in seeking unconscious causes of behavior. On this level of argument, there certainly can be no common understanding between the two schools with respect to this matter. If one looks to the dynamic implications of this conception, however, one finds an area in which there can be a great deal of common agreement.

What is significant for caseworkers in Freud's concept of the unconscious is not the question of whether the mind is split into two parts or not, but rather the idea of oppositeness, or polarity, which is a basic proposition in the dynamic understanding of physical as well as psychological phenomena. Freud and Rank were not in disagreement about this, nor are the present-day diagnostic and functional schools, except in so far as they believe that they must be in disagreement about everything. Rank, it is true, discarded the conception of conscious and unconscious mind, but he substituted will and counter-will, which certainly are polar conceptions. The truth is that both Freud and Rank were dynamically oriented, as indeed their successors must be, unless their practice is to be a mere matter of mechanics.

The idea of unconscious motivation for all that one does not completely understand can be used mechanically, as the idea of will can be. Either conception can become a convenient repository for all that one does not know. What is significant to any dynamically oriented worker, in either of these conceptions, however, is not how they can be used to explain what he does not understand, but rather what value they have for explaining what takes place when one person tries to help another. This is a situation in which there is very often concealed *oppositeness,* a fact which is recognized by both diagnostic and functional schools. This concealed oppositeness exists within the person who consciously seeks help. He wants to be helped, but at the same time he wants not to be helped. He seeks out the helper, but wishes he did not have to do so. Now it does not matter whether one says he consciously wants help and unconsciously resists it, or whether one says he has a will to get help but a counter-will not to take it. The one significant fact is that this oppositeness exists within the individual and must be recognized before any real helping can take place.

In any dynamic approach to the client, therefore, one starts with recognition of the duality implicit in the request for help. Furthermore, one does not act as if the opposing trends in the personality of the client, or for that matter the worker, were not there. The dynamically oriented worker knows, to start out with, that just as his client wants help and resists it, so does the worker wish to help but also must recognize the point where he really does not want to do so. One is limited by the oppositeness within himself, if by nothing else.

In this very oppositeness is to be found enormous potentiality

for helping. It is significant that before Freud's development of
the concept of unconscious mind, there was very little psychological helping, and that since acceptance of this concept there
has been so much. The reason for this is that dynamic helping
first became possible when the fundamental oppositeness in
human personality was recognized. For once one proceeds in
any helping process with a recognition of that side of the personality in the client which wants not to be helped, and with
recognition, too, of that side of the personality in the helper
which does not want to help, then those important factors which
can block either a true giving or a true taking of help, lose some
of their concealed power. The opposite forces, those which must
be equated with wanting to take and to give help, can come into
the ascendancy and helping can actually take place.

The process by which this occurs must be a dynamic one.
There must be interchange between client and worker in which
the worker recognizes the forces in the client's personality which
are opposed to taking help and the client recognizes that even
the helper has his limitations and cannot do it all. A sense of
mutuality must be established, through a recognition of certain
mutual weaknesses. Different strengths will be found in one
person and in the other, and the forces of one personality may
complement those of the other. Under such circumstances, inherent dynamics can come into play with one another. They
cannot in an atmosphere of identity or oneness. They will do
so in a situation in which opposite forces become free to interact
with each other.

For the dynamically oriented worker, therefore, there is a philosophy of help implicit in the Freudian conception of the unconscious. This conception was originally meant to be a dynamic
one, and it has served those who are willing to see its potentialities in precisely that manner. For those who would insist on
making of the unconscious a kind of repository from which
long-discarded items of experience are simply to be extracted,
the conception can have no more than mechanical significance.
For those who are interested, however, in the way unconscious

forces operate in the helping situation, that is to say, the way they affect the behavior of client and worker, and the way in which opposing and complementary forces in the one person meet with those in the other, the concept of unconscious mind lends itself to endless development. No two helping situations are viewed as identical when the concept is used in this way. In every situation there will be a distinct conscious approach to help and an equally distinct unconscious one. In order to understand what takes place, one will look to the interplay of conscious and unconscious forces in the individual and also between the two individuals involved. How does conscious expression on the part of one person meet with and fit into conscious expression on the part of the other? How does it meet and fit into unconscious feeling and attitude? These are the questions which must be understood for help to take place in a dynamic manner.

2. *Ambivalence*

The individual who seeks help is necessarily in conflict. This is a proposition on which both diagnostic and functional schools can agree. Whether or not the conflict should be called ambivalence is of no consequence, although those who have a need for a different terminology do object to the use of this term. Regardless of affiliations, however, it is recognized by all that what one is confronted with in any kind of psychological helping is *conflict*, that is to say, opposite feelings and attitudes within the same individual. Without this conception it is impossible to help except in the most mechanical manner. With it, however, one is inevitably faced with a dynamic situation. For a question arises, in relation to whatever the client is expressing, regarding the side of the conflict which is not being manifested. Does the expression of one side of the conflict lead inevitably to the expression of the other side, or can the worker put in something which will lead to this type of development? The concept of ambivalence, which is a highly dynamic concept, implies that the individual will shift in his feeling and that he can do so

if left to himself. In the helping situation, however, he is not
left to himself — at least not in any truly dynamic situation.
Here, movement from one phase to another can be facilitated by
recognition of what is being expressed, and by the willingness
to share, which is inherent in the role of the helper.

The dynamically oriented worker, therefore, does not sit
idly by as the client experiences and re-experiences his own conflict, but instead recognizes that whatever he does or says will
have one effect or another upon the client's ambivalence. It will
fortify one side of his feeling, cause him to repress one side,
make it clear that the unexpressed will be understood, and so
forth. In other words, the worker's response to the client's ambivalence can serve as a dynamic, and the worker must remain
aware of this fact. This means that he will observe the effect of
what he puts in upon the client's ambivalence. Does it produce
fuller expression or help the client bring out the other side of his
feeling? Does it tend to substantiate one side? Does it give the
client a feeling of freedom? Does it help him to see the naturalness of his own two-sidedness?

The worker who recognizes the full implications of the concept of ambivalence is willing to apply this concept to himself
as well as to his client. He knows that in his own helping attitude
there are real possibilities for conflict and that he cannot be
an automaton in his helping activities. He must be a human
being, which is to say, he must experience conflict. How much
of the client's negative expression does he really want to take —
particularly when it is directed toward himself? How much dis-
ciplining of his own self is he willing to impose? Every worker
who is honest with himself knows that he has ambivalent feelings
within himself with respect to those inevitable requirements
which are made of him in any helping situation. In a dynamic
approach to the client's ambivalence, the worker must remain
aware of his own, where this exists, and he must so handle his
own feeling that it will not interfere with the client's opportunity for full expression of the opposites within himself.

Those who practice casework or counseling mechanically have

no need to relate to the ambivalence of the client and still less need to recognize their own. The dynamically oriented worker, however, sees the client's ambivalence as the very medium with which he works. If his diagnosis is to have any dynamic character at all, it will be concerned with the client's ambivalence and whatever shift occurs within it, and if he has a function to present he will observe the client's ambivalent reactions to it. Whether diagnostically or functionally oriented, he cannot practice effectively unless he is attuned at all times to ambivalence in the client and in himself.

3. The Past

A great deal of controversy has raged over the question of whether or not it is necessary to know the client's past. The diagnostic school has held, on the whole, that knowledge of the client's past is valuable in arriving at a diagnosis, while the functional school has maintained that knowledge of the past is quite unnecessary. Many questions have been raised in this connection, including the following: Is it possible to know anything about another person? Can reliable information regarding the past be acquired? Assuming that scientifically verifiable information is obtainable, is it necessary to have it in order to make valid judgments about the client's character and potentialities?

What we are concerned with here is not epistemological argument, but rather the relation of theory to practice. Anyone who has ever practiced in a helping profession knows that most clients are very much interested in telling about past experiences. Many do so spontaneously, and others willingly respond to any eliciting of past experience when they know of the worker's interest in it. This is an empirical fact which is readily verifiable. It is pertinent to ask, therefore, why the client has this kind of interest. What value is there for him in speaking of the past? Here we must recognize that it is possible to avoid present problems by telling about the past and that some clients do this when the worker is engrossed in history *as such*. It must be recognized, too, that any mechanical or dry factual approach to the client's history will lead only to a recital of events which will have neither diagnostic nor treatment value.

In a dynamic approach to the past, however, there is no mere recital of factual data, but rather a vivid and varied type of feeling response to the worker's interest. There is no reason why the worker who is convinced of the value of present experience, and who wishes to see his client face present problems in the present, need limit himself to this, particularly when the client himself wishes to talk of the past. The questions which then arise are: What kind of feeling and attitude does this historical content carry? What is its meaning to the client? How does his recollection of past experience tie up with his present relationship to the worker? What use is being made of this recollection, by the client and by the worker? What can the worker do with it to make it not just the past, but living, dynamic experience? These are the questions which the dynamically oriented worker will raise and they are the questions which must be substituted for the epistemological ones which have been raised in the diagnostic and functional controversy.

The dynamic point of view recognizes that past, present, and future are related to each other and that one cannot be separated from the others. The significant question, therefore, is how they are related. In what ways does the past affect the present, and what transformations of the present will affect the future? Human beings live in this manner. They come for help so that the future may be different from the present. They naturally see the present as a product of the past, and they want to influence the future, in so far as they can, through present experience. All three, past, present, and future, are aspects of a single dynamic continuum. The past cannot be picked out of this continuum without reference to the present, nor can the present be abstracted from it without recognition of the fact that it is a continuation of the past.

It is an unsatisfactory past which brings the client to the worker. Out of a sequence of unsatisfying experiences arose the desire for help, a desire which serves as an initial dynamic factor in the helping situation. This desire does not exist as an entity in itself. It is bound up in many ways with the unsatisfactory experience of the past and must be unloosened, as it were, from it. The worker cannot do this unloosening. All that he can do is to help the client achieve it. This means that the worker will bring out likeness and difference between the past and the present. In order to do so, however, he must show interest in both. He will recognize, moreover, that the present, of which he is a part, will become the past and that it is the essential aim of the client to make this so. The client will be motivated by future considerations, not just past or present. The future does not yet exist except in the mind of the client. There, however, it serves as a most significant motivational force. It is his image of the future and his desire for the attainment of it as actual experience which brings the client to the worker and keeps him coming.

The dynamically oriented worker, therefore, deals neither with the past alone, nor the present alone, but with past, present, and future as aspects of one continuum. He becomes a part of this continuum, and it is important for him and for the client to recognize what part he actually is. Discovery of how he fits into this continuum of experience is one of the essential therapeutic tasks.

4. *The Transference*

Another area of great dispute between the diagnostic and functional schools is the Freudian conception of transference. The Freudian worker is prone to think in terms of transference between the client and himself, by which he means an attachment characterized by feelings of love or hate. Originally held in relation to parent-figures, these feelings of affection or dislike are transferred to the worker, who can respond in a different and more objective way than the persons who were the original objects of the feeling. The worker's response to such feelings is a non-entangling one, and the client therefore has a unique opportunity to understand why he feels as he does. Gradually he overcomes this tendency to transfer his feelings onto the worker and learns to express them appropriately in the real world.

The Rankian worker is more likely to think in terms of a casework relationship with the client and sees no need to think in terms of a transfer of love feelings to the worker. What he sees as predominant between client and worker is the expression of will, and the client's expressed feelings of love or hate are viewed as a manifestation of the client's will to control the relationship. What he requires, therefore, according to the functional view, is not an understanding of his love or hate, so much as it is the need to give up an inappropriate use of feeling which stems from the way his personality is organized. The functional worker therefore puts his stress on the reorganization of personality which comes about when the client enters into a relationship with him where he has an opportunity to work out his will-conflict.

When one goes to the actual experience of both functional and diagnostic workers, one thing emerges quite clearly: namely, that the helping relationship is one in which *strong likes and dislikes* play an exceedingly important role. It is clear too that these strong likes and dislikes not only are presented to the worker, but are actually projected onto him. In other words, it is the helper who becomes the object of strong like or dislike. This occurs inevitably and invariably in any true helping relationship. The client cannot look upon the helper as a mere object, although one can have strong likes and dislikes for an object too. The helper is regarded, however, as another human being to whom one is related, that is to say, toward whom one has many feelings. One can easily like or dislike a clerk in a store with whom one has the most fleeting contact. With the helping person, however, contact is not fleeting, even when it is of short duration. Even what is known as "a short contact" is relatively long. And since it is centered on the person himself rather than things about him, it is natural and inevitable that he should respond with feelings for or against the other person who is involved in the contact.

Whether or not one calls the feelings of like or dislike "transference" — whether or not one sees the origin of these feelings in the original parental situation — there can be no question of their existence. Not only do they exist, but they become the substance of the relationship. The helping relationship as a whole consists of many components, including concrete social services where the client comes for casework help. However, the concrete social services, to which both client and worker must be related, represent just one part of the relationship considered as a whole. The concrete service plays its part in a feeling medium — one which has a great deal to do with the helper himself. The client either likes or dislikes the worker — he is never neutral. The degree of his liking or disliking may vary. In one case it will be quite intense, and in another, much less so. In all instances, however, the tie between client and worker will be a feeling tie, composed of a variety of elements but always involving like or dislike. The worker cannot act as though this were not so. If he does, he subjects his client to misunderstanding and he tries to make of the relationship what it cannot be, namely, a dry, impersonal type of contact, drained of all humanity.

The dynamically oriented worker, therefore, does not act as though there were no such phenomenon as "transference." Instead, he regards the feeling tie between the client and himself as the warp or woof of a many-colored fabric and just as indispensable. This does not mean that the worker immediately proceeds to interpret everything that takes place as transference of an original set of feelings toward the parents. What it means is that the worker will direct attention toward the discovery and the realization of the true nature of the feeling which the client has toward him as the worker, recognizing that this will not be identical with the feeling that the client might have toward some other helping person. The dynamically oriented worker accepts the fact that he is a distinct human being with distinct virtues and limitations. He recognizes that the client is reacting to *him* and not to someone else. Whatever the client thinks, feels, and does in this relationship is meant for him, and not for someone else. Moreover, since he is a human being himself, he reacts, too, with feeling for or against the client. He does not pretend to maintain any kind of absolute objectivity himself, but knows that just as the client identifies with or projects onto him, so he must, if the contact is going to be a human one at all, do his share of identifying and projecting. Both his identification and his projection will be professionally oriented and disciplined. But he will be identifying and projecting in the relationship, if it is to be a relationship at all.

This means that the dynamically oriented worker must be aware of two streams of feeling which move in opposite directions — one on the part of the client toward him and one on his part toward the client. He must be aware of the way these streams of feeling dam up sometimes or shift their courses, and he will be particularly conscious of the effect of any new factor upon both streams. If he puts in a requirement, let us say, or if the client has had an opportunity for positive expression of himself outside of the relationship, the flow of these two streams of feeling will necessarily be affected. If he is concerned with dynamics, therefore, the worker will watch the way this new factor in the relationship operates dynamically. He will ask, assuming that he knows what new occurrence has taken place, just how this new factor affects the client's feeling and what it does to his own. In other words, what does it do to the transference? In this approach the worker is oriented not just to the past, but to a moving present of which he is part and to a future which arises out of the present. He sees himself as a participating part of shifting streams of feeling, and it is his business to keep aware of the way the two streams of feeling shift.

The dynamically oriented worker, however, tries to keep aware not only of how the streams of feeling shift, but also of what causes the shifting. Some of it he will cause himself, some of it the client will cause, and some of it will be due to extraneous factors. Changes will take place, however, and the worker must keep attuned to them. Since the transference is not an entity for him, but rather a matter of ever-shifting streams of feeling, he will be concerned with an analysis of what changes occur and why. Through this manner of inquiry, he will not perpetuate the "transference-relationship" indefinitely, nor will he disrupt it prematurely. He will allow it to take its course, so to speak, and at the same time he will not hesitate to play his part in it.

5. Resistance

The type of relationship pictured above is not one in which all is smooth and serene. In such a relationship there are rough spots and these are likely to occur as a result of interpretative activity on the part of the worker. The relationship is not one in which either client or worker is the mere passive recipient of whatever is put forth by the other. Each reacts to what the other has to offer, and sometimes does so in a strongly resistant manner. Sometimes it is not just the content of what the worker is saying which is not acceptable to the client, but the fact that this content is presented in a manner which is out of tune with the feeling which emanates from the client himself. One cannot completely identify with everything which comes from the other person, nor should one. When one does not identify, a feeling state develops which is best known under the name of "resistance." In a resistant frame of mind, the client shuts out that which comes from the worker, and, of course, the shutting-out can also be done by the worker. When this occurs, the resistance is sometimes known as "counter-resistance." With the existence of one or the other, there cannot be a free flow of feeling between the two persons, and something must be done about this.

In the hands of the unskilled it is always the client who is considered responsible for the blocking, and he either is blamed for it or is left totally to his own devices in overcoming it. The skilled worker, however, recognizes that resistance is a force — not just a negative obstacle which needs to be overcome, but a potentially positive force with many dynamic potentialities. Given a basic identification between client and worker, the resistance will not be treated as a failure of the other person to comprehend, nor will it be handled as an impasse which the client must break, but will be seen instead as a signal for re-examination. Who is resistant to what? Wherein lies the cause of the resistance? What does the client seek which the worker is not giving? Can he give it? Will the client's purpose be accomplished if he does? Only when such basic questions regarding the resistance are raised can it be worked through.

Resistance, in other words, is an opportunity for stock-taking. No part of the whole helping process is more important than the stock-taking phase, and it is resistance which presents such an ideal opportunity for this. The analysis of resistance must be mutual. In talking about it, client and worker have an opportunity to examine the very nature of the relationship itself, its purpose and its objectives. The direction in which the relationship is developing, as contrasted with the way in which it was meant to develop, can be brought out, and a turn in direction will often take place, if this is indicated.

In other words, resistance is approached not as something which is wrong in the relationship, but as the truly dynamic factor which it can be. Resistance is a motive-force. It is one of the tensions in the relationship which causes it to move. It will not do this, however, if it is left untouched. The resistant frame of mind must be recognized and it must be subjected to analysis. Through analysis it may be transformed so that it no longer acts as a block but becomes a source of power which can be harnessed for attack upon the problem itself.

In the dynamic approach to resistance, therefore, the worker does not treat this phenomenon in relationship as an unchanging entity but rather as a force which has positive as well as negative potentialities. It is true that as long as the client resists he does not take help. But it is equally true that when he meets with understanding of why and how he resists, he can give up resisting and move on to a new phase of relationship. No client ever just resists. He resists for an ascertainable reason which he himself can participate in discovering. The resistance must be analyzed. When it is, it turns out to be no longer resistance. For in the analysis, if it is a mutual one, there will be a shift of feeling, very often, on the part of both parties to the relationship. Resistance must be seen, therefore, as one of the vital moving forces which make the wheels of the helping relationship go round.

In order to handle resistance in this way, the worker must be alert to any shift of feeling in client or in himself. He must know and recognize resistance when he meets with it, and he must be able to discover it under many assumed guises. When he does so, he will not be disturbed by the fact of resistance, and therefore develop counter-resistance of his own, but will see it as an opportunity to work through a stage of the relationship and to move on to a new phase. He will accept the naturalness and the inevitability of the resistance, and he will make full use of the opportunity which it affords for both client and himself to come to terms with an essential factor in the relationship.

We thus see how these five fundamental Freudian conceptions lend themselves to the development of a dynamic philosophy of helping. This is true not only for the Freudian principles, however, but will be found to hold for the Rankian ones as well. Let us therefore turn to the five fundamental Rankian concepts.

The Five Rankian Concepts

1. *Will*

One of the most dynamic of all psychological concepts is that of will. The word suggests nothing whatever that is static in nature and a great deal that is forceful, moving, and changing. Synonymous with wish, desire, and choice, the word has met with rejection from many who would not hesitate to use these other terms. Whatever the reasons for the rejection might be, however, the will remains a highly useful concept which contributes much to a dynamic philosophy of helping.

In order to appreciate the significance of will, one must see first of all that it is not a *part* of the person who is being helped, but the *whole*. This does not mean that there is no such thing as partial help. There is indeed, but partial help can be taken only by a whole person. It is the whole person who takes or rejects partial help and it is the whole person who *wills* to accept or reject it. One cannot carry out an act of will without exerting one's total self. For will is the term which is used popularly, as well as psychologically, to indicate the mobilization of the whole personality toward a given end.

When we speak of mobilizing a whole personality toward a given objective, we of course skip over a great deal which must take place in this mobilization. A great deal must take place to reach this end, and what takes place can be understood in dynamic terms. This is especially true in the helping situation where mobilization of the personality is the desideratum. Here it is possible to see clearly that the process of willing must take place within a context of thought, feeling, and attitude. No client can come and present his will as if it were an entity in itself. What he presents is the self as it is at the moment, with all its diverse feelings and rationalizations. Within these more easily presented aspects of the self, a "willing" process is going on. The client comes to decisions. He in fact decided to come for help. It is through his decisions, the product of his willing, that a person can reach and make comprehensible what his own will is like.

In its very nature, will is a hidden process. This does not mean that it is a mystical or an occult one, any more than is unconscious mind. What it means is that "willing" is an internalized process — one which is not readily accessible. One must reach it through its products or end results just as one reaches any unconscious process. Just as the dream and free association reveal what goes on in the unconscious mind, so the *decision,* and the associations with it, reveal what kind of willing the individual is doing.

In any helping process one works from and toward decision. The willing which goes on between the initial decision to come for help and the final decision to leave it must make up much of the substance of the helping process. This takes place whether one calls the effort to arrive at decision "will" or something else. It is obvious, of course, that if one does not even recognize this decision-making process enough to give it a name, one will do comparatively little with it in the therapeutic process. If one does recognize, however, that this aspect of the psychology of the individual is worthy of the same kind of attention as other aspects of the personality, then willing becomes just as much a concern as thought, feeling, or impulse. Will is not abstracted then as an entity to be dealt with in itself. It can exist only in a rich context of thought, feeling, and impulse, and it must be treated in this context. It should be *differentiated* from thought, feeling, or impulse, but in reality it cannot be *separated* from them.

In dynamic helping, therefore, willing is dealt with not in skeletal form, but as one aspect of a warm and full-blooded psychology. Feelings surrounding it, thoughts and rationalizations which support it or emanate from it, impulses which are easily confused with it — all are explored, and out of such exploration there develops a realization of the character of the willing which the individual is doing. This realization constitutes a synthesis. In it the individual can see himself *as a whole*, and not just as so many parts.

This is what makes will such a useful concept for the dynamically oriented worker. In working dynamically, it is necessary to deal not merely with surface manifestations but with what goes on below the surface. This must be done in terms of the way the whole person acts, beneath the surface, and not just in terms of this or that hidden thought, feeling, or impulse. Understanding of an isolated feeling is of no great consequence. It is understanding of the drive, direction, and bent of the whole person which is significant.

2. *Counter-Will*

Of equal significance to the dynamically oriented worker is the Rankian opposite number to will, namely, counter-will. The focus of interest for the dynamic worker is the helping relationship, and it is in relationship, primarily, that counter-will is manifest. In all of Rank's philosophy a great deal of emphasis is given to oppositeness, and in the concepts of will and counter-will Rank recognized that, when human beings participate in relationship, there will necessarily be a great deal of feeling and opposite expression. The will of one, in other words, often will be met by counter-will on the part of the other. Rank recognized that not only is there oppositeness in the individual himself, but that in relationship there inevitably will be two individuals, each of whom acts as a whole person. Each expresses his own will, and this sometimes means that there will be clash between the two wills. The clash will be much greater in some instances than in others. As a result, the interplay of will and counter-will may not be observed at all in those instances where the clash does not obtrude itself. But this does not mean that a dynamic interaction between the will of the one person and the counter-will of the other is not taking place.

Such a dynamic interaction between the two wills — one influencing the other — does take place, invariably, and it is the business of the dynamically oriented worker to discover what effect the will of the client is having upon him, and what effect his own will is having upon the client. This concept of the worker-client relationship presupposes that the worker has a will — professionally disciplined, it is true, but nevertheless a will. It does not make of the worker an automaton or an inhuman creature who is not expressing himself at all in his work. It rather recognizes that the worker is human too, and that only through his humanity can he be of help to the other person.

The worker has a will — a will to be helpful, and he expresses it in a variety of ways. The client also has a will — a will to be helped, and he expresses it in many ways. It is this will which brings him to the worker in the first place. After he comes, however, he finds that the opposite side of his will — namely, the will not to be helped — begins expressing itself. The worker wants to help, but when he meets with this opposition he reacts humanly, that is to say, with his own will, or in some instances, with counter-will too. Meeting with counter-will or resistance from the client, he may become insistent. He will be particularly apt to do so if he has no understanding of how his own will operates professionally. If he is skilled, however, he will recognize and understand the interplay of opposite forces here, and he will share this understanding with the client. Mutuality will then in all likelihood take the place of oppositeness. There will be a dynamic shift, and this will take place on the basis of the worker's understanding of the way will and counter-will necessarily interplay with each other in the therapeutic relationship.

In any genuine process of help two wills must be engaged with each other. Two whole persons must relate to each other in such a manner that the willing which takes place in the relationship will be conscious and accepted willing. It is the willing of the client which must be predominant, but the worker too must not deny his own will. From both functional and diagnostic writings, it would sometimes appear that the worker is a being without will, which simply is not so. If will is characteristic of every human being it must be of the worker too. The important questions therefore are: What does the worker do with his own will? What form does it take in the helping situation? Can he subordinate it to the will of the client? Where does he want to make it known? Obviously the worker must follow the will of the client. It is just as obvious, however, that his role cannot be solely a following one. With respect to certain matters, he must take the initiative. He cannot allow the client to come at any time of the day or night, nor will he see the client at any place. He sets a certain fee as appropriate, or a certain sum of financial assistance as legitimate. These conditions of the relationship come from the worker, not the client, and they represent what the worker is doing with his own will. The client's will, with respect to all of these conditions, may be different from the worker's. In fact, the two wills seldom coincide. If there is mere assertion of one will against the other, there can be no therapeutic development. If struggle takes place, it ought not to be struggle for the sake of struggle. In itself, struggle has no value. When client and worker become engaged with each other in working on a difference, however, there is an opportunity for dynamic development. Neither must end necessarily with what he puts in at the beginning. Out of opposites can come a synthesis, and in the synthesizing there can be much consciousness of the will which one is putting into the situation.

The dynamically oriented worker gives attention to the way will and counter-will interact. He stands on the side of synthesis and he works toward it. His will, in other words, must be constructive. He watches for every opportunity to recognize will or counter-will, and to bring these into interplay with his own thoroughly disciplined approach, that is to say, with his own will. This means that he must distinguish between those instances where the client is engaged with him and those where this is not so. Talking to oneself is not therapy, nor is talking to another. Talking *with* another can be. In the engagement of will and counter-will, one talks *with* the client. The way in which discussion tends to develop is observed, especially in terms of the client's will to have it develop in a certain manner. What the worker must deal with here is not what is on the surface, but rather the will or counter-will which the client puts into the discussion. He must relate to this dynamically. In order to do so, however, he must be observant of all manifestations of will or counter-will, and he must be aware of what he does to elicit them. The dynamically oriented worker makes this kind of observation in the beginning, and he continues to do so throughout the helping process. He is not content with mere observation, however. In addition to observing, he recognizes, interprets, and substantiates the will of the client wherever it is possible for him to do so.

Through inadequate understanding of the role of will in relationship, some have pictured the worker on the one hand, as "holding to" a position once stated, and the client, on the other hand, as "yielding" to the inexorable rightness of the worker. This is an undynamic view of will which limits what must be done in relation to will and counter-will in the helping situation. The client does yield at times. If the worker functions dynamically, he also yields. He yields to the strength and the rightness of the client's will and he yields to the necessities of a situation when these are apparent. The example which he sets in his ability to yield to the will of the client often makes it easier for the client to give in. In any case, a fluid, moving, and dynamic situation results when the worker is in possession of his own will to this extent, and when he is secure enough so that he does not need to "hold to" a stated position, when doing so will only block, rather than facilitate, movement of any kind. The dynamically oriented worker is free in the use of his own will and in his receptivity to and his reactions to the will of the other. His freedom facilitates the expressions of will and counter-will, which, once expressed, shared, and understood, often no longer need to attach themselves to the same objects in the same way. In a dynamic helping process, therefore, will and counter-will are expressed as freely as possible and they meet with the greatest possible responsiveness.

3. *The Present*

In Rank's philosophy, the present takes priority over either the past or the future. Rank believed that psychoanalysis, which had developed originally as a therapeutic method, tended to become research because of its emphasis on the past, and that if therapy was to be the aim, emphasis would have to be shifted to the present, which was the only place, as he saw it, where therapy could take place. In recent years, many non-Rankian therapists have accepted this aspect of Rank's philosophy, and the functional school of casework has built up its own philosophy, using this Rankian principle as one of its foundation stones. Rank, it might be mentioned here, was not a functionalist. His followers in the field of casework, however, adopted certain of his principles and on this basis developed the system which is now known as the functional school of thought.

Prominent in this system of thought is an emphasis on present experience as the source of help. With this concept as a basis, the functional school has developed several corollary ones, to some extent, and these corollary conceptions must be understood in relation to the primary one upon which they are based. These corollary conceptions are the following: (*a*) difference between client and worker as a source of help; (*b*) the structure of the agency as a factor in helping; and (*c*) the use of limitations. None of these conceptions can be developed without reference to the others to which they are related.

As we have indicated, the functionalists are not the only ones who have found it desirable to put emphasis on the present relationship as a source of help. It is obvious, too, that no matter what the philosophy of the helping person may be, unless the person seeking help can relate *to him* as an individual, no help will take place. Help cannot be forced on anyone. The one who is to take it must believe that the person carrying the helping role really can help. This is a prerequisite in any developmental experience. Given this prerequisite, the helping person must then so conduct himself as to warrant the faith which has been put in him by the one who seeks help. This, of course, can take place only in the present, not in the past, nor in the future. It is the present relationship — in other words, a relationship of merited trust — which lies at the base of the help-taking and help-giving situation, and nothing else can take its place.

Difference Between Client and Worker as a Source of Help. In this relationship of fundamental trust, certain instrumentalities, personal and non-personal, are used by the helping person. One of these is a meticulous honesty which requires that the worker express his *difference* with the client where he actually feels it and where it seems to be of importance to him. The client, for example, might insist on presenting a member of his family in a certain light. If it is obvious to the worker that this member of the family could not possibly be as admirable, let us say, or as hateful as the client would have him, then the worker will not hesitate to present his own different view of the situation. In an utterly passive approach, the client would be allowed to go on stating his projections and exaggerations. In a more dynamic one, however, the worker's "difference" is expressed, and in this expression the client has an experience of a dynamic character. He may resent the worker's view, he may try to cast it off, he may reflect on it, he may agree to some of it and yet try to defend his own. In any case, through this present experience with the worker, there is an opportunity for *new* experience; that is to say, what was the present a moment ago, has been transformed through interaction between two persons, and a new present (from the point of view of the old one, a future) comes into being. A highly dynamic situation is created, in other words, through the expression of difference, and in this situation the emphasis is on the present.

The worker in this situation might be very much interested in all of the past experience which causes the client to see a present relationship in a certain light, and the client might have a need to talk about past experiences. The situation becomes a dynamic one, however, at that point where the trusted one expresses a different view. Merely expressing difference, however, and then dropping it, is neither dynamic nor helpful. For the expression of difference leads to consequences. There must be a reaction to it on the part of the client, a resistant reaction, for example, a partially accepting one, an ignoring one, a fearful one, a placating one, or the like. And such reaction must be observed and in turn must be reacted to. This is what is meant by dynamic interaction. To action there must be reaction, which in turn stimulates further action or reaction on the part of the original actor. A chain of events is started *in the present,* through the expression of difference in a situation involving mutual trust and respect. On this basis, action and reaction, give-and-take, become the order of the day, and through this give-and-take a therapeutic development takes place.

While this is what emphasis on present experience can mean,

however, it is not what is always done with the philosophy of
the present. For an emphasis on the present can lead to a kind
of justification for a mechanical rather than a dynamic approach
to human beings, and this is precisely what happens in the hands
of the unskilled. Focused on the present to the extent where they
cannot see its relation to the past or the future, some workers
handle themselves in this mechanical manner, and in so doing
cut off rather than open up opportunities for growth and development. The reaction of the client means nothing to such workers,
who are much too preoccupied with their own difference to be
able to see, or to react to, what the client is doing with it. The
dynamically oriented worker does not maintain his difference
in this manner. Instead he expresses it because he feels it, and
because he believes it can have value for the other person. Once
having expressed it, however, he moves, as the client generally
does. What *was* the present, he recognizes, is now the past and
what *is* the present will become the past. His attention is directed toward the moving present — toward the future. A static
present has no meaning for him, but a moving present offers innumerable opportunities to him — and to the client.

The Structure of the Agency as a Factor in Helping. Another
corollary concept which lends itself to both mechanical and dynamic usage is the concept of *structure*. The functionalists have
used this concept a great deal, in some instances giving it dynamic meaning, and in others, using it as a kind of panacea. In
the latter case, the worker "holds on" to structure, that is, to the
agency policies and procedures with which he is identified. When
he holds to structure, maintaining and sometimes repeating insistently that this is the way it must be, the client supposedly
yields to the unbending nature of the structure, or else "chooses"
not to use it, and in the latter case, the worker need have no
further concern. This "take-it-or-leave-it" philosophy has no place
in dynamic helping.

When structure must be used for the worker's protection, or as
a way to avoid identification with the client's problem, it can
have no therapeutic value whatever. When, on the other hand,

it is used as an opportunity for the client to experience a present reality, different from his original picture of the helping situation, but nevertheless clearly a helping one, it can have enormous meaning and value for both client and worker. In coming to an agency for help, the client meets with a situation different from that involved in going to a private practitioner. He meets with an agency structure, a set of policies and procedures which are determined by no single person, but rather by the agency board, administrator, and others. The agency's structure is societally determined, so to speak, and the client should have a societal experience in coming to an agency, as contrasted with the more personal one of going to a private practitioner. Anything societal in character must be structured, that is to say, organized. We meet with social organization in many phases of our daily activity, but our reactions to it are largely unconscious. In going to an agency for help, however, one cannot deal in an unconscious manner with the organization one meets. The organization of the agency — its structure — can be a matter of much consciousness; that is, it can become a significant part of the *present experience* of the client.

Structure is of no value where it is not experienced, and it can be experienced only when it is used dynamically. The worker must believe that there is something good about the structure of his agency, and he must also believe in the client's capacity to make use of it. Above all, however, he must be willing to follow up the use his client makes of it and to adapt his own responses to the changing reactions of the client. Structure is presented, then, not in a spirit of "Here it is, take it or leave it" — but rather with the assumption that the client will meet something new and different from his own image in the experience with the agency, and that there will be an opportunity in this present experience for dynamic development.

The Use of Limitations. Quite a similar concept is that of *limitations* which are also associated with present experience. The limitations which the client experiences in functional casework are primarily the limitations of structure. If certain rules of eligibility, let us say, are formulated by the agency, the client will come up against them. He will react to them with any of a variety of feelings. He may feel that they are unfair and not at all adapted to his situation. He may resent them. He may docilely accept them. He cannot do anything about them, however, until they are presented to him. When they are, he reacts to them, often with a characteristic pattern.

If the case is a continuing one, this reaction is not likely to be a one-time event. The client will come face to face with this limitation, or another similar to it, again and again. He should not be treated, therefore, as though he were having a single isolated experience. To handle limitations as isolated experiences is to mechanize them, whereas what needs to be done with them is to vitalize them. The limitation in itself is of no value. It is the limitation experienced and reacted to. The reaction must be shared with another person, namely the worker, who can make it comprehensible. When this occurs, it is not just a limitation, to be resented, mastered, circumvented, or whatever the individual might be inclined to do with it. Instead it is part of a total experience which takes on moving and dynamic quality.

Aside from structural limitations, of course, there are limitations in the client's ability to make use of help and in the worker's capacity to give it. The help which any individual receives or gives cannot go beyond these human limitations. Two persons are involved and each has his own limitations. These not only should be recognized, but they should be used. Coming to terms with limitations is wholesome. However, a great deal goes into the "coming to terms." The client should not be asked, as he sometimes is in functional casework, to do this by himself. In that there is no help. The coming to terms should be a shared process. It should be an experience shared with the worker who understands what the client goes through in coming to terms with a limit in himself, in the helping person, or in the agency. Such a worker will not attempt to bring about the coming to terms at one fell swoop, but will be ready and willing to respond to any aspect of the difficult experience which the client wishes to bring to him. The experience of coming to terms with a limit must be broken down and dealt with in parts. Only in this manner will it have any significance as present or living experience.

4. Separation

One of the distinguishing characteristics between Freudian and Rankian philosophies is the emphasis on togetherness in the former (as, for example, in the transference) as contrasted with the emphasis on separation in the latter. Rank's philosophy of individuality is based on the proposition that the individual can achieve a sense of freedom only by separating himself from the one to whom he was formerly attached. The functionalists, following Rank, have made much use of this proposition. It should be mentioned that Rank also recognized the need for togetherness before separation could take place, while some of his disciples apparently have seen value in separation without such togetherness. In the dynamic outlook, both union and separation are essential. One cannot take place without the other, and the dynamically oriented worker therefore looks for both in every helping contact.

When a client comes to seek help, he generally does not have much idea of how he is going to get the help he wants and needs. That is something which the worker supposedly knows. Most people know today, however, that it will be necessary to enter into an extended relationship with the helping person. There are short-time contacts, of course, and in these the relationship cannot be thought of as extended. In even what is considered a short contact, however, there will be many of the elements of relationship, encapsulated, as it were. But in most casework or counseling contacts, the relationship must go on for a period of months and most clients today know this.

What they do not know, however, is just what the relationship will consist of and what forms it will take. Through popular literature, lectures, and other media of information, they may have some understanding of transference and they may expect that hostility will be accepted. They do not know, however, what personal qualities they will find in the helping person, just what his professional conduct will be like, how much need he may have to keep them attached and dependent on him, how much respect for individuality he may have, or, on the negative side, how much need he may have to get away from them. They must trust that he has an understanding of human relationship which they do not have, and that he will use this understanding wisely on their behalf.

There are many aspects of relationship to be understood. By far the most important, however, are two we have referred to here as union and separation. No real helping can take place without some uniting; and the more uniting there is, the more need there will be for a carefully worked out separating experience. For those who are well disposed toward others, the uniting generally is not too difficult a phase. On finding sympathy, understanding, and acceptance on the part of the worker, the client will generally respond with positive feelings of his own, and a true getting together will take place. This does not mean that there will be no problem in developing complete trust in the helping person, or that once the togetherness is achieved it can be forgotten. True togetherness is momentary and many minor separations occur in even the most positive relationship. The only way any true union can take place, however, is on the basis of trust, and trust must be merited. There are no techniques which the worker can use to achieve this. Only his own integrity and his own disposition to unite, perceived by the client, will lead to any kind of true togetherness. Once this state of relationship is achieved, however, there will still be innumerable moments of withdrawal, and the necessity for this too must be understood and appreciated.

The dynamically oriented worker is attentive to every bit of union or separation which takes place between the client and himself, and he frequently helps the client to move from one phase to the next. This is particularly true toward the end of treatment, where the client naturally has great difficulty in giving up that which formerly had great value for him.

The process of helping the client separate himself from the relationship has been given much more stress by the functionalists than by others, and on the whole, the functional helping process is a much shorter one than others. In some instances it is undoubtedly too short, and this is due to the fact that the functionalist worker sometimes puts so much stress on separation that he loses sight of the necessity for significant union before the separation can produce any kind of real freedom. The diagnostic worker, who allows more time for the development of the transference (by which he means essentially the same thing as the functional worker who speaks of the sense of union between the client and himself), is perhaps less prone to end the relationship prematurely. Workers of either school who practice dynamically, however, recognize that there must be enough good feeling between client and worker, and sufficient exchange of significant feeling, so that each one can feel he has met with an important person in his life. Each must be aware of the fact that he is a participant in an important relationship; each must value the relationship and contribute something toward sustaining it. The relationship must be lived out and it must be lived out together. One person cannot retire from it and let the other one live it out. For only when there is a contribution from both sides is there any such thing as a significant relationship. Both persons must let themselves go, so to speak, and allow this relationship with each other to come to fruition. This is the essential factor in "union," "transference," or whatever else one might wish to call it.

Separation can have significance only in relation to such a development of mutuality between client and worker. Some clients, and some workers, too, are literally so much afraid of this kind of togetherness that they hasten the move toward separation in order to escape the fearful uniting. The worker who is this much afraid of a positive relationship certainly cannot help the client to develop and sustain one. The one who can welcome new experience, however, will encourage the client through his own willingness to enter into both the uniting and the separating.

The worker who practices dynamically is afraid neither of the

uniting nor of the separating. He himself puts into both phases
of the relationship a careful analysis of what is actually taking
place, and in doing so, brings a dynamic factor into play which
otherwise would be missing. In many everyday relationships, or
even in many professional ones, such as teaching, the uniting and
separating take place almost unconsciously and seldom with any
analysis of what is going on psychologically. In the helping relationship this need not be so, and in fact will not be, if the
worker is dynamically oriented. In this type of helping one always shares. One shares understanding of the uniting which
takes place, as well as of the separating. Because it is the more
difficult, one must have great understanding of the conflict which
is expressed in separating, and efforts must be made to work out
this conflict dynamically.

In such a working out of the conflict over separation, the
worker will do nothing to hasten it, but instead will rely on the
client's own necessity to separate, knowing that in many instances
he will do so, the more willingly, if he is not forced from the
outside. The worker who fully understands the separation experience will therefore approach the end phase of the relationship in an experimental spirit and will permit the client to try
functioning on his own, in some instances for greater and greater
periods of time. He will substantiate independent action of any
kind, while at the same time he recognizes the client's need to
maintain the security which he has found outside of himself, that
is, in the worker. As the client sees that there is security in himself, he will have less need of the outside source of security.
While he still experiences a need for it, however, the worker will
not cut him off from it. Instead he will work with the client on
the problem of how much he may be needed, and for what he
may be needed, and in this way put a special significance on this
end phase of the relationship.

When this is done, separation is not just a negative experience.
It is a constructive one — in fact, it may be the most constructive
phase of the relationship. Great consciousness will go into this
kind of separation and great regard for the other person. An

opportunity is at hand in this kind of experience to see the other more as he really is and less on the basis of one's own projections. By the time the client has reached the point of separating, he has much less need to project than he did initially, since the whole helping process is directed, in a sense, toward understanding his projections, as such. By the time he is about ready to separate, his projections — including those centered on the worker — are recognized as *his own,* and the client therefore can enter into a different phase of relationship with the worker. This is nevertheless a most difficult phase, and the client still needs the worker's help. He needs it primarily because the separating is rather a fearful experience: the faith in himself which he has built up by this time, together with the faith of the worker in his capacity to separate, sustains him. In the separating phase, therefore, the worker himself must manifest freedom from fear and genuine respect for separateness, that is to say, for the individuality of the other. The separation then will not just happen, nor will the worker force it to happen. Instead it will be worked out delicately, which means with much feeling for the other person, and dynamically, which means in a step-by-step manner.

5. *Creativity*

Rank's concept of creativity is in no sense a narrow one. It is not to be confused with artistic creation alone, or that which requires special talent, but is rather to be thought of as an attitude toward life or a way of adjusting to living problems. In neurotic adaptation, Rank found that the creative impulse, or the impulse to transform some aspect of the outside world, is stifled, whereas in creative expression the outer world is perceived as less threatening and more malleable. Not that the outer world presents no difficulties. The creative individual, however, is more willing to attack problems and to express himself in relation to them. This means expressing *himself* and not someone else's self, or what someone else thinks he should express. In creativity there must be individuality, and in individuality there must be separateness. It is the creative frame of mind, therefore, which one works toward in all helping. If the individual happens to possess talent or an adaptability to the arts, he may express his creativity in this manner. If he does not, however, there will be nothing to keep him from a creative frame of mind and creative living, assuming of course that the helping person directs himself toward the achievement of these ends.

Rank's philosophy is thus an extremely positive one. But not all adaptations which have been made of it are as positive. In fact, in the approach of certain functional workers, what one finds is the antithesis of what is implied in Rank's concept of creativity. Those workers who feel that they must "hold to" structure, and should therefore approach all problems and all persons in the same way, negate the conception of creativity and make of all helping a mere mechanical procedure. All the worker has to do in such an instance is to sit tight and let the client do whatever moving is to be done. The worker who appreciates what is involved in creative living, however, will not practice in this manner.

In neurotic adaptation, the client stands in his own way, and he does this with the worker as well as with others. In creative adaptation, he does not block himself nor will he be blocked by others. This does not mean that the creative person recognizes no limitations or that limitations cannot be used in working with him. It does mean, however, that limitations alone will not help him. What is needed to bring out creative potentiality is not the challenge of a limit so much as it is the recognition of power within the individual himself. The individual who comes for help generally feels much more subject to outside forces and limitations than he needs to feel. Constructive or creative forces within himself are tied up and must be loosened. Limits will not unloosen them. A creative attitude, however, on the part of the helper himself will do so.

The most important implication in Rank's concept of creativity is that the helper himself must be creatively oriented. If he is, he will seek and bring out the potentialities for creativity in his client. If he is not, he can easily block creativity in the client through a mechanical holding to rules and procedures. The creative helper is of necessity dynamically oriented. He is interested at all times in transformation and he therefore follows development in feeling and attitude. Because he does not hold onto the old himself, he does not expect his client to do so, and this disposition naturally contributes to change. Any necessity on the part of the helper to hold onto the old himself, that is to say, to repeat himself, brings out similar tendencies in the client and leads to the blocking rather than the encouragement of creativity. Creative attitude on the part of the helper leads to moving and growing disposition on the part of the client. It means that the worker never stops with what he puts into the contact initially, but watches the effect of his own activity and makes adaptation after adaptation on this basis.

The Rankian conception of creativity therefore is full of implication for dynamic casework and counseling. It gives point and purpose to this type of helping, and it even holds profound implications as far as method is concerned. The method of dynamic helping is a method which involves what Arthur Miller has aptly called "the creative thrust forward." [1] All creativity involves such a "thrust forward" and so does all dynamic living or development.

The Integration of Theory and Practice

Through this type of examination of Freudian and Rankian concepts, it is possible to see that both Freud and Rank have contributed indispensable ideas for the development of a dynamic philosophy of helping. As the original sources of both diagnostic and functional thinking, their contributions deserve honor and great respect. Unfortunately, what has happened in the development of the diagnostic and functional schools is that a kind of sectarianism has arisen, in their names, which does neither justice nor credit to either of these original and thoroughly creative thinkers. Their principles have been taken as antithetical rather

[1] "Many Writers, Few Plays," *New York Times,* August 10, 1952.

than complementary, and a stultifying opposition has arisen which can lead only to a dead end. The way to avoid this dead end — and the way which it seems to me the profession must take sooner or later — is to turn away from futile opposition and to look to the contributions which have come from both sources. In this manner a fuller and more satisfactory philosophy of help can be built up and a method developed which will rest on the primary contribution of both, namely, the dynamic principle which is inherent in all of their thinking and in all of modern psychology — as indeed, in all of modern science.

There is only one direction in which either of these two schools can develop, and that is to become more dynamic. The principles which both schools have set forth in the past decade do not need restating. What is required is analysis of their implications in dynamic terms. How are these principles applied in actual practice? Are there some which play a much more limited part in practice than would appear to be the case when they are discussed theoretically? There is only one way to determine this and that is to submit actual practice to scientific scrutiny. Verbatim case records must be examined from the standpoint of what the worker does and says rather than from the standpoint of the client's movement alone. What principles does the worker actually use? Are they in keeping with his philosophy? How dynamic is his approach? Does it reflect clear-cut *inter*action between client and worker? Or is the movement which takes place in the case one-sided? Is it movement which takes place in spite of the lack of facilitation rather than because of facilitating activity on the part of the worker? Such questions cannot be answered on the basis of principle. They can be answered through inductive research, however, and when such inductive research is actually carried out, contributions to theory will inevitably flow from it. Certain theoretical propositions of each school which are given a great deal of emphasis may well be found to play a minor role in the actual activity of practitioners, and others which now receive comparatively little emphasis may well take priority.

In any case, both schools, if they can bring themselves to the point of allowing such study of their practice as related to their principles, will find, I venture to predict, that much too little use has been made of the dynamic principles which are inherent in their respective philosophies. There is much practice being carried on today by representatives of both schools which is utterly mechanical and undynamic in character. For dynamic application of principle, one must go to the actual work of those practitioners who are dynamically oriented. Their work must be studied scientifically, and out of such study will come an interrelated dynamic theory and practice.

Toward this end the following chapter is devoted. In it a verbatim interview is presented and analyzed in terms of the fundamental concepts of both the diagnostic and the functional schools. Dynamic factors at work in the interview are observed and examined from the standpoint of their theoretical significance.

7

ANALYSIS OF A COUNSELING

INTERVIEW FROM A DYNAMIC

STANDPOINT

Throughout this book we have put a good deal of emphasis on the need for inductive research. The data of actual practice, we have said, must be examined and this must be done scientifically. What a worker actually does, rather than what he thinks he does, or says that he does, must be analyzed. The ordinary type of descriptive record which is kept in social agencies does not serve this purpose, and in order to carry out such research it is necessary to use data procured by mechanical means. This is no simple task, since the electrical recording machine or any other device used to secure reliable data must itself have some effect upon the interview. If neither client nor worker knew of the existence of the recording device, perhaps this could be avoided. Such a procedure, however, would certainly be unethical and is not likely to be accepted in social work practice.

The only sound procedure, it seems to me, is to use the mechanical recorder with the full knowledge of both client and worker, recognizing that the presence of the device will have its effect on both of them. From my own experience, I should be inclined to say that the effect of the recording is much greater in the beginning, when it tends to make worker and client more cautious than they might otherwise be. When both become accustomed to it, however, and when both really feel that a worthwhile purpose is being served, the effect on the content of the interview seems to be minimal.

The interview cited here is one held after a good many sessions in which an electrical recording device was used. The client is an intelligent and well-educated person who fully understood its purpose. As the content of the interview demonstrates, it did not seem to deter him from speaking of his innermost thoughts and feelings. I do not mean to suggest that the electrical recorder can be used with any and every client without causing difficulty. Many clients of social agencies, who come to be helped, and not to participate in research, would resent the intrusion of such a device. Certainly every client should have the right to feel assured of complete confidentiality, just as he would in going to a private therapist. Certain persons, however, are willing to contribute to research in this manner, and this was true in this particular instance.

The client in this instance is a man of thirty-four whom we shall call Mr. Mann. He is a person of unusual sophistication who several years previously completed a long period of psychoanalysis. After the completion of his analysis, he established himself as a consulting engineer. Previously he had devoted himself exclusively to sculpture, in which field he had shown a great deal of ability. It was difficult to make a living as a sculptor, however, and he decided to go into engineering, for which he also had training, in order to earn an adequate living for his wife and children.

Although his decision was a firm one, Mr. Mann resented the fact that he had to make it, and as a result he harbored a good deal of negative feeling toward his family, particularly his wife.

Before proceeding with the interview itself, perhaps a word should be mentioned about the choice of this particular interview for presentation. As indicated earlier, it is my belief that the field of counseling represents the area in which the two schools of thought — functional and diagnostic — come closest to each other. Because of the absence of any concrete service, attention is necessarily focused on the problem aspects of the situation and the personality of the client. Agency-centered discussion is therefore minimal. This fact emerges clearly when one compares placement interviews, let us say, with those in child guidance or family counseling interviews with those in public assistance. Counseling interviews are centered primarily on the person and his problems, and there is comparatively little discussion of a pure functional nature which can take place within such interviews. Even when the counselor is functionally oriented, he must shift his center of interest from his function to the client and his problem, in the counseling situation. This is where the attention of the diagnostically oriented counselor is also focused. Likenesses and differences between the two therefore emerge quite clearly whenever a counseling interview is considered. For this reason it seems most appropriate to look into an actual counseling interview and to examine it from the standpoint of its functional and diagnostic content.

Perhaps a word should be mentioned too regarding the type of person with whom the counselor works in this instance. This client's educational and economic background, as well as the fact that he completed a long analysis and therefore had a certain familiarity with the helping situation, might be regarded as unusual in social agency experience. With the development of counseling on a fee basis, however, more and more clients with similar background do avail themselves of agency help. In this particular instance, the agency is known in the community as one which provides both concrete social services and counseling. Both types of help are offered to all economic groups. The agency's clientele therefore is not limited to the economically disadvantaged. Mr. Mann, in fact, is not at all atypical as a client of the agency. He is a rather vivid personality, and his understanding may exceed that of many other clients. The counseling experience which he had, however, is not generically different from that of many other clients.

Transcript of Interview [1]

(Good morning.)

How are you?

(Fine. How are you?)

Not bad, but not good. *Laughter.* Coming down here, I sort of got an idea as to what is happening in my coming here. Not that any — not that any of it is my business, but — *Laughter.*

(It certainly is your business.)

Well, I know when I first came — the first six sessions or something like that — I realized that this is the way things went — you saw that I not only was willing to improve my outlook, but to change it — not only to try to change my outlook, but really my development. I suddenly find I'm starting to change it, and it's unpleasant too!

(Only unpleasant?)

Yes, it's unpleasant. After all, if you build up an image of yourself, regardless of what the image is, the resistance to change is fantastic! If you change anything in your daily life — if, for in-

---

[1] Except for a few editorial changes to make it more readable and a few changes in identifying data, the verbal content of the interview is presented here as it occurred. The counselor's part is given in parentheses.

stance, you're used to brushing your teeth a certain way and somebody tells you of another way — I mean, I know you can be resistant as hell — everything, I mean, in any kind of change there's resistance. Human beings are like that. They like to make habits, good, bad, or indifferent. So I don't find it so easy to change either — I'm like anybody else. Somehow I got a certain amount of satisfaction from the image of myself I had built up. It was better than what I had had before . . . it was progressive, in a way. But it was static too in that it didn't tend to make for self-improvement. So I found myself this week back in an old pattern without even knowing it. It wasn't until yesterday that I began to become aware of it. After last week, I felt — I not only felt good, but I felt that I would try to, you know, *do things.* There were certain things that I was going to do. I had a definite feeling of what I would call relatedness to people. I felt generally more related — I didn't feel, you know, uppity — you know — high and mighty — or feel the need for isolation, and so forth. Things conspire against you, though, it's funny, things work out the wrong way or the right way, you might say. So — I don't waste time, and I've got a lot of guts, and it was a satisfaction . . . I don't know what it was, to tell you the truth, I don't know what it was. Maybe it was a relatedness with regard to the children or someone who works for me — I don't know. It's just a question of being on a simple level of existence and destroying an intellectual illusion about having to — let's say — having to dislike television, because I wanted to be an intellectual, for example, which a lot of people do . . . you know?

(Yes.)

I dislike it anyhow — I don't look at it, but I made too much of a point of it, which is typical of intellectual snobbery. So I began to — so I felt that if I wanted to look at it, I could look at it without having to feel guilty that I was not being an intellectual snob — after all — an artist . . . So I sort of felt pretty good and I tried to settle a lot of things — nothing was either taboo or not taboo. I really got some things settled.

(Yes.)

So along came Saturday night and we were to go to a small party at somebody's home which included my wife's pet hate, whom you probably know.

(Yes, I do.)

So she finally said, "I'm not going." Well, I'm in my expansive mood and I said, "Well, I'm going to go. I feel like a party and maybe a few drinks. Maybe it'll be a good party, who the hell knows?" So she said, "All right, go." So I went and I had a helluva good time. *Laughter.* I had a helluva good time. I'm a terrific dancer and there were people there that I could dance with. So I danced all night. I drank a lot and I sang a lot — which for me is a pretty good release. I can get a lot out of it. I sort of go into it pretty completely when I do. Most parties are deadly dull — more or less — but at this one there was a combination of things and it went all right. It wasn't just that I enjoyed it, but everybody — it was a pretty good party — and everybody seemed to be more or less in the mood, for some reason. And Claire wasn't there, which made it easier for me, so that I didn't have to look at her to be unhappy, you know — that would make me unhappy and self-conscious and in some way guilty . . . So, the next day, we got into an argument about it . . . She may not have done anything — I don't know — I can't separate it — I don't remember well enough what happened. I may have been only too ready to fall into a pattern of getting rid of shackles, so that I could really have more fun, you know, be a little bit wilder, be a little more expressive, you know, so that I can't tell now whether I interpreted what she said, or what you said, or what she said I said — you know? I don't know. I don't really know. I can't really remember. Anyway it was not so much an argument, but I retreated completely. I didn't talk to her for practically three days. Hardly at all. Wouldn't have anything to do with her. Wouldn't go near her. And I felt justified all the time. I felt here's somebody holding me down. Somebody who was dead and didn't know enough to lie down. Somebody who had no real emotions — just a person full of denial. She won't do what there is around to do, but she won't do anything about it, which is partly justified, because I suppose she can only move as fast as she can move — so, that's how I'm supposed to be — *Laughter* — or expect myself to be. When you live with somebody, you have to make compromises and adjustments. But I didn't want to. I was at the point, I felt actually at the point — ah, Jesus, I'd just as soon give her money and live someplace else. The hell with the whole business. I didn't like it. I'd only be held down. I can't all of a sudden get rid of her. I still feel tied down — imprisoned, even though I've gotten rid of the — I still am carrying around the feeling that I'm being held down, and that I'd like not to be held down. It doesn't have anything to do with her or anything else, actually. But it's funny that it didn't go away as much as I thought it would, this time. It started to break up, but it hasn't really gone away yet.

(All of which means something to me. It means a great deal, really. Tell me, what did she do when you went to the party?)

She stayed home.

(Just stayed home. Did nothing at all?)

No.

(Just what occurred the next day?)

I don't know. Nothing really. Let me see if I can recall. I started talking to her in bed in the morning, and I told her I had a good time, and mentioned several other things that happened there, and somehow it came about that she said that I was trying to force her to accept this woman (her pet hate) and these people. That when she couldn't have a good time I was trying to make her and I've always been trying to make her — force her to accept this girl. There wasn't any argument or anything. I just got angry and I moved out — you know. I just clammed up and wouldn't say anything further.

(Was she angry about your going to the party in the first place?)

I claim that she was. She absolutely denies it. I claim that she was. I don't know — I just say that she was. She said it wasn't true at all — that she didn't feel that way at all. She may or may not have been. I don't know. I felt — I think I felt an anger in the morning — a resentment, or whatever you want to call it. I think I did. But I don't remember. I don't know what the hell it was. You know, it got blurred in that terrible anger that followed for three or four days. Till yesterday — so I can't separate it. It gets lost, gets tangled in the strain of anger. It's lost, I don't know what happened, exactly. I don't think I can recall what happened exactly. I doubt if I can recall. I can't see in what way it's related to feeling good the day before and getting this terrific reaction from — I mean, there was no need for myself to get that kind of reaction. I didn't need it. It was a reaction which had actually taken hold of me so that I had no control. I also broke it up, but I was surprised that I had that amount of control, and that amount of anger. It really wasn't real anger. It wasn't anger in a very definite sense. It didn't burn me up. It didn't burn me up. It was a cold, calculating anger, you know. Not in the usual — I usually get very intense — you know — inflamed. It wasn't that. It was cold. Unusual for me, as a matter of fact. It just doesn't connect up.

(Tell me, do you have any feeling for what it's like for a woman to be left alone while the man she is interested in is having a good time with other women, or some one other woman particularly — in this case, a woman whom she has a great deal of feeling about?)

Well, man or woman — I think that unless a person, and this has happened to me often enough, is free enough to want the other person to have a good time, or feels that he should have a good time, which has happened to me often enough, in regard to things that Claire has done which I wouldn't do — it didn't bother me. I was satisfied that she went, you know. Any good time that I had in relation to the party was not in relation to her. It was in relation to what was doing there. Not as far as she was concerned though.

(You said man or woman — do you feel it's the same for both, is that it?)

Well, as far as I can see, yes. I can't see that there's much difference. I can't feel any difference, if that's what you mean. I
wouldn't know if there's any difference. I'm not a woman.

(No, but you are a sensitive person, and you are able to capture
feelings of other people. You see, according to my way of
thinking, there is a tremendous difference in the way it seems to
a woman and the way the same experience seems to a man.
In fact, it's not really the same experience. It's a totally different
kind of experience.)

That's obvious. I mean a woman is a different person. I wouldn't
expect her to feel the same way I do. But a person, at any rate,
the woman part, I don't know.

(How would *you* expect her to feel?)

Well I'll tell you how I felt on such occasions.

(Would you expect her to feel as you did?)

Yeah, I certainly would expect her to feel as I did.

(You would?)

I mean, why not? Under the circumstances, wanting the other
person to have a good time, yes. That's the way I felt, I think.
Why shouldn't she sometimes be able to feel that way too, maybe
not all the time. But under specialized circumstances, I would
expect her to — I don't see why she should be unhappy about
the fact that I'm having a good time.

(Well, now that's all very logical, but it really is very un-under-
standing, especially so for you, it seems to me. It doesn't really
recognize what is different about your wife from yourself.
You're asking in effect, that she respond to a situation exactly
as you would.)

No. I mean on occasion she could. No, I don't mean — I mean
on specific occasions she should. I say this, being a specific occa-

sion . . . if I said, shall we say, "Well listen, stay home, I'm
going out, I'll be back" . . . I can understand she'd feel lousy —
Where is he going, what is he going to do — who knows? But
just visiting people, she knew it was just a party where people
are gathered together, there's nothing threatening, really threatening — you know what I mean? There was nothing really
threatening as activity. I know I'm being logical again, but it
seems to me I can't — I wouldn't even say that she should feel
good about it — I don't say she should feel good about it, but
I wouldn't expect her to feel horrible about it! — Nor would
I expect her to have a tremendous reaction to it, because it was
just —

(Let's look at your feeling about her and about your relation
to her. Do you know what it is?)

Yeah. Well, the only thing is — I appreciate the way she feels,
and on the other hand, she has been with me for now going on
a year in different groups where Anne (her pet hate) has been.
She has been there enough to gain a certain amount of confi-
dence and feeling about my behavior, especially in view of my
attitude and my discretion toward Anne, you know what I mean,
to gain a certain amount of satisfaction that there is nothing
in it that should in any way involve a threat. No, I think that
she is carrying this thing too far. I think that she is holding on
to it just terribly. That's all. She keeps on giving a person,
a weak, fantastic person, the most terrible power over her all
the time. I'm not going to deny that she still feels that way.
She does still feel that way. She didn't know any more than
I knew that Anne would be there, as a matter of fact. She didn't
know. I didn't know — she just happened to be there. No, I
know it's not the best kind of circumstances in the world, no —
I mean, it's not ideal. Ordinarily, I wouldn't even go. I just
happened to be feeling good. Felt like going. It's not often that
I feel as positive about going, you know. But I felt positive
about going, you see. Very rare. But I'm very glad I did go.
Anyhow, I don't give a damn about how Claire felt. That's the
way she felt — O.K. — you know? I'm only worried about the
way *I* felt. I mean — I can understand the whole — I'm sensitive

enough to feel all the differences she felt — but I still would do it. So she had to suffer because I felt good. I'm not concerned with that. That's her business — her problem. I'm concerned that I should have such a reaction to the way she felt about it. I don't give a damn about that. That's her business. She's happy about it or she's unhappy about it — most times, I would take this into account, but if I don't feel like taking it into account, I won't take it into account and I'll take the responsibility for it. But I won't take the responsibility for it and then she says some harsh words and I laugh it off — O.K.? But all right, if she says some harsh words, I shouldn't laugh it off? That I don't get. That's what bothers me. That I should go back into the old pattern and that I should break up everything because I don't like one thing, or because I feel that it's going to tear me down and allow me, no — I mean the very thing you said just brought an antagonism to me. It made me mad. The idea that I felt, well, if that's so, then I always have to take into account the fact that she feels that way. I would therefore certainly not go out. I would be so sensitive to the way she felt that I wouldn't do anything about it. I would just stay home.

(You mean that's what I was implying?)

Well, that's what I felt you were implying. So it's like saying the hell with sensitivity if it's going to hold me back too much.

(Maybe what's happening is that what I've been doing this morning is something like what she did, and you're reacting to it the way you did to her.)

Could be.

(You *are* sensitive to her really.)

I don't think I reacted to her at all. I think the reaction is too close. It was entirely within myself. As I say, there was no argument — nothing got cooked up, you know. Just walked out the door, nothing violent, which is unusual!

(When you called it anger before, I wondered a bit, since it wasn't expressed as anger and since it remained with you so long — wasn't it guilt in a way?)

Well, I don't know. I can see elements of guilt in it, but —

(Guilt over having a good time —)

That could be true. It's funny. There's something quite mixed up in it. Not so much having guilt about having a good time because that is something which I have not been able to recognize. Let's put it this way. It's guilt over not feeling guilty about having a good time.

(*Laughter.*)

I mean it. It's much closer to that than it is to the other. Perhaps it doesn't make any sense — it isn't logical — it isn't reasonable — but that's the closest to the way I felt — I don't feel guilt. I still feel happy about the good time I had — still do.

(I can accept that, strange as it may seem!)

It does seem strange — it doesn't make sense to me.

(No. This is what it means to me. It means that a side of yourself, the — if you like — the more masculine side, the less considerate side, the less identifying side, expresses itself in this situation in opposition to the other side of yourself — the sensitive side — the identifying side — the part that can see the way the woman really feels in that kind of situation. Whether it is justified or not isn't the question. You see that's the way she *feels* . . . You feel to some extent along with her. Now that side apparently was squelched in this whole episode. Right?)

It makes a little sense, it's just that — well, yes, for the most part it seems like that. But that particular feeling of guilt in relation to guilt — guilt in relation to non-guilt, rather, is a part of the feeling which prevented me from becoming angry in an overt way. And the other thing, side by side with it, is an infantile kind of an expression of wanting-to-break-away-from-the-mother business, you know. Not wanting to be told what to do. Very raw terms! I don't want to be told what to do — I don't want to be held down — I don't want to — and again I bring up the word — be castrated, in a sense. I don't want to have any part that feels good and living to be cut off. That's why I felt castrated.

(What you did here was, if you like, a little bit of self-castration, that is, in being true to one part of yourself, the assertive part, you were being untrue to the other part of yourself, the part that could see her side of it.)

Well, how can you live with two people like that?

(*Laughter.* But you *are* two people like that, really. Your problem is how to make one out of those two.)

Yeah. I can't see that the two will necessarily agree. One has to go. *Laughter.*

(*Laughter.*)

Because as I say — as I said before, I realize the whole problem, and I could go and do something and not be — not get a reaction from it. I mean, fine — I would have done it and that would be the end of it — I would have done it with a clear knowledge of what I was doing, and not be disturbed by it, and also not be angry with the other person for any reaction that he or she might have.

(So you see it intellectually really. But you haven't achieved it in the sense that these two selves have been brought together. They haven't yet —)

No, I wouldn't destroy that feeling in me. I wouldn't have that same aggression — aggressive feeling, if, say, I were sorry. It's still lingering slightly — it doesn't want to depart. It's hanging on with a good deal of life, for the fear of being drowned, or something.

(You know, there's a part of this that has nothing at all to do with her, and it has, as you can begin to see this morning, an awful lot to do with being held down here. In the beginning, this was going to be something that one would toss off — do it quickly, get it over with . . .)

Correct a few minor defects.

(Yes.)

Just getting a machine to work a little smoother.

(Now I was, and would be, willing to have it that way, but you apparently wanted —)

Something else —

(Something beyond.)

Yeah. I was aware that I must have wanted something beyond or it wouldn't actually have turned out the way it did.

(But then when you do get deeper into things, particularly into yourself, you have this natural and inevitable feeling of being tied down here. You go out and you have what feels like a good living experience to you, but you've got to come back and talk about it afterward. You have to break it up somehow. You have to present it to somebody who, you know beforehand, is not going to see eye to eye with you on it. You really knew before telling me about it this morning, didn't you, that I was going to differ with you?)

I didn't think in terms of sympathy. I didn't think in terms of agreement. I really hadn't. I mean there was no indication of any agreement. No. No. I'm pretty clear. No question about it. I didn't even think in terms of agreement. I didn't expect agreement. I didn't even think in terms of agreement or disagreement. I was mostly interested in solving it as a problem which had disturbed me. I wasn't interested in anything else. No. I'm not that mixed up. I don't get those things mixed up any more. No, to me it was a problem which I felt should not have existed and to me, as I say, it was a return to some other state — which I felt was somehow way back, you know, on a previous level of existence. It reminded me of myself fifteen or twenty years ago, not now — you know what I mean. That was what bothered me. No, I only came here in the interests of solving a problem. I have admitted to myself and to Claire that there was nothing reasonable about what I did . . .

(Nothing? —)

Reasonable — I mean that it was just an irrational reaction. I admitted it to Claire yesterday. At first, I tried to get away with that. But I finally admitted it. I tried to put the blame on her as being the person who was dead and the ghoul who will beat me to the grave with her. You know what I mean, that kind of thing. But that didn't worry me. I didn't try too hard either —

(*Laughter.*)

So I finally admitted that it was completely irrational and I didn't have to hold onto any kind of anger against Claire. It had spread to too wide a base by then, you know. Lost its individual character — whatever individual character there is in anger. Like today — it existed no longer. I no longer feel individually angry at Claire, because she's an image which merges into something so big that I can't see it as a person. A parent, a mother, and a — you know — several non-objective things like anchors and lead weights and whatnot.

(It feels to me though, that while you don't feel it toward her, you really do feel it toward me this morning, don't you?)

Only in relation to the thing that you said that she might have felt, or only in relation to feeling sensitivity. It's a reaction

against sensitivity, or the feeling that why should I be sensitive
— why shouldn't these two people get together and work together. To me it became "I don't want to have anything to do
with this sensitive character." To hell with him. Let him fend
for himself. I'm tired of being sensitive. I don't want the responsibility of sensitivity. I don't want any part of sensitivity.
I don't want it to be part of me, except if it's a part of me that
I don't know anything about. I don't want to be known as a
sensitive person. I don't want to have it. — That's part of the
thing I lost this week, or that I was willing to give up, as a
matter of fact. That's part of it. To lose this kind of image
of myself as being particularly sensitive, because it meant an
obligation to myself in some way, which I shouldn't feel, but
that I personally had to uphold, which if it was there, should
be — I don't know — I guess I'm not making myself clear —
I wasn't willing to go along with this picture of myself as a
definite, sensitive, artist image, because it meant — began to
mean to me, putting on a certain kind of show, which I wasn't
willing to do. I was willing, this week, to reidentify myself with
the man in the street. I was willing to reidentify with anybody.
I want to be close to somebody. I want to be able to see anybody, not be the odd one. You know what I mean?

(Yes.)

Well, this was an image I was definitely trying to get rid of.
I wanted to be a laborer or something, not the opposite. I
wanted to be sensitive to character and life, and not be a name
which I endowed myself with, "an artist."

(Do you know how opposite this is to the way you saw it all
last week?)

No.

(If I were to play back the recording of last week's session —)

Don't do it! *Laughter.*

(— it would be hard for you to believe that it was the same person talking today who spoke last week.)

Well, I —

(What you asserted last week was quite the opposite. What you asserted then was something that you may want to get rid of at times, and something that does need toning down, but you are the artist — You can't stop being the artist!)

Well it does make sense to me. I don't deny that. I just say that it should be integrated into me and not be separated from me — that I should not be conscious of being an artist and a sensitive person *and* something else.

(Now, I do want to applaud your interest this week in the man on the street, and your willingness to be ordinary. That's fine. But the two do have to be combined.)

I agree.

(The two can be combined. Last week, you were busy concentrating on the one, and this week you have been busy concentrating on the other —)

Next week maybe I can concentrate on both. *Laughter.* No, it's all right. It doesn't bother me. It seems perfectly logical, perfectly reasonable to go from one extreme to another in the search for myself. So what! It makes sense, and I'm not denying it. I just want one to take its place and the other to take its place. I have a feeling — I'm also quite aware of my sensitivity in many, many ways. In simple little ways. Not in complicated ways. I don't have to look for ways of being sensitive. I'm sensitive to music, for example. I'm sensitive to dancing, very much so. I dance well because I have a terrific sensitivity to it. Everybody wants to dance with me, because I'm a good dancer, and because I'm sensitive and what you call creative. It's funny, I can only see it in simple ways. I don't see it in regard to my sculpture, which I don't do very much these days anyway . . . It gets a little mixed up, but I see it in regard to my work too, in a simpler way. There I will attack a problem and solve it well and that takes sensitivity and imagination.

(Yes.)

But I'm not so sensitive in regard to people, except in an analytic kind of way, you know? I have sort of conquered most of it, I imagine. It's — no, it isn't that — But to return to a general relationship to retirement, I mean where I had opened myself up to a reaction against Claire, a reaction to sensitivity, a reaction against everybody, a retirement into a loose and vulnerable position. It's just a sort of running back and getting caught in a closet and . . . Maybe it wasn't such a good idea. I got into trouble right away. Probably deliberately got into trouble . . . I stuck my neck out, or like a small boy I deliberately do something knowing mother is going to get mad at me for it, and do it anyhow so that mother will get mad at me, so I can get mad at mother! I don't know, it gets sort of complicated. As I say, I feel this very deeply —

(Yes, I think you really feel it.)

Yeah. I do, in a way because I feel it goes back pretty far into me. You know, far back, and things way back in the head that make a sort of connection. I don't know exactly . . . But I had to make some kind of a connection with this long-ago-familiar and long-ago-disturbing (but it's not as disturbing as it was) and it didn't burn me up like it once would have burnt me up. You know, in some way, I got rid of the need to retire completely. The retirements previously weren't successful. I never did retire successfully. In effect, I didn't retire completely this time, and I didn't retire with real anger, and I didn't retire even in feeling, you know what I mean? I still felt connected. I just resisted any connection. I didn't want it to be — I wanted somebody else to make the connection. I wanted Claire to make the connection. I wanted — That doesn't really make any sense.

(Why doesn't it?)

Well, it's as I say, I wanted her to prove that she wasn't dead.

(While acting as though you were!)

That's right. That's why I say it doesn't make sense — it's childish —

(I see what you mean.)

Very childish. I mean, I can see a child doing it. I can see myself as a child doing it.

(It's not easy to cut off the past, is it?)

No. It's not easy to reformulate anything once you get it set pretty strong. I mean after I had left, I mean after I had left, after I had left that analysis that I had, I first attempted to build an image — then I had none, I had nothing. I saw that I had to do something for myself. I saw that I wasn't going to get anything from anybody. You might put it that way. I saw that I wasn't going to get any help and I had to do something about it. It was then I began to feel as though there never would be any self that would operate, that would at least co-operate.

(Yes.)

And that was my problem. I didn't have any image about co-operating. Previously I operated, and then there was this not being able to do anything at all. You know, complete immobilization. I did have depressive moods before then, and during the analysis I had terrible depressions, but I got rid of the depressions, and I got rid of the immobility, and I really had something that would work, and that's how I went into my present work. I was, you know, I was just floundering for years.

(Yes.)

So I built up something that would move.

(Yes.)

It's hard to break it down, except to make another one that will move better.

(When you came here then — was it in order to fortify something, to build up or to integrate parts of this image that weren't quite put together —)

Yes. Definitely. That's why I said earlier that I only came to have the machine fixed up a little so it would run a little smoother. I didn't intend to build a new machine.

(Yes.)

Although it feels like I'm building a new machine, not repairing the old one.

(Yes.)

Well, I mean I wasn't satisfied with the old one, but I could have used it, you know. Evidently I wasn't satisfied with the old one, but one doesn't control those things. If I was satisfied, I would have stopped — I would have gotten a few little things maybe that may have made it run a little smoother — who knows? I don't know myself.

(I think you'll find before we stop that it's not building a new machine — starting fresh — something that has nothing to do with the old at all, but rather that it's putting together the parts of the machine which are all there, a bit like a jig-saw puzzle, all the parts are there and they're good and they'll make a whole. It's a question of getting these parts to fit into the right places, so that they are integrated — you can feel them as being integrated.)

I suppose so.

(I don't know just how long it's going to take you to do that, or how many experiences like this one, this week, you must have in order to do it. I expect not too many, and I also think that it's not going to take you years and years and years to achieve this objective. It might be a comparatively short time.)

Well, for one thing, you know, I'm conscious of my own power. Very definitely conscious of this power — of my own power, what do you call it, of my own dynamics, and the consciousness — now I very definitely am conscious of my creative sense — a self-created sense, which is also difficult to reckon with, because it's only applied in a small way. It still doesn't operate completely. No, it's very narrow and it demands a lot more than it gets. Let's put it that way. It demands or leaves me — usually dissatisfied — something more that I want than I have. I'm not satisfied with my life as it is. It's got to work out better. Actually I've got a sense of, a feeling — a more definite desire to see results of my creative processes, whatever they are, whether it be in sculpture or something else . . .

(Well, for the time being, you've turned all of this creative energy, if you like, on yourself. You're busy creating a self, a life, rather than a piece of sculpture —)

You think that's so — I mean, do things work like that really?

(Sure they do.)

I don't know — I mean I would have no knowledge of that really, I suppose —

(The same kind of energy goes into this as into the other, and some of the same kind of pain, is that not so?)

Laughter. I'm sure of that.

(*Laughter.*)

Sure. There's no growth without some kind of pang.

(Well maybe we've done as much as we can, for one morning.)

I think so . . . *Pause.* You know Claire isn't strong at all, and she could benefit by my strength, you know, if I'm able to be strong, and usually I am. I felt that I was her protector all this time. That was another reaction I had, actually. I'm sick of protecting her, I'm sick of keeping her under my wing, you know. I wanted to let her fly herself a little bit! I'd like to see her fly. I would be proud of it if she could fly. But she refuses to fly as far as the corner. She still plays it pretty certain. But I expect she'll change. Maybe the satisfaction, even the fact of her not going to the party is a step in the right direction, a step toward doing something for herself.

(Yes, and I think as change occurs within you, it will have its effect upon her too.)

Yes. I suppose so. Maybe I deliberately hold her down — you know.

(Yes.)

Keep things from her . . . *Pause.* Same time next week?

(Yes. Just let me look at the calendar to check — Yes.)

*   *   *   *

Let us now consider the applicability of our five Freudian and five Rankian concepts in understanding this interview.

Application of Diagnostic (Freudian) Concepts

Unconscious Mind

It is quite obvious that one does not deal directly in this interview with manifestations of unconscious mind as such. Mr. Mann does not, for example, bring dreams for interpretation, nor is there free association. Does this mean, however, that understanding of the unconscious has no relevance whatever to the interview? I do not think so. In fact, if the counselor did not understand that part of his personality which Mr. Mann tries to conceal from himself (which after all is the essential meaning of unconscious mind) this interview would have been impossible. Much of the counselor's activity is directed toward helping Mr. Mann understand himself *fully*. This understanding must be more than intellectual. There must be a realization and a possession of the whole self which Mr. Mann does not manifest initially. It is as though he accepts and asserts half of himself, without owning up to the other half. One half, so to speak, is conscious; the other half, unconscious. The counselor's purpose here is to make both halves conscious and to bring about a state of wholeness.

Obviously the concept of unconscious mind permeates the counselor's thinking here, and when translated into activity, serves as one of the essential dynamics of the interview. One does not need to talk about the unconscious motivation. One must be oriented to the whole self, and if one is, a question will arise in connection with almost anything the client presents as to whether the whole self (conscious and unconscious mind) is being represented, or only partial self (conscious mind only). Whatever questions are asked or observations made by the counselor, will stem from this basic interest.

Ambivalence

Mr. Mann is essentially an ambivalent person. No other word perhaps, describes his general mental state so well as does the term "ambivalence." With all of his conflict, however, he has made a reasonably good adaptation from a vocational standpoint and from the standpoint of his family life. As compared with many creative personalities, he has done perhaps a good deal better than average in making adaptations to reality. Nevertheless, the degree of his ambivalence should not be minimized. If Mr. Mann were to go again for psychiatric treatment as such, at this point in his life, it would be his ambivalence which would represent the essential psychiatric problem.

Mr. Mann does not come for psychiatric treatment as such, at this time, but instead for a limited kind of psychological help, which he hopes will make him more comfortable in his family life. For this kind of help, as well as for psychiatric help, it is necessary to understand the inherent personality factors at play, and in order to do so, one must make use of the conception of ambivalence. No matter what terms might be used to describe what goes on in Mr. Mann's mind, the central and pervading factor in his case is ambivalence.

The Past

It is certainly important for the counselor to know that Mr. Mann had been through a long period of analysis in which he explored a great deal of his childhood experience. The understanding which came out of this undoubtedly helped him to make the kind of adaptation he did before coming to the counselor. It is significant to note also that Mr. Mann knew, before coming to the counselor, that no effort would be made to delve into his past all over again. In interviews preceding this one, Mr. Mann did describe the general nature of his relationship with his father, mother, and siblings. Understanding of his early family life, however, was not necessary in order to comprehend the nature of Mr. Mann's present problem.

The key to an understanding of Mr. Mann's problem lies much more in the concept of ambivalence than it does in the past, and it is possible to fully comprehend his ambivalence without knowing his past. This is no argument against spontaneous presentation of past experience, nor even against inquiry into the past. It is an argument, however, against any mechanical approach to the client's past, or any assumption that knowledge of the past can be equated with genuine helpfulness. Even if one fully understood his past ambivalent experiences, one would not necessarily understand his present ones, and it is only through understanding of his present ones that he can be helped *now*. Mr. Mann gives the counselor an opportunity to inquire into the past when he speaks of "a return to a previous level of experience" and comments that he is "reminded of himself fifteen or twenty years ago." The counselor responds, however, only in terms of how difficult it is to cast off the past.

The counselor's whole approach to Mr. Mann is an approach which emphasizes the present. Mr. Mann must have a present experience, different from any he has had in the past, and in this experience he must realize and possess parts of himself which he initially represses or denies. In order to come to this type of self-understanding, he must undergo a dynamic experience, one where he lives through a relationship with the helping person in which *shift of feeling* about the past, the present, or the future, about the self or about others, is a constant focus of interest.

In speaking of shift of feeling, we of course refer to the essential dynamics of the interview. Feeling does not shift automatically. It shifts as a result of *new* experience. In any kind of helping situation, the helper must so conduct himself that the person being helped will have new experience. His center of interest, in other words, will be dynamic. The shifts of feeling which occur in a therapeutic process are the result of the interaction which takes place between the two persons involved. One person must bring his spontaneous feeling and the other must bring his understanding of the situation. If his understanding is centered on the past, he will be less likely to bring any questions or observations with dynamic import than if he is really concerned with the dynamics of the relationship itself.

The Transference

This brings us to the transference, which must be recognized as one of the dynamic factors operative in the interview. Mr. Mann does not speak of feeling for the counselor, positive or negative, except at the point where he is annoyed with the counselor's expressed identification with his wife's feelings. However, transference implies identification (literally, "making the same") and Mr. Mann most certainly would like to make the counselor's outlook the same as his own. This effort to make the counselor's outlook identical with his own serves as one of the dynamics of the interview. Just as the analyst cannot become father or mother in the transference situation, so the counselor cannot become Mr. Mann. The assumed identity must be broken up, and is when the counselor brings in a rather sharp difference of outlook.

Underlying all of this, however, is enough basic identification to make it possible for Mr. Mann to bring his problem and to work on it with the counselor in a spirit of trust and genuine mutuality. Without this, the interview never could have taken place. With it, unlimited possibilities are opened up.

Even those who are opposed to the use of the term "transference" must recognize that it is only in a relationship of a distinct character that there can be truly dynamic interplay or influence. The client must bring something to the relationship in the way of faith in the helping person, and the latter must bring something too in the way of disposition to merit that faith. Whether one calls the resulting relationship transference or something else is immaterial. There can be no understanding of the dynamics of therapeutic situation, however, without a thorough and sensitive comprehension of what is best known under the name of transference.

Resistance

Perhaps the outstanding characteristic of the interview is Mr. Mann's strongly resistant attitude toward the counselor's view of the situation. It is true that the resistance is broken up rather quickly so that Mr. Mann can come, at the end of the interview, to feel and say that perhaps it is not his wife who ties him down, but rather he who has held her from doing what she would like to do. This transformation of attitude does not take place automatically, but is rather the result of a variety of factors which are at play simultaneously. Not the least of these is the counselor's sympathetic understanding of the resistance itself. Mr. Mann is quite conscious of his resistance to change and speaks of this at the beginning of the interview. He is also conscious of his resistance to the counselor's interpretation. The helping person, however, must be attuned to resistance and must feel it as Mr. Mann himself does. ("It is still lingering slightly, it doesn't want to depart.")

Mr. Mann's comment that he is conscious of his own "dynamics" is especially interesting in this connection. Being as sensitively introspective as he is, Mr. Mann can consciously *feel* his resistance to the influence of others. He can strongly feel his own impulse to change and his counter-impulse to preserve his present state of mind. The resistance in other words, is not unrelated to his fundamental ambivalence. This is what requires interpretation, and it is this which receives most stress from the counselor.

From this brief analysis in terms of the five "diagnostic" concepts it is clear, I think, that there can be much understanding of what actually takes place in an interview through the use of these conceptions. If we turn, however, to the "functional" counterparts of these concepts, we shall find that a parallel type of understanding is possible through the use of supposedly opposite conceptions.

Application of Functional (Rankian) Concepts

Will

Let us first look at the applicability of the concept of will to this interview. Mr. Mann must be recognized as a person with a will of his own. There is purpose, direction, and organization in what he does and says. He knows what he wants and can act in order to achieve it. In the interview he manifests some consciousness of will, but there is much more that is implicit. The implicit can be captured, so to speak, and fully understood only as a result of the attention given to it by the helping person. When Mr. Mann says, for example, that he settled a few things for himself and decided that he was now going to try to "do things," what he is talking about is a manifestation of developing will. Again, in his decision to go to the party alone, since his wife had expressed a will of her own, there is a similar expression of developing will.

As in many instances, however, what Rank called "the will-guilt complex" comes to the fore. Indeed the guilt which Mr. Mann manifests after going to the party may be taken as evidence of will in conflict. What Mr. Mann needs therefore is substantiation of his will, which does not mean total acceptance of the form which it momentarily takes. Unless one recognizes, however, that there is something *good* in the willing, which can be seen as an attempt at self-fulfillment, there can be only the sense of guilt and frustration.

Will does not exist in a vacuum. It is an exceedingly important aspect of Mr. Mann's psychology and requires full affirmation. It must remain under the influence, however, of other aspects of his total outlook, including his capacity to identify with others and to act on the basis of such identification. Will, in Mr. Mann's case, must be tempered with identification, and it is toward this end that much of the counselor's activity in the interview is directed.

The very term "will" is a dynamic one and there can be no doubt of the dynamic role which it plays in this interview. Mr. Mann, like every other person who comes for help, must do a certain amount of lifting himself by his own bootstraps. The helping person can only *help*. He cannot do that which must be done, in the last analysis, through exercise of the individual's own will. Will is that aspect of the personality which can work on itself, so to speak. It is creative power, and is recognized as such by the counselor at the end of the interview.

Counter-will

Just as the helping person should look for the manifestations of will, so he should be aware at all times that will is accompanied by counter-will and be prepared to recognize the opposite form of will when it expresses itself. With a person who has so much fundamental oppositeness within him as Mr. Mann, this is not a particularly difficult task. Mr. Mann's counter-will can be clearly observed throughout the interview, especially if one is mindful of the interview which preceded it. In the preceding interview, he had expressed strong interest in being sensitive and understanding, in co-operating, as he put it, in the present interview. The counselor brings this to him rather forcefully, and although he doesn't want to recognize it, he does realize the extent to which he has departed from his position of just a week ago. In the reaction, as he puts it himself, he began to feel that sensitivity was a burden and that he should cast it off. ("I am tired of being sensitive.") Mr. Mann recognizes, however, that in his assertion against sensitivity he is reacting excessively, and he is beginning to wonder how he can combine the sensitive and assertive sides of himself.

This movement from one pole to the other is not solely a will phenomenon. But where will is being expressed, such movement can be anticipated. Through the "making conscious" of this oppositeness in the self, there can be much therapeutic development. Acting on this principle, the counselor helps Mr. Mann to become aware of the two kinds of will within himself and thus opens up possibilities for integration.

It may be well to note here that the same oppositeness within the personality, which can be thought of in terms of ambivalence, may be recognized and dealt with in terms of will and counter-will. The latter two terms are essentially dynamic in their connotations, and suggest an extremely important aspect of personality not connoted by the term "ambivalence." As we have noted elsewhere, however, the term "ambivalence" is also a dynamic one with significant implications for the understanding of personality. The usefulness of all three terms, "will," "counter-will," and "ambivalence," in understanding the interview with Mr. Mann, seems apparent.

The Present

As indicated previously, the counselor, despite Mr. Mann's references to the past, concentrates on his shifting feeling in the present. While recognizing that Mr. Mann's present attitudes with regard to others and himself are the product of past experience, the counselor is concerned with the *transformation* of continuous experience on the basis of new influence which is assimilated by the client. The emphasis, in other words, is on the influence from the outside that is being exerted upon the inner psychological stream, which encompasses past and present and moves on into the future. Just as it is believed that outside influences had an effect upon the development of personality in the past, so it is assumed that outside influences can affect the personality pattern which is active now. Mr Mann's father and mother did have profound influence upon the development of his personality. But in great part, he has grown beyond their influence and now seeks stimulation from other sources. In serving as counselor, the worker takes responsibility for being this kind of stimulus, and Mr. Mann responds on this basis. He wants and expects the worker to stand in such a relationship to him, and he makes it clear that he intends to take advantage of such influence as the worker is willing to have upon his future development.

Separation

The factor of separation is paramount in this interview. Mr. Mann, in fact, lived out some of his own separating tendency in relation to his wife only to find that he does not want too much separateness. ("I want to be close to someone.") Nevertheless, he struggles in action and in words to separate himself, and the counselor sympathetically recognizes the nature of the struggle in terms of Mr. Mann's feeling of being tied down, not only by his wife and family, but by the counselor too. The fact that he need not remain tied in his relationship to the counselor is stressed and this has a freeing effect.

Mr. Mann uses the relationship with the counselor to separate himself, to whatever extent possible, from his past. He is moving on to a new stage of personal integration and he can achieve a satisfying adjustment through the uniting and separating in a relationship different from any which he has experienced in the past. Here the uniting and the separating are conscious and understood. They are in no sense accidental. Instead, they are willed and fully comprehended.

A true separating experience must be a dynamic one. It must be lived through step by step. In it the inner will of the individual and the outer influence of the helping person come into play with each other to produce a new consciousness and a new level of adaptation to the outside world. This interview represents the beginning of such a separating experience for Mr. Mann.

Creativity

It is interesting that the interview ends with a discussion of creative energies and what Mr. Mann is doing with them. The fact that Mr. Mann is an artist of considerable accomplishment makes the discussion more appropriate and more meaningful than it might be with a less creative person. But in any instance a true therapeutic experience must have the quality of a creative one.

The creativity of a therapeutic experience is mutual. As the counselor indicated with Mr. Mann, the same energies which go into the creation of an artistic product can go into the re-creation or the transformation of the self. The client must do his own creating; the helping person cannot do it for him. There is much creative spirit in the art of helping, however, and any true helper will put into the therapeutic situation his own creative or constructive interest. The creative attitude or disposition on the part of the helping person permeates every interview and serves as one of the essential dynamics. In the interview with Mr. Mann, the creative capacity of the artist meets with the creative disposition of the helping person, and the application of energies to self-transformation is encouraged. The counselor's interest in the creative, however, is matched by his recognition that creativity alone is not sufficient for the kind of balanced living which Mr. Mann wishes to achieve. One can be creative without being well adjusted to one's personal environment. Mr. Mann wants to achieve both — creativity and adjustment — and it is the counselor's business to try to help him attain such a goal. In so doing, the counselor must recognize that a good personal adjustment might be accompanied by less artistic creativity. The counselor should stand for the balanced adjustment despite his own creative interest, and in the interview with Mr. Mann he does so.

Thus, although creative interest permeates the interview, it is subsidiary to the goal of balance adjustment. Mr. Mann's creativity and the counselor's combine to achieve this essential goal, and in this respect, the interview has the same elements in it as might be found with a much less creative client. However, the emphasis on the creative is much more in evidence with a sensitive, artistic person like Mr. Mann. This was true not only in the interview transcribed here, but in preceding and subsequent ones where Mr. Mann discussed the relation of his creative activity to his family life.

We thus see that the five fundamental Rankian concepts also lend themselves very satisfactorily to description of what takes place in the interview. Let us turn, however, to several other factors which must be taken into consideration, if we are fully to understand the dynamics of this interview. Let us ask ourselves an important question: What does *the counselor* put into the interview to become a part of the total dynamics?

Analysis of Dynamics

There are, of course, non-verbal dynamics which are at work in this interview but these cannot be analyzed on the basis of the verbal content available in transcription. Using the actual tape recording, one might pick out the factors of empathy and identification which are apparent in tone of voice, laughter, and so forth, and if a motion picture were available other factors would be observable such as the quality of attention manifested in facial expression, muscle tone, and gestures. By examining the counselor's verbal responses to the client's presentation, however, it is possible to analyze some of the significant dynamic factors, in terms other than those which we have used so far.

After the exchange of greetings at the beginning of the interview, Mr. Mann states that he has been trying to figure out "what is happening in my coming here — not that it is any of my business." The counselor responds to this with a positive statement, "It certainly is your business." Obviously, several responses to this comment of Mr. Mann's were possible. The counselor might have raised the question why Mr. Mann said it was not his business, or he might have responded non-committally. In this instance, however, the counselor chooses to take a positive stand and one which is diametrically opposite to what Mr. Mann is saying, although obviously not to what he has been feeling or doing. Why does the counselor take this opposite stand? Why does he affirm that it *is* Mr. Mann's business to examine what has been happening in coming to see the counselor? What is the effect of this oppositeness?

It would seem from Mr. Mann's next comment reviewing his interest at first in only a little bit of change, and then in more, and ending with an expression of his consciousness of change and the resistance which he feels toward it, that the counselor's affirmative comment, "It is your business," simultaneously gave sanction to Mr. Mann's interest and stimulated him to project further his feeling about changing. When Mr. Mann comments that it is unpleasant, the counselor proceeds along the same lines by raising a question as to whether it is only unpleasant. Mr. Mann responds to the provocative factor in this by affirming that it is unpleasant and that he is like anybody else in his resistance to change. He had built up a pattern of living, he says, and it was more satisfactory than what he had before, but not enough so. He was determined, therefore, that he would try to change it. This meant destroying intellectual illusions and substituting a simpler way of living, one involving "more relatedness," a phrase which may have been used by the counselor in a previous interview when he recognized that this was what Mr. Mann seemed to be seeking.

While Mr. Mann projects all of this, the counselor simply listens. After the initial expression of difference, he shifts to a passive, accepting role while Mr. Mann continues to put out the thoughts and feelings which are uppermost in his mind. The counselor's passivity, however, is blended with the difference which had been established when the counselor in the beginning expressed some oppositeness to Mr. Mann. The expression of oppositeness had a stimulating or provoking effect, and the passivity which follows has a permissive effect. Once a sense of oppositeness is expressed, neither Mr. Mann nor the counselor need to stick with it. Likeness can then be expressed, and is in Mr. Mann's reference to his becoming more related and less pretentious, which is affirmed by the counselor with a simple "yes."

Following this, that is, after talking about the progress which he has made, Mr. Mann is able to move on to an account of the problem he experienced during the week in his relationship with his wife, which is the reason for his coming at this point, and which represents the essential focus of this counseling interview. Here, Mr. Mann tells of his feeling of being held down, supposedly by his wife, and expresses his desire for a sense of freedom. He acts in keeping with this desire, but then feels guilty for reasons that he cannot understand. Throughout the discussion the counselor brings in his own interest in the wife and her part in the separating incident. Mr. Mann is quite annoyed at this. He doesn't care what his wife thinks or feels — it is his own feelings which are important, and not hers. The counselor will not allow Mr. Mann to concentrate exclusively on his own feeling (as one might conceivably do in pure therapy) but instead brings in the external reality. His wife is a person with feelings which are not to be denied, and the counselor, a bit insistently, brings her into the picture. In so doing, the oppositeness between Mr. Mann and the counselor is re-established. Mr. Mann is not left with his own feelings or his own rationalizations, but must conjure with those of another person. It is more difficult, however, to deal with the possible feelings of a third person than it is to recognize the way one feels toward the person one faces at the moment. In this case it is the counselor that Mr. Mann now faces with annoyance, rather than his wife, and when it is recognized that Mr. Mann feels tied down by the counselor as well as by his wife, he responds positively to this. ("What I have been doing this morning is something like what she did, and you are reacting to it the way you did to her.") Mr. Mann responds to this, saying, "Could be," and then proceeds to examine his own part in the difficulty with less projection and with more attempt to understand himself and his way of relating to others.

Throughout this discussion it again is *difference* between Mr. Mann and the counselor which serves as the principal dynamic. This difference, however, does not have the character of argument. Mr. Mann naturally defends himself when the counselor indicates some identification with his wife, but the difference once again is tempered with recognition of the way Mr. Mann himself feels. An interpretation is added to this recognition, in the form of a question as to whether it was anger or guilt which Mr Mann felt, and this interpretation serves as an additional dynamic. Mr. Mann works on the source or the basis for the guilt which he feels, and the counselor joins him in this inquiry, adding a further interpretation regarding his denial of one side of himself, the sensitive, identifying side. This leads to Mr. Mann's question: "How can you live with two people like that?"

When Mr. Mann reaches this point in the interview, he is quite beyond the need to project blame onto the other. He can now permit something beyond the expression of difference by the counselor, or simple recognition of what he is saying. Interestingly enough, Mr. Mann turns to the historical at this point. "It reminds me of myself fifteen or twenty years ago," he says. The historically oriented counselor might here ask Mr. Mann what he was really like at that time, and this would undoubtedly stimulate a good deal of recollection. The question which the counselor faced at this point, however, was whether to stimulate recollection or to concentrate on an understanding of Mr. Mann's present feeling toward his wife and the counselor, both of whom are identified as tying him down. As indicated earlier, one consideration which probably made for a veering away from the historical in this instance was the fact that Mr. Mann had done a great deal along such lines in his analysis. What seemed more important, therefore, were his conflicting feelings toward his wife and his use of the counselor to resolve these feelings.

Either line of inquiry could serve a dynamic purpose. Concentrating on Mr. Mann's present feeling toward the counselor, however, led to perhaps the most significant part of the interview, namely, Mr. Mann's wish to deny rather than to assert the sensitive part of himself. There is a part of him which would rather not be the sensitive person he is — the same part which wants to throw off the shackles. In almost the same breath, however, Mr. Mann must assert his need for the other side of the coin: ("I want to be close to somebody.") The counselor accepts Mr. Mann's present denial of the more sensitive part of himself, but will not affirm it. Instead he reminds Mr. Mann that just a week ago he spoke in quite an opposite vein. He recognizes the comments about not wanting to be an artist as denial of a real part of Mr. Mann's make-up and corroborates that part of the client which is being withheld ("You are the artist.") This is combined with recognition of the value of what Mr. Mann is doing in wanting to slough off any false artistic interest or temperament.

Following this, the client and counselor came together in recognition of the fact that both selves need to be combined. The genuine identification here between client and counselor serves as an additional dynamic making for movement. Mr. Mann now thinks that the idea of *cooperation* is essential in living and that the achievement of it begins at home. The change required is tremendous, like "building a new machine." He is conscious of his own power, however, and he expresses the desire to apply it to the development of a new pattern. The counselor expresses the thought that Mr. Mann does not have to "build a new machine" but rather to put the parts of the present one together.

This is accepting, but still involves some expression of difference.

The interview ends with the expression of Mr. Mann's wish that his wife would need less of his strength and protection, and his reflection that perhaps it is he who is holding her down and keeping things from her. This is quite the opposite of what he started with and represents a kind of summation of all that took place in the interview. It is the product of no one element in the interview, but rather of all the dynamics which are at work.

The additional dynamic factors which should be recognized, then, as playing an important role in this interview are the following:

1. Projection by the client.
2. Expression of difference by the counselor, tempered with identification.
3. Recognition, acceptance, and corroboration by the counselor.
4. Interpretation.

These dynamic factors are all intermingled in the actual interview but it is of value to try to separate them for purposes of understanding. Let us, therefore, look at each one a bit separately and *as if* it were not combined at all times with other dynamic factors.

Projection

What is the significance of the projecting which the client does? Obviously the counselor would have nothing to react to if the client did not "put out" something which represents his mental state at this particular time. Everything the client says might be called "projection." There is a clear-cut difference, however, between one type of content in this interview and another. When Mr. Mann blames his wife early in the interview for holding him down, but reflects toward the end that he may be holding her back, what he is "putting out" in the two instances differs appreciably. In the first instance he is attributing his problem to another person, and in the second, he is taking the responsibility for it himself. The one kind of "putting out" or projecting is very different from the other.

The second kind of projecting could not have occurred without the first. The first, in fact, is a pre-condition for the second. Once Mr Mann has done the first kind of projecting, blaming the other person for his problem — and once he has met with a response from the counselor which does not agree with this projection, but which instead actually asks him to do some identifying with the very person he is blaming, Mr. Mann can then bring some of his feeling of resentment into the immediate situation and see that it is not only his wife, but the counselor too against whom he is fighting. He is doing the same thing with two different persons, both of whom are important to him, and neither of whom he can be content to blame for all of the problem. He therefore looks to himself and acknowledges the problem as his own.

Difference and Identification

Projection in itself has no great dynamic quality. When it meets with a neutral response it takes on more. When projection meets with objective difference, however, it becomes a powerful force making for change. In other words, it is not the mere putting out which has any real therapeutic value, but the meeting with difference which occurs as a result of the putting out. The difference must be objective. It cannot have the same quality as the original putting out. Projection meeting with projection does not produce change. It only leads to further projection. But projection meeting with its opposite — with neutrality or objective difference — tends to transform itself.

The role played by Mr. Mann's projection in this interview was of this character. He put out his genuine feeling of the moment, which was largely one-sided, representing the masculine side of himself, but denying the feminine. The creative side of himself and the need to be individual is also denied. The counselor responds to this denial with a reminder of the existence of the other and with a reminder that the masculine side itself is not enough. Mr. Mann must live with others, particularly his wife, and to do so he must do some identifying with her. He is quite capable of this, although his verbal expression of the moment might make it seem doubtful. Aware of the importance of identification in Mr. Mann's case, the counselor attempts to stimulate it in a variety of ways. It is safe to say, in fact, that this interview could not have taken place without a basic identification between Mr. Mann and the counselor. Let us, therefore, look to the dynamic role played by identification in the interview.

It is clear that the relationship between Mr. Mann and the counselor is one which permits Mr. Mann to feel that the counselor is with him, even when the counselor finds it necessary to differ with him regarding some of the content which he presents. There is a basic identification which sustains Mr. Mann in his basic struggle with himself. He knows that the counselor is deeply interested in him as a person and as an artist. He knows the regard which the counselor has for his wife, too. While he can feel the counselor's presence and support, however, he also knows at all times that the counselor will not see eye to eye with him. Along with identification, there is a sense of difference, since identification, like projection, can have no therapeutic value in itself. When combined with difference, however, it becomes a true dynamic factor making for movement within a relationship.

Recognition, Acceptance, and Corroboration

Mr. Mann's consciousness of the sense of relatedness, which he gives expression to in this interview, stems from the identification he has experienced in his relationship with the counselor. This was a subject of discussion in previous interviews, and Mr. Mann is now ready to seek a similar sense of relatedness elsewhere — with his children, with his employees, with the man on the street. Along with the development of this sense of relatedness, he feels a pull in the opposite direction — into "retirement," as he puts it. However, the retirements are never successful. He must be related, and the counselor recognizes, accepts, and corroborates his interest along these lines. Momentarily, Mr. Mann has found it necessary to separate himself in feeling from his wife, and indeed, he wishes to do so from the counselor too, but by the end of the interview his sympathetic feelings toward his wife have come to the fore, and as he leaves, there is a spirit of identification between Mr. Mann and the counselor.

The active identification of the counselor in this situation enables him to see and accept the ambivalent feelings which Mr. Mann has toward his wife and toward the counselor too. These two persons are the principal subjects of both Mr. Mann's identification and his tendency to withdraw. One cannot live, normally at least, solely by identification any more than one can live solely by projection. What is required is balance, and the effort to achieve balance often involves a great deal of struggle. Recognition and acceptance of both the identification and the struggle is called for, and when it is forthcoming, movement out of the struggle is facilitated. In counseling, as in any helping process, all is not struggle and difference. Both are essential, but so are the positive factors of recognition, acceptance, and corroboration. The activity of the helping person must have a balanced quality, and it is through these positive factors that the important negative factor of difference is balanced.

Interpretation

This balance was achieved in this particular interview because the underlying spirit of identification between Mr. Mann and the counselor made it possible for the difference which the counselor stressed to be taken in by the client. This "taking in" is no direct and simple process. It is, rather, a roundabout one. The counselor offers two types of interpretation in this interview. In one he gives expression to his own identification with Mr. Mann's wife when Mr. Mann himself is complaining about her (the counselor asked whether Mr. Mann can imagine what the experience felt like to his wife). The other is in the nature of interpretation of the direct relationship with the counselor. The latter is the easier for Mr. Mann to take. The former he meets with strong resentment. He doesn't see how his wife feels, he says. He is a man and should not be expected to identify with the feelings of a woman. It is important that he have a sense of freedom. Why does she hold him back? Why does the counselor expect him to be sensitive to her feelings — that only makes him feel antagonistic toward the counselor too. Mr. Mann's assertion of his feeling — an assertion against what the counselor stands for at this point — does not stop the movement of the interview. Instead, what it actually does is to facilitate movement. Through full expression of the negative, Mr. Mann is left free to express the positive, which he does as soon as his negative feeling is recognized as an acceptable part of the relationship with the counselor. It is this recognition which transforms it into a dynamic factor in the interview.

The Dynamic Focus

If one is interested in the "diagnostic element" alone in this interview, it is obvious, I think, that the counselor is oriented to *dynamic diagnosis,* that is to say, to the shifts in feeling which take place within the interview and to change taking place within the relationship. The counselor must lend a diagnostic eye to this throughout every part of the interview, just as the member of an orchestra must take his cues from the conductor while he is simultaneously attentive to a variety of other factors. Gross diagnosis — the categorizing of the client — does not take place in this interview. It is only through constant *observation* that the counselor can adapt himself to the movement taking place. A diagnostic orientation is necessary, but fixed or static diagnosis is not.

As far as the pure "functional" component is concerned, there is one element in the interview which may be identified as functional, namely, the counselor's orientation to Mr. Mann's attempt to free himself. This may be thought of as stemming from functional philosophy, although it is quite obvious that the term "functional" is a misnomer as applied to this element. Mr. Mann's movement toward an ending is something which should be observed by the diagnostic worker and something which need not be by the functional one. With a dynamic orientation, however, the worker of either school will necessarily give attention to it. He will recognize its validity, appreciate the difficult experience which the client must have in such movement, and contribute his share toward the successful achievement of this objective.

The factor of difference, to which we have given so much attention here, may also be thought of as stemming from functional philosophy, and indeed is one of the indispensable factors in the functional approach. There is nothing in the use of difference, however, which is antithetical to the diagnostic approach, nor is there anything in it which makes it the exclusive property of the functionalists. In any truly dynamic approach to human problems, the part played by difference is a great one. As we have observed in this interview with Mr Mann, the difference which the counselor brings to him repeatedly serves as a stimulus and interacts as a dynamic with other factors, contributed both by the client and by the counselor, to make for a total dynamic situation.

We thus see, in this instance, that a fully dynamic situation exists only when the presentation of the client meets with a potentially dynamic response from the counselor. The two potentials combine in a facilitating atmosphere and comprise a dynamic factor making for movement and change. But no one dynamic factor operates by itself. In any instance a number of such factors function simultaneously, and in the actual interview it becomes difficult to separate one from another. The fact that it is difficult to isolate the factors at work in an interview, however, should not be allowed to stand in the way of analysis of actual interviews from the standpoint of the dynamics involved. In the carrying out of such analysis one is necessarily limited by the basic deductive concepts which one uses to understand what goes on in the helping process. One is limited, in other words, by one's philosophy of help.

The essential value of such analysis, however, lies in what it can contribute to the modification of an existing philosophy or the development of a new one. In the present instance, it is obvious, I think, that the factors which are most significant from a dynamic standpoint are the property of neither school, and are in fact common to both, despite all conceptual divergences. Further analysis of actual interviews from a dynamic standpoint undoubtedly would disclose many such factors common to the actual practice of both schools, but given a minimal role in the theory which each school has developed. On grounds of principle, the two schools have grown further and further apart. On the basis of such study of actual interviews, they would undoubtedly come closer and closer together.

We thus return, by way of this analysis of an interview, to our thesis concerning the coming stage of development in casework and counseling theory and practice. This must be a stage in which emphasis shifts from diagnosis and function to dynamics. In such a shift of emphasis the two schools will find a common meeting ground, and they will do so particularly if they are willing to examine practice, scientifically, and to orient themselves to a preponderantly inductive rather than a deductive approach to the problems of social work philosophy. This is now possible. Interviews can be electrically recorded and compared. They can be examined from the standpoint of diagnostic, functional, and dynamic content, and theory can be compared with practice. It is possible to ascertain now how much diagnosing the diagnostically oriented practitioner actually does in an interview, and what kind of diagnosing. It is likewise possible to ascertain how much use of function the functionally oriented practitioner actually makes. How much of the activity of both is neither diagnostic nor functional in character? An objective study of this question will lead to the transformation of both schools of thought and will place social-work philosophy on a new and firmer footing.

Although the practice of casework and counseling is an art and not a science, there is no reason why this art cannot be practiced with genuine scientific orientation. Just as the art of medicine is the actual living expression of medical science, so the practice of casework or counseling can be the translation into action of a body of scientific knowledge. It is not unfair to say that during the past half century there has been no such thing as a science of social work. However, fifty years of experience, based upon conviction and principle rather than science, have brought us to the point where the profession can develop along genuine scientific lines. The first step in such a development must be the study of scientifically reliable data, such as those provided by the electrical recorder. The next step must be what Miss Richmond called "the comparison and weighing of evidence." Through the sifting and weighing of data, there will develop an evaluation of the "evidence" examined. In such evaluation, principles which have been found to have practical utility will be substantiated. Those which have no practical value will be discarded or fall into desuetude. The examination of actual practice may well lead to new points of emphasis and even to the development of new principles. This frequently happens in the course of development of a scientific process, and there is no reason why it cannot take place in the field of social work. The development of such principles will represent a third stage of scientific progress.

For the time being, however, we have not reached such a stage. In fact, the profession as a whole has hardly begun to take the first step, which is to submit the data of *actual* practice to scientific scrutiny. Interviews such as the one presented here must be compared with those representing different orientations. The presentation and analysis of a single interview may have certain values in itself. The comparisons provided by many such interviews, however, will yield much more. If such comparisons are made from the standpoint of the dynamics involved, the possibilities for scientific inquiry will be endless. The pursuit of such inquiry is indeed a task worthy of the profession.

SUPPLEMENTARY READING LISTS

Chapter 1

1. Adler, Alfred. *Individual Psychology.* New York: Harcourt, Brace, 1929.
2. Bosanquet, Helen. *Social Work in London, 1869–1912.* London: J. Murray, 1914.
3. Boylan, Marguerite. *Social Welfare in the Catholic Church.* New York: Columbia University Press, 1941.
4. Brackett, J. *Supervision and Education in Charity.* New York: Macmillan, 1903.
5. Brisley, Mary S. "An Attempt to Articulate Process," *The Family,* 5:157–161 (October, 1924).
6. Bruno, Frank. *Trends in Social Work.* New York: Columbia University Press, 1948.
7. Colcord, Joanna. "Relief," *The Family,* 4:13–17 (March, 1923).
8. DeSchweinitz, Karl. *England's Road to Social Security.* Philadelphia: University of Pennsylvania Press, 1943.
9. Devine, Edward T. *When Social Work Was Young.* New York: Macmillan, 1939.
10. Dexter, Elizabeth. "The Social Case Worker's Attitudes and Problems as They Affect Her Work," *The Family,* 7:177–182 (October, 1926).
11. Family Service Association of America. *Scope and Methods of the Family Service Agency.* New York: Family Service Association of America, 1953.
12. Farrington, Benjamin. *Science in Antiquity.* New York: Oxford University Press, 1947.
13. Fink, Arthur E. *The Field of Social Work.* Rev. ed. New York: Henry Holt, 1949.
14. Freud, Sigmund. *General Introduction to Psychoanalysis.* New York: Liveright, 1935.

15. Freud, Sigmund. *History of the Psychoanalytic Movement.* New York: Nervous & Mental Disease Monographs, 1914.

16. Freud, Sigmund. *The Basic Writings of Sigmund Freud.* New York: Modern Library, 1938.

17. Frisch, Ephraim. *A Historical Survey of Jewish Philanthropy.* New York: Macmillan, 1924.

18. Goldenweiser, A. A., and William F. Ogburn. *The Social Sciences.* Boston: Houghton Mifflin, 1927.

19. Gurteen, S. H. *A Handbook of Charity Organization.* Buffalo: The Author, 1882.

20. Hollis, Florence. "Some Contributions of Therapy to Generalized Casework Practice," *The Family,* 15:328–334 (February, 1935).

21. Horney, Karen. *Our Inner Conflicts.* New York: W. W. Norton, 1945.

22. Jung, C. G. *Two Essays on Analytical Psychology.* London: Routledge and Kegan Paul, 1953.

23. Karpf, Fay B. *The Psychology and Philosophy of Otto Rank.* New York: Philosophical Library, 1953.

24. Karpf, M. J. "Towards a Source Book in Jewish Philanthropic Origins," *Jewish Social Service Quarterly,* 12:324–336; 12:396–410; (March–June, 1936).

25. Kropotkin, Petr. A. *Mutual Aid.* New York: Alfred A. Knopf, 1925.

26. Lecky, W. E. H. *History of European Morals.* New York: Appleton, 1913.

27. Lowrey, Lawson G. *Orthopsychiatry 1923–1948.* New York: American Orthopsychiatric Association, 1948.

28. McCormick, Mary J. *Principles of Thomistic Philosophy in Social Casework.* New York: Columbia University Press, 1948.

29. Mullahy, Patrick. *Oedipus Myth and Complex.* New York: Hermitage Press, 1948.

30. Murphy, Gardner. *Historical Introduction to Modern Psychology.* New York: Harcourt, Brace, 1950.

31. Niebuhr, Reinhold. *Contributions of Religion to Social Work.* New York: Columbia University Press, 1932.
32. Puner, Helen Walker. *Freud, His Life and His Mind.* New York: Howell Soskin, 1947.
33. Queen, Stuart A. *Social Work in the Light of History.* Philadelphia: Lippincott, 1922.
34. Randall, John Herman, Jr. *The Making of the Modern Mind.* Rev. ed. Boston: Houghton Mifflin, 1940.
35. Rank, Otto. *Art and the Artist.* New York: Alfred A. Knopf, 1932.
36. Rank, Otto, *Modern Education.* New York: Alfred A. Knopf, 1932.
37. Rank, Otto. *Will Therapy and Truth and Reality.* New York: Alfred A. Knopf, 1947.
38. Reymert, Martin L. "The Organization and Administration of a Child Guidance Clinic," Paper in the *Handbook of Child Guidance,* Ernest Harms, ed. New York: Child Care Publications, 1947.
39. Richmond, Mary E. *Friendly Visiting Among the Poor.* Charities Review, 1914.
40. Richmond, Mary E. *Social Diagnosis.* New York: Russell Sage Foundation, 1917.
41. Richmond, Mary E. *The Long View.* New York: Russell Sage Foundation, 1930.
42. Robinson, Virginia P. *A Changing Psychology in Social Casework.* Chapel Hill: University of North Carolina Press, 1930.
43. *Social Work Yearbook;* Articles on Catholic, Jewish and Protestant Social Work. New York: American Association of Social Workers, 1954. (Also, previous editions published by Russell Sage Foundation.)
44. Sullivan, Harry S. *The Inter-Personal Theory of Psychiatry.* New York: W. W. Norton, 1953.
45. Taft, Jessie. "The Relation of Psychiatry and Social Work," *The Family,* 7:199–203 (November, 1926).
46. Tsu, Yu Yue. *The Spirit of Chinese Philanthropy.* New York: Columbia University Press, 1912.

47. Ulhorn, Gerhard. *Christian Charity and the Ancient Church.* Edinburgh, 1883.
48. Watson, Frank D. *The Charity Organization Movement in the United States.* New York: Macmillan, 1922.
49. Weber, Max. *The Protestant Ethic and the Spirit of Capitalism.* New York: Scribners, 1930.
50. Witmer, Helen. *Social Work; An Analysis of a Social Institution.* New York: Farrar & Rinehart, 1942.
51. Wittels, Fritz. *Freud and His Time.* New York: Liveright, 1931.
52. Zilboorg, Gregory, and George W. Henry. *A History of Medical Psychology.* New York: W. W. Norton, 1941.

Items 2, 4, 8, 9, 12, 13, 19, 25, 26, 30, 33, 34, 39, 40, 41, 42, 46, 47, 48, 49, 50, and 52 are recommended to the student who wishes to acquire familiarity with the pre-professional phases of development in social work.

Items 3, 17, 24, 26, 28, 31, 43, 46, 47, and 49 are recommended to those students who are interested in the relationship of private social work and religion during earlier phases of development. Ideational and practical differences are delineated in these works.

Items 1, 14, 15, 16, 18, 21, 22, 23, 29, 32, 35, 36, 37, 39, 44, 45, and 51 will provide background for the student who is interested in the influence of the different schools of psychotherapy.

Items 5, 6, 7, 10, 11, 13, 38, and 42 will help the student to trace developments and changes within the field of social work, and more particularly, social casework.

Chapter 2

1. Alexander, Franz, and Thomas M. French, eds. *Psychoanalytic Therapy.* New York: Ronald Press, 1946.
2. Allen, Frederick H. *Psychotherapy with Children.* New York: W. W. Norton, 1942.

3. Aptekar, Herbert H. *Basic Concepts in Social Casework.* Chapel Hill: University of North Carolina Press, 1941.

4. Aptekar, Herbert H. "The Significance of Structure in the Practice of Casework," *The Family,* 24:375–381 (February, 1944).

5. Boggs, Marjory. "Present Trends in the Caseworker's Role in Treatment," *The Family,* 13:158–162 (July, 1932).

6. Book, Dorothy L. "Meeting the Pressure," *The Family,* 12:21–22 (March, 1931).

7. Burpee, Dorothy G. "Further Aspects of Relief, an Extended Review of Grace Marcus's *Some Aspects of Relief,*" *The Family,* 11:58–61 (April, 1930).

8. Dawley, Almena. "Diagnosis, The Dynamic in Effective Treatment," *Journal of Social Work Process,* 1: 19–31 (1937).

9. Day, Florence R. "Changing Practice in Casework Treatment," *The Family,* 18:3–9 (March, 1937).

10. Family Service Association of America. *A Comparison of Diagnostic and Functional Casework Concepts.* New York: Family Service Association of America, 1951.

11. French, Thomas M., and Ralph Ormsby. *Psychoanalytic Orientation in Casework.* New York: Family Service Association of America, 1944.

12. Garrett, Annette. "Historical Survey of the Evolution of Casework," in *Principles and Techniques of Social Casework,* Cora Kasius, ed. New York: Family Service Association of America, 1950.

13. Hollis, Florence. *Social Casework in Practice: Six Case Studies.* New York: Family Welfare Association of America, 1939.

14. Hollis, Florence. "Some Contributions of Therapy to Generalized Casework Practice," *The Family,* 15:328–334 (February, 1935).

15. Hollis, Florence. "The Function of a Family Agency," *The Family,* 12:186–191 (October, 1931).

16. Kasanin, J. "A Critique of Some of the Newer Trends in Casework," *The Family,* 16:35–39 (April, 1935).

17. Lowry, Fern, ed. *Readings in Social Casework, 1920–1938.* New York: Columbia University Press, 1939.

18. Marcus, Grace. *Some Aspects of Relief*. New York: Charity Organization Society, 1929.

19. Reynolds, Bertha C. "Can Social Casework Be Interpreted to a Community as a Basic Approach to Human Problems?" *The Family*, 13:336–342 (February, 1933).

20. Reynolds, Bertha C. *Learning and Teaching in Social Casework*. New York: Farrar & Rinehart, 1942.

21. Robinson, Virginia P. *A Changing Psychology in Social Casework*. Chapel Hill: University of North Carolina Press, 1930.

22. Robinson, Virginia P. "Psychoanalytic Contributions to Social Casework Treatment," *Mental Hygiene*, 15:487–503 (July, 1931).

23. Taft, Jessie. "Function as the Basis of Development in Social Work Processes," American Association of Psychiatric Social Workers, *Newsletter*, Vol. 9 (1940), No. 1.

24. Taft, Jessie. *The Dynamics of Therapy in a Controlled Relationship*. New York: Macmillan, 1933.

25. *The Journal of Social Work Process* (Philadelphia: Pennsylvania School of Social Work), Vols. 1, 2, 3 (1937, 1938, 1939).

Items 11 and 13 represent the "Freudian" approach in social casework.

Items 2, 8, and 24 are basic contributions in relationship therapy.

Item 1. Certain similarities between relationship therapy and one type of practice in psychoanalysis will be found in this volume.

Items 5, 6, 7, 14, 15, 16, and 18 will give the student a broad understanding of the stage of conflict between relief-giving and therapy.

Items 3, 4, 23, and 25 represent the functional approach to social casework.

Item 10 contains concrete descriptions of diagnostic and functional casework.

Items 9, 12, 17, 19, 20, 21, and 22 give a generalized picture of social casework during the period treated in this chapter.

Chapter 3

1. Alexander, Franz, and Helen Ross, eds. *Dynamic Psychiatry*. Chicago: University of Chicago Press, 1952.
2. Aptekar, Herbert H. "Casework with the Child's Own Family in Child Placing Agencies," in *Six Papers on Child Welfare Problems*. New York: Child Welfare League of America, 1953.
3. Austin, Lucille. "Trends in Differential Treatment in Social Casework," in *Principles and Techniques of Social Casework*, Cora Kasius, ed. New York: Family Service Association of America, 1950. Pp. 324–338.
4. Boehm, Werner. "Clarifying Terminology of Social Casework," in *The Social Welfare Forum 1954, Proceedings of the National Conference of Social Work*. New York: Columbia University Press. Pp. 113–130.
5. Cockerill, Eleanor E., Louis J. Lehrman, Patricia Sacks, and Isabel Stamm. *A Conceptual Framework for Social Casework*. Pittsburgh: University of Pittsburgh Press, 1953.
6. Dawley, Almena. "The Distinctive Area of Social Work," *American Journal of Orthopsychiatry*. 19:6–13 (January, 1949).
7. Faatz, Anita. *The Nature of Choice in Functional Casework*. Chapel Hill: University of North Carolina Press, 1953.
8. French, Thomas M. *The Integration of Behavior: Basic Postulates, Vol. I*. Chicago: University of Chicago Press, 1952. *The Integrative Process in Dreams, Vol. II*. Chicago: University of Chicago Press, 1953.
9. Gomberg, M. Robert, and Frances Levinson, eds. *Diagnosis and Process in Family Counseling*. New York: Family Service Association of America, 1951.
10. Hamilton, Gordon. *Theory and Practice of Social Case Work*. 2nd ed. rev. New York: Columbia University Press, 1951.
11. Hollis, Florence. "The Techniques of Casework," in *Principles and Techniques of Social Casework*, Cora Kasius, ed. New York: Family Service Association of America, 1950. Pp. 412–426.

12. Kasius, Cora, ed. *Principles and Techniques of Social Casework*. New York: Family Service Association of America, 1950.

13. Perlman, Helen Harris. "Social Components of Casework Practice," in *The Social Welfare Forum, Proceedings of the National Conference of Social Work, 1953*. New York: Columbia University Press, 1953.

14. Posner, William. "Case Work Process in a Private Residence Program for Older Persons," *Journal of Social Work Process*, 4:9–28 (May, 1953).

15. Pray, Kenneth L. M. "A Restatement of the Generic Principles of Social Casework Practice," *Journal of Social Casework*, 28:283–290 (October, 1947).

16. Robinson, Virginia P. *The Dynamics of Supervision*. Philadelphia: University of Pennsylvania Press, 1949.

17. Sterba, Richard, Benjamin H. Lyndon, and Anna Katz. *Transference in Casework*. New York: Family Service Association of America, 1948.

18. Taussig, Helen P. "Treatment as an Aid to Diagnosis," *The Family*, 19:289–294 (January, 1939).

19. Towle, Charlotte. "Client-Centered Casework," *Social Service Review*, 24:451–458 (December, 1950).

Items 3, 5, 10, 11, 12, and 18 will contribute to the student's understanding of diagnostic method.

Items 7, 15, and 16 are functionally oriented.

Items 1, 8, 16, 17, and 18 will contribute to the student's understanding of dynamics in related fields.

Items 2, 4, 6, 9, 12, 13, 14, 17, 18, and 19 provide background for understanding of the dynamic problem in casework.

Chapter 4

1. Aptekar, Herbert H. "Casework, Counseling, and Psychotherapy — Their Likeness and Difference," *Jewish Social Service Quarterly*, 27:163–171 (December, 1950).

2. Aptekar, Herbert H. "The Use of Private Psychiatrists in a

Social Agency," *Jewish Social Service Quarterly*, 25:381–394 (March, 1949).

3. Axline, Virginia. *Play Therapy — The Inner Dynamics of Childhood.* Boston: Houghton Mifflin, 1947.

4. Bowers, Swithun. "The Nature and Definition of Social Casework," *Journal of Social Casework*, 30:311–317, 369–375, 412–417 (October, November, December, 1949).

5. Brodsky, Rose. "Family Relationships and Multiple Service," *Jewish Social Service Quarterly*, 27:192–198 (December, 1950).

6. Brody, Celia. "Counseling Help to a Borderline Schizophrenic Adolescent," *Jewish Social Service Quarterly*, 30:264–277.

7. Brody, Celia. "Helping a Client Move into Psychiatric Treatment through a Counseling Process," *Jewish Social Service Quarterly*, 27:265–277 (March, 1951).

8. Coleman, Jules V. "Distinguishing between Psychotherapy and Social Casework," *Journal of Social Casework*, 30:244–252 (June, 1949).

9. Family Service Association of America. *Diagnosis and Treatment of Mental Problems.* Eight articles reprinted from *Social Casework* (1950).

10. Gomberg, M. Robert, and Frances T. Levinson, eds. *Diagnosis and Process in Family Counseling.* New York: Family Service Association of America, 1951.

11. Green, Rose. "The Treatment of Parent-Child Relationships," *American Journal of Orthopsychiatry*, 18:442–446 (July, 1948).

12. Hamilton, Gordon. *Psychotherapy in Child Guidance.* New York: Columbia University Press, 1947.

13. Hofstein, Saul. "Inter-related Processes in Parent-Child Counseling," *Jewish Social Service Quarterly*, 26:286–300 (December, 1949).

14. Hollis, Florence. *Women in Marital Conflict.* New York: Family Service Association of America, 1950.

15. Levinson, Frances. "Counseling in the Family Agency," in *Proceedings of National Conference of Social Work*. New York: Columbia University Press, 1947. Pp. 270–278.

16. Marcus, Grace. "Family Casework in 1948," *Journal of Social Casework*, 29:261–270 (July, 1948).

17. Mudd, Emily H. *The Practice of Marriage Counseling*. New York: Association Press, 1951.

18. Reynolds, Bertha C. "Can Social Casework Be Interpreted to a Community as a Basic Approach to Human Problems?" *The Family*, 13:336–342 (February, 1933).

19. Rogers, Carl. *Client-Centered Therapy*. Boston: Houghton Mifflin, 1951.

20. Rogers, Carl. *Counseling and Psychotherapy*. Boston: Houghton Mifflin, 1942.

21. Rose, John A. "The Relationship of Psychotherapy to Counseling," *Jewish Social Service Quarterly*, 27:278–284 (March, 1951).

22. Shapiro, Violet R. "Factors in Determining the Focus of Treatment in Parent-Child Counseling," *Jewish Social Service Quarterly*, 26:255–269 (December, 1949).

23. Taft, Jessie, ed. *Counseling and Protective Service in Family Casework*. Philadelphia: University of Pennsylvania, School of Social Work, 1946.

24. Taft, Jessie, ed. *Family Casework and Counseling*. Philadelphia: University of Pennsylvania Press, 1948.

Items 1, 2, 5, 7, and 13 contribute to the definition of counseling as a special form of personal help.

Items 7, 10, 15, 17, and 20 are interesting exemplary articles on the present status of counseling.

Items 3, 6, 7, 9, 10, 11, 12, 14, 15, 17, 19, 21, 22, 23, and 24 are of much interest in connection with the overlapping of therapy and counseling.

Items 4, 8, 16, and 18 are helpful in defining casework.

Chapter 5

1. Cockerill, Eleanor E., Louis J. Lehrman, Patricia Sacks, and Isabel Stamm. *A Conceptual Framework for Social Casework.* Pittsburgh: University of Pittsburgh Press, 1953.

2. Faatz, Anita. *The Nature of Choice in Functional Casework.* Chapel Hill: University of North Carolina Press, 1953.

3. Family Service Association of America. *A Comparison of Diagnostic and Functional Casework Concepts.* New York: Family Service Association of America, 1951.

4. Family Service Association of America. *Scope and Methods of the Family Service Agency.* New York: Family Service Association of America, 1953.

5. Frings, John. "Function and Operation of a Research Program," in *Diagnosis and Process in Family Counseling,* M. Robert Gomberg and Frances T. Levinson, eds. New York: Family Service Association of America, 1951.

6. Gomberg, M. Robert. "Criteria for Casework Helpfulness," in *Diagnosis and Process in Family Counseling,* M. Robert Gomberg and Frances T. Levinson, eds. New York: Family Service Association of America, 1951.

7. Hamilton, Gordon. *Theory and Practice of Social Case Work.* 2nd ed. rev. New York: Columbia University Press, 1951.

8. Herzog, Elizabeth, and John Frings. "A Proposed Next Step in the Diagnostic-Functional Issue," *Social Casework,* 33:140–147 (April, 1952).

9. Hollis, Florence. "Casework Diagnosis — What and Why?" *Smith College Studies in Social Work,* Vol. 24, No. 3 (June, 1954), pp. 1–8.

10. Hunt, J. McV. and Leonard S. Kogan. *Measuring Results in Social Casework.* New York: Family Service Association of America, 1950.

11. Marcus, Grace. "A Leap to Conclusions," *Trends in Social Work* (June, 1951).

12. Perlman, Helen Harris. "The Parable of the Workers in the Field," *Social Service Review,* 23:21–24 (March, 1949).

13. Rogers, Carl. *Client-Centered Therapy.* Boston: Houghton Mifflin, 1951.

14. Taussig, Helen P. "Treatment as an Aid to Diagnosis," *The Family,* 19:289–294 (January, 1939).

15. Teicher, Morton I. "Anthropology and the Functional-Diagnostic Controversy," *Social Service Review,* 27:55–61 (March, 1953).

16. Witmer, Helen. *Social Work, An Analysis of a Social Institution.* New York: Farrar & Rinehart, 1942.

Items 3, 8, 9, 10, 12, 14, and 15 are of special interest in connection with the problem of the functional-diagnostic controversy.

Items 5, 6, 10, and 13 should be read by the student interested in research.

Items 1, 2, 4, 7, and 9 exemplify distinct points of view bearing on the functional-diagnostic problem.

Item 16 provides background for understanding the role of social work as a social institution.

Chapter 6

1. Allen, Frederick H. *Psychotherapy with Children.* New York: W. W. Norton, 1942.

2. Alexander, Franz, and Thomas M. French, eds. *Psychoanalytic Therapy.* New York: Ronald Press, 1946.

3. Alexander, Franz, and Helen Ross, eds. *Dynamic Psychiatry.* Chicago: University of Chicago Press, 1952.

4. Dawley, Almena. "Diagnosis, the Dynamic in Effective Treatment," *Journal of Social Work Process,* 1 (1937), 19–31.

5. Gomberg, M. Robert, and Frances T. Levinson, eds. *Diagnosis and Process in Family Counseling.* New York: Family Service Association of America, 1951.

6. French, Thomas M. *The Integration of Behavior: Basic Postulates, Vol. 1.* Chicago: University of Chicago Press, 1952.

7. Mullahy, Patrick. *Oedipus Myth and Complex.* New York: Hermitage Press, 1948.

8. Perlman, Helen Harris. "Social Components of Casework Practice," in *The Social Welfare Forum, Proceedings of the National Conference of Social Work.* New York: Columbia University Press, 1953.

9. Rogers, Carl. *Counseling and Psychotherapy.* Boston: Houghton Mifflin, 1941.

10. Rogers, Carl. *Client-Centered Therapy.* Boston: Houghton Mifflin, 1951.

All of the above items are recommended as contributing to an understanding of the dynamic theory and practice.

C D E F G H I J — R — 7 3 2 1 0 / 6 9 8 7 6 5

INDEX

Abreaction, 43
Activity, in casework, 114, 115
Adler, Alfred, 23, 24
Administration, of concrete services, 1, 16, 131
Agencies, agency-determined dynamics, 130; placement, 64; policies and procedures, 116; practices in, 1; private, 59, 123; public, 59; role in casework, 118; role in counseling, 116
Agency purpose, 119
Agency service, 117
Agents, of charity organization societies, 4
Ambivalence, 27, 165, 169, 222
Analytical psychology, 23
Aptekar, Herbert H., 57, 107
Assistance, public, 57, 60
Associationism, 36
Attitudes, in casework, 19; of client, 15; of worker, 84; reflected in history, 150

Boggs, Marjory, 55
Book, Dorothy L., 56
Bowers, Swithun, 107
Burpee, Dorothy G., 54

Case examples, 45, 73, 156, 201; in public assistance, 60, 61
Casework, 1, 3, 39, 40, 64, 86, 105, 109, 114; definition of, 107; distinguished from counseling, 115 et seqq.; functional factors in, 130; origin of, 3; responsibility in, 115; role of agency in, 116
Casework process, 19, 157 et seqq.
Catharsis, 43
Causal factors, in diagnosis, 7, 44

Causality, in science, 91; relation to control, 91, 92
Charity Organization Movement, 4
Child guidance, 114, 119, 121, 122, 127
Child placement, 65, 112
Classification, in diagnosis, 69
Cockerill, Eleanor, 71, 141
Colcord, Joanna C., 22
Compensation, concept of, 23
Conceptual framework, 72
Conflict, 84, 87, 100, 101, 168
Content, diagnostic, 81; functional, 81, 116; in casework, 113, 155; of the unconscious, 26, 81
Control, distinguished from responsibility, 95
Counseling, 1, 3, 39, 40, 105; definition of, 108; distinguished from casework, 115 et seqq.; dynamics in, 125; interview, 201; marital, 121, 122, 130; parent-child, 117, 127; responsibility in, 115; role of agency in, 116; skill in, 130
Counter-will, 32, 165, 182, 227
Creativity, 34, 165, 195, 230

Day, Florence R., 55
Denial, concept of, 32
Departments in agencies, 1, 2
Dewey, John, 5
Diagnosis, 4, 5, 6, 19, 70, 72, 73, 87, 89, 140, 143 et seqq.; causality in, 72, 144; classification in, 70; evidence in, 8; formality in, 7, 146; inference in, 8; method in, 10, 141; need for, 68; problem of, 139; process in, 18, 140; psychological factors in, 72; stages in, 8

Diagnostic approach to casework, 19, 20, 25, 72, 73, 123, 142 et seqq., 240; method, 71; summary, 7

Diagnostic-functional controversy, 16, 17, 35 et seqq., 70, 132 et seqq., 142, 167

Diagram, on evolution of casework, 37; on types of help, 120

Difference, concept of, 186, 233; as a factor in helping, 237

Differentiation in types of help, 1, 2

Duality, in casework and counseling, 167

Dynamic concept, 38, 39, 40, 78; counseling, 125, 128, 129, 131, 231; helping, 79, 83, 98; orientation, 82, 85, 86, 88, 89, 93, 94, 97, 99, 101, 102, 168; problem, 71 et seqq.; theory and practice, 165

Dynamic passivity, 42, 43, 52, 53, 63; case example of, 45 et seqq.

Education, 5, 12

Electrical recording, 163, 200

Eligibility, in casework, 130; in public assistance, 57, 58

Environment, in casework, 14

Evidence, in social diagnosis, 8

Evolution, professional, 1, 3

Evolutionary point of view, 134, 135

Faatz, Anita, 153

Family agency, 123

Family cohesion, 9

Family Service Association, 15, 55, 140

Farber, Arthur, 157

Father-figure, 26, 45, 155

Fees in casework and counseling, 94, 128

Focus, in helping, 2, 53, 80, 84, 121, 122, 126, 240

Formality, in diagnosis, 7, 146

Free association, 26

Friendly visiting, 4, 5

Frings, John, 134

Freud, Sigmund, 5, 23, 25, 26, 28, 31, 41, 165, 166

Freudian conceptions, 25 et seqq., 72, 165, 166 et seqq.

Function of agency, 59, 60, 66, 70, 93; clarification of, 63; in placement, 67; origin of interest in, 58, 59, 60; skill in use of, 67; use of, 62

Functional approach, 19, 20, 25, 63, 66, 69, 75

Functional-diagnostic controversy, 16, 17, 35 et seqq., 70, 132 et seqq., 142, 167

Future, concept of, in casework and counseling, 172

Generic elements in counseling, 123, 127

Goldenweiser, A. A., 31

Gomberg, M. Robert, 106, 163

Hamilton, Gordon, 71, 152

Helping process, 92; phases of, 93

Herzog, Elizabeth, 134, 163

History, 9, 28, 44, 149; attitudes reflected in, 150; relation to counseling, 149; relation to diagnosis, 147, 149; use of, 148, 150, 165, 172

Hollis, Florence, 54, 141

Hunt, J. McV., 163

Hypnosis, 26

Identification, as a factor in helping, 237

Individual psychology, 23

Inference, in diagnosis, 8

Inferiority, concept of, 23

Influence, personal, 1, 2, 4

Information, in diagnosis, 14

Insight, 30

Integration, in dynamic helping, 102, 103; of observations, 89; of theory and practice, 197

Interaction, of client and worker, 47, 78, 80, 99
Interpretation, 9, 30, 236
Investigation, 13

James, William, 5
Jung, C. G., 23, 24

Karpf, Fay B., 31
Kasanin, J., 56
Kasius, Cora, 133
Kogan, Leonard, 163

Lehrman, Louis J., 71, 141
Levinson, Frances, 106, 163
Limitations, 186, 189
Lindeman, Eduard, 103
Love-hate object, 29

Marcus, Grace, 53, 54, 134
Murphy, Gardner, 36

Ogburn, W. F., 31
Oppositeness, in casework and counseling, 167, 168

Parent-figure, 29, 45
Passivity, in casework, 154
Past experience, 28, 149, 165, 171, 223
Patterns of behavior, 15
Perlman, Helen Harris, 134
Personality, 67, 79, 81, 87, 179; growth of, 123; in psychotherapy, 117
Placement, 67, 85, 112, 116, 126, 127, 128; of elderly persons, 157 et seqq.; visiting regulations in, 130
Polarity, 93
Pray, Kenneth L. M., 90, 91
Present, concept of, 33, 165, 185, 229
Problem, in counseling, 117, 127; of self-determination, 13, 16, 17, 18; meaning of, 6

Procedure of agencies, 65, 116, 117, 155
Process, conditions of, 94; in diagnosis, 8, 10, 11, 18, 19, 80, 91; dynamically oriented, 40, 97, 126; dynamics in, 123
Profession of social work, 104, 135
Professional casework, approach, 11; evolution of, 3; origin of, 3 et seqq.
Professional synthesis, 136
Projection, as a factor in helping, 236; in transference, 29; upon the therapist, 24
Psychiatric understanding, 68, 69
Psychiatry, influence on social work, 20, 21, 23, 53, 56; relation to other disciplines, 111
Psychoanalysis, 23
Psychological change, 97
Psychological interest, in casework, 13
Psychology, 36; in social casework, 41, 42; of placement, 81, 84, 86, 88
Psychotherapy, 107, 111, 112; definition of, 110; likeness to counseling, 123
Public assistance, 57, 59
Public relief, 57, 59; training problem in, 58

Rank, Otto, 23, 24, 25, 31, 33, 34, 41, 42, 57, 165, 166
Rankian conceptions, 30 et seqq., 144, 165, 174, 179 et seqq.
Rankian orientation, 57
Recognition, as a factor in helping, 236
Relationship, 9, 10; in dynamic helping, 101, 175; nature of, 150; therapeutic, 129; union and separation in, 193
Relationship therapy, 48, 51, 53, 58, 63; defined, 49, 50
Relief, 22, 23, 54, 94; public, 58, 59, 63

Repression, 26

Research, in casework, 156, 200; need for, 161; problems, 138, 161

Resistance, 29; as a force in casework and counseling, 177, 178, 225; associated with transferences, 45

Responsibility, distinguished from control, 95; in casework, 115; in counseling, 115; in dynamic helping, 90, 93, 94, 95; of worker, 65

Reynolds, Bertha, 55, 106

Richmond, Mary, 4, 5, 6, 7, 8 *et seqq.*, 20, 25, 41, 68, 72, 80

Robinson, V. P., 21, 41

Rogers, Carl, 106, 156

Sacks, Patricia, 71, 141

Schools, of psychology, 35, 36; of psychotherapy, 24; of social work thought, 20, 132

Scientific attitude, 137

Scottish school, of psychology, 36

Self-determination, 11, 12, as a problem, 13, 16, 17, 18

Separation, concept of, 33, 67, 82, 165, 191, 229; dynamics of, 82

Skill, generic and specific, 121; in counseling, 130

Social Diagnosis (Mary Richmond), 4, 5, 6, 9, 10, 20, 21, 68

Social services, 1, 2, 108, 109, 113, 119

Sociatry, 15

Sources, of help, 15; of information, 9

Specialization, 113

Stamm, Isabel, 71, 141

Structure, as a factor in helping, 64, 188; concept of, 51, 93, 186; in various fields, 65

Struggle, in casework, 154

Synthesis, in dynamic helping, 102, 103, 104

Taft, Jessie, 49, 57, 106

Taussig, Helen P., 146

Teicher, Morton, 134

Theory, of casework, 155, 167; dynamic, 165

Therapeutic factors, in counseling, 131

Time limits, 93, 128

Transference, 29, 44, 45, 165, 173, 224

Treatment, 14, 20, 72, 73

Types of help, 1, 2, 3

Unconscious, the, 25, 27, 56, 165, 166, 221

Union, in casework relationship, 193

Visiting regulations, 130

Will, concept of, 16, 31, 165, 179, 226; definition of, 31; in relationship therapy, 50, 51

Will struggle, 52, 58, 61, 62

Witmer, Helen, 135